BOOT SALE

Also by Nige Tassell

The Bottom Corner: Hope, Glory and
Non-League Football
Three Weeks, Eight Seconds: Greg LeMond, Laurent
Fignon and the Epic Tour de France of 1989
Butch Wilkins and the Sundance Kid: A Teenage
Obsession with TV Sport
Mr Gig: One Man's Search for the Soul of Live Music

Nige Tassell

BOOT SALE

Inside the Strange and Secret World of Football's Transfer Window

YELLOW JERSEY PRESS
LONDON

1 3 5 7 9 10 8 6 4 2

Yellow Jersey Press, an imprint of Vintage
20 Vauxhall Bridge Road
London SW1V 2SA

Yellow Jersey Press is part of the Penguin Random House
group of companies whose addresses can be found at
global.penguinrandomhouse.com.

Penguin
Random House
UK

First published in paperback by Yellow Jersey Press in 2019

www.vintage-books.co.uk

A CIP catalogue record for this book is available from
the British Library

ISBN 9781787290327

Typeset in 11/14.5 pt Minion Pro
by Integra Software Services Pvt. Ltd, Pondicherry

Printed and bound in Great Britain by Clays Ltd, Elcograf S.p.A.

Penguin Random House is committed to a sustainable future for our
business, our readers and our planet. This book is made from Forest
Stewardship Council® certified paper.

To Keith and Nick,
the boys on the touchline

'For your popular rumour, unlike the rolling stone of the proverb, is one which gathers a deal of moss in its wanderings up and down'

      – Charles Dickens, *The Old Curiosity Shop*

'I've just seen Vengloš in Rock Ferry buying energy drinks / He's deffo taking over'

      – Half Man Half Biscuit, 'This One's For Now'

Contents

Preliminary Talks

The past is a foreign country. They do football transfers differently there.

Forty years ago, on 9 February 1979, English football's most sensational transfer of the entire twentieth century was announced. It was not so much about the player, nor the direction of travel. Moving from relegation certainties Birmingham City to league champions Nottingham Forest was a perfectly logical career step for England international Trevor Francis. No, the disquiet was all about the money.

One million pounds.

The fee demanded by Birmingham, and cheerily paid by Forest, was an extraordinary escalation of the British transfer record. Just one deal had previously crossed the half-million threshold, and that was only when David Mills had swapped Middlesbrough for West Bromwich Albion a matter of a few months before. Francis, still only twenty-four despite eight headline-making seasons at St Andrews, was certainly a premium player. His availability was, in the words of the *Guardian*'s correspondent, 'like a Rembrandt coming on to the open market'.

Birmingham's insistence that Francis would only be sold if the million-pound valuation was met may have raised eyebrows in most quarters, but two of the game's more unorthodox characters – Forest's Brian Clough and Coventry's managing director Jimmy Hill – had no qualms about attracting scorn in coming up with the cash. They knew a Rembrandt when they saw one.

For those not alive or too young to follow football back then, it's surely difficult to grasp the seismic rumbles the transfer provoked. Newspapers ran stinging editorials decrying the ridiculous price tag, while the transfer made the headlines on the early-evening news, a rare event in English football's more moribund years. The journalist Duncan Hamilton rightly called it 'football's equivalent of breaking the sound barrier'.

The amount now sounds paltry. After all, these days middle-ranking academy players routinely attract seven-figure fees. However, what is likely to sound extraordinary to younger ears four decades on is the manner in which such a high-profile transfer was forged.

At the start of February 1979, Birmingham had amassed just eight points all season and were staring the old Division Two right in the face. This wasn't a prospect that Francis was prepared to countenance. He had submitted the first in a series of transfer requests back in 1976. A full three years later, his manager Jim Smith finally demurred, understanding that Francis deserved a better arena for his talents than the misfiring, almost-certainly-doomed Blues. The size of the transfer fee demanded by the club, and their insistence on not budging on the figure, would be decent compensation.

No restrictive trading periods existed back then, with managers free to buy players right up to the third Thursday in March. But Clough didn't bother playing it cool and chose not to bide his time – Jimmy Hill was lurking with a counter-offer, after all. Accordingly, there was little brinkmanship involved, with Clough happy to pay the fee (although he would later insist that the final figure was a pound short of a million. The VAT applied to the fee ensured it wasn't).

Francis – understandably preferring to move to the league champions than to Coventry, whose last piece of silverware was the Second Division title back in 1967 – was summoned to the City Ground. There, he, Clough and Peter Taylor shut themselves away for a four-hour meeting to thrash out terms. Back then, phrases such as 'sell-on fee' and 'buy-out clauses' weren't part of football's lexicon. There was also a distinct lack of agents, advisers and directors of football adding their two-penneth. It was the way Clough liked to work: 'man-to-man, cards-on-the-bloody-table plain dealing'.

Not that there was anything especially unusual about the set-up; this was largely the way transfers were negotiated at the time. The Dutch midfielder, Arnold Mühren, once told me that the first he knew of Ipswich's interest in him back in 1978 was when Bobby Robson himself turned up at his house in Volendam. Robson set out the terms of the deal right there in Mühren's kitchen, with no protracted, multilateral discussions to muddy the waters. Lawrie McMenemy signed Charlie George during the same season. The negotiations involved the Southampton boss picking up George in London and driving him back to the McMenemy homestead in Hampshire where the striker stayed overnight. The contract discussions began between just the two of them the following morning after breakfast.

Transfer negotiations have long since not been such intimate affairs. We live in the age of the entourage. 'Sign a player today,' says Harry Redknapp, 'and you sometimes need to find a bigger office just to accommodate all the people who are brought along to do the deal. Agents, advisers, lawyers, PR experts, uncles, aunts and mates …'

Even if Francis's record-breaking move had taken place in the era of agents and entourages, Clough would surely have given any representatives extremely short shrift – and almost certainly an extended interrogation over how the agent could possibly justify any sizeable personal recompense for what they'd contributed to the deal. As it was, without any agent's cut, Francis reportedly banked £50,000 himself as part of the deal.

Being the most expensive British footballer didn't accord Francis any special privileges, though. When he was presented to the clamouring press, it was Clough who hogged the limelight. Arriving in gym kit and brandishing a squash racquet, the manager was clearly impatient to get to the courts at Trent Bridge Cricket Ground, just around the corner. The mildly shambolic proceedings undermined Francis, who had arrived at the City Ground in his Jaguar with his glamorous wife Helen, described by eyewitness Duncan Hamilton as 'looking like a catwalk model from Paris, swathed in a massive fur coat'.

Clough's reluctance to treat Francis like a high-value commodity continued as soon as the press conference was over, with the new arrival being dealt with in a manner that a twenty-first-century player would not remotely recognise. First, Francis was pitched straight into a Midland Youth League game on a local parks pitch. Then, unavailable to play in Forest's European Cup campaign unless they reached the final, he was placed on tea-making duties during the quarter-final against the Swiss side Grasshoppers, forced to serve hot beverages to his teammates at half-time.

While not exactly suggesting that Francis was on his uppers and had been forced into a life of servitude (he had, after all, topped up his regular earnings the previous summer by trousering another fifty-grand lump sum for turning out nineteen times for Detroit Express in the North American Soccer League), the story comes from a time when clubs held most, if not all, the cards. It wasn't until the mid-nineties that the tables were turned, thanks to legal action taken against the Royal Belgian Football Association by an unremarkable midfielder who played for RFC de Liège.

The ruling that colloquially took the name of the plaintiff – Jean-Marc Bosman – had a profound effect on British and European football that's near impossible to measure. In December 1995, a ruling was finally made on a five-year legal battle. Earlier in his career, with his contract having expired, Bosman had hoped to move across the French border to Dunkerque, but found that RFC de Liège were refusing to release him. Believing such an action to be in contravention of EU freedom of movement legislation, Bosman took his case all the way to the European Court of

Justice, who found in his favour. Football transfers would never be the same again: players now had the right to run their contracts down and move for free once their current deal had expired.

* * *

The implementation of the transfer window was a by-product of the Bosman ruling, a way for the football authorities to try to clip players' wings to curtail their growing power and to guard against a transfer free-for-all. Talk of its introduction in English football, though, was first heard a few years before.

In 1992, the nascent Premier League, the swanky, strutting new kid on the block, gave encouraging words to an idea circulating around some of the more progressive managers of the time that sought to curb the ability of richer clubs to buy their way out of trouble, or to buy success, as late as three-quarters of the way through the season – that third Thursday in March. By reducing the trading period, the argument suggested, you'd be levelling the playing field. And certain managers were keen from a personal standpoint. Terry Venables, in particular, believed it would shrink the burden on his brethren's shoulders. 'Terry's idea is that managers ought to be coaches,' explained Rick Parry, the Premier League's first chief executive, 'spending time with their players and not looking around for new signings or fending off agents.'

By the end of the decade, UEFA issued plans to limit and standardise the transfer market across Europe by implementing a six-week window between mid-December and the end of January. By now, the Premier League – buoyant and increasingly rich – was against the proposal, and they were joined in this by the Bundesliga.

The following couple of years, though, changed the landscape. With the whole system of European football transfers increasingly being interpreted as in contravention of the Treaty of Rome (the treaty which set up the European Economic Community and outlined the concept of a European single market), FIFA proactively drew up compromise proposals. These included accepting the need for a twice-yearly transfer window. With the Premier League the only dissenters across the entire continent, English clubs found themselves under insurmountable pressure from UEFA to adopt the proposals.

'It reduces the flexibility for clubs to be able to sell players throughout the season,' moaned Arsenal's vice-chairman David Dein. 'For some clubs, that can be a matter of survival. We were robustly opposed to it, but were advised by UEFA that we had to comply and we have no alternative but to comply against our will.'

On the eve of the 2002–2003 season, the first with the new trading limitations in place, observers were suspicious of what was to come. Writing in the magazine *When Saturday Comes*, Adrian Chiles let off both barrels. 'It would be more accurate to call it a transfer wall or a transfer ban. We're all sleepwalking into this. It comes in on August 31st and it's going to fundamentally change the way football is run in this country. If I was a tabloid editor, I'd be having sleepless nights now, because what sells stories but transfer speculation? And I'd be having even more sleepless nights if I was a Second or Third Division club, because my understanding is that they won't be able to sell.'

A few months later, in the same magazine, a more conciliatory tone was set by the writer Barney Ronay, who declared that the new system 'might just turn out to be exactly what English football – bloated, cash-strapped and cripplingly hungover after partying up to the hilt of its credit limit – is in need of.' Ronay was a rare, semi-positive voice. 'The transfer window might just be a staging-post on the way to saving football's skin.'

Managers, looking more at short-term survival for their clubs rather than long-term sustainability for the sport, weren't convinced. Venables, that early advocate, was now singing from a different hymn sheet, moaning that having a limited trading was 'a bit like a greengrocer only being open on Mondays'. Ronay tackled the logic of this observation. 'The analogy doesn't work. A greengrocer's job is selling apples, whereas a football club exists to play football, not to buy or sell players. A more accurate comparison would be greengrocers being encouraged to grow their own apples rather than buying someone else's, in the hope that the quality of produce will improve and fewer of them will end up going out of business. Manchester United and Arsenal may not agree with the idea of a transfer window, but then neither would Tesco or Sainsbury's.'

As the window established itself, other managers were in harmony with Venables. 'It detracts from the game as far as I'm concerned,' grumbled Sam Allardyce to the *Manchester Evening News*. 'It's such a frantic period that can only cause panic, frustration and inflation of prices. I'm not a lover of it whatsoever.' His exasperation was mirrored by Gary Megson, speaking to the *Telegraph*. 'The transfer window is rubbish. It is unfair and I would like to see it challenged in court. Look at other businesses. If a haulage company wanted a new lorry and someone said in September, you cannot have one until January, you are not allowed to do those kind of things.' Arsène Wenger joined the criticism. 'It makes no sense. What is the expression? Act in haste and repent at leisure.'

While John Barnwell, the then head honcho of the League Managers' Association, argued in 2004 that 'FIFA's imposition of the transfer window has left the media with too many column inches to fill during the six months with no player movement'. This could, and would, have consequences for his members. 'The newspapers had to find something other than player movement to write about. The trend is to turn the focus more onto the managers and how they are faring.'

Within a couple of years, though, Barnwell appeared broadly supportive of how the window was shaping English football, telling the *Guardian* he believed it to be 'vital for the game's future. It demands foresight and continuity, and provides a level playing field for clubs. Teams are now unable to rely on financial power and buy their way to success. They can no longer buy a new centre-forward in March to score the goals to seal promotion or stave off relegation at the expense of a less wealthy club. In the past, clubs have simply bought new players when injuries, suspensions or poor form have a negative effect on results.'

If Barnwell's words now sound somewhat naïve and idealistic, he couldn't, of course, have envisaged the torrent of money that would completely reshape English football, in particular, the influx of enormous overseas investment. Clubs might have been disqualified from buying players late in the season, but deep-pocketed owners simply bought ready-made replacements ahead of those injuries, suspensions and poor form. The stockpiling of players – their personal ambitions softened by eye-popping salaries – allowed inequality between clubs to resurface. The playing field revealed its bias again.

*   *   *

The panic alluded to by Sam Allardyce had already shown its face during English football's very first transfer window in January 2003. Only this wasn't panic-buying. It was panic-selling. Leeds United, in gross financial straits despite reaching the semi-finals of the Champions League less than two years earlier, had to cash in on several of their prize assets. Without the longer trading period, the club's hand was forced into speedily jettisoning players for whatever prices they could muster. As the *Daily Mail* later pointed out, 'the other clubs had Leeds over a barrel. They knew they had to sell.'

Despite having despatched Rio Ferdinand to Manchester United the previous summer for a record-breaking £30m, Leeds still needed to cut costs and recoup more cash by offloading further talent. Lee Bowyer was next to go, heading to West Ham as the first-ever permanent signing during an English transfer window. On the eve of the first deadline day, Robbie Fowler went to Manchester City for £6m, while Jonathan Woodgate was the subject of the biggest deal of the final twenty-four hours, signing for Newcastle for £9m. Deadline day would, in time, become known as the day when over-valued purchases were made and ludicrous sums paid. This first one was defined by a single club trying to clear its decks, and its debts, by selling off the family silver for whatever it could get.

This wasn't the only difference. There were no Sky reporters hogging the pavement outside training grounds and stadiums during that first window, no clumps of supporters noisily forcing themselves on camera in the background. It wasn't much of a spectacle at all. Back then, no one had foreseen its appeal and thus its value.

Since then, though, the transfer window has taken on an identity and a character all of its own. It's a pop-up mini-industry that takes centre stage twice a year, a complete distraction to both those operating within football and those looking in from outside. The sideshow casts a long shadow; in mid-season, it can eclipse the January fixtures. For that month, at least, it appears bigger than the matches themselves.

The transfer process is a much different dance these days, one now led by players – or, at least, by their repre-sentatives. These agents are not the only new faces. The window has made the names of certain broadcasters and journalists inextricably connected with it. The same goes for certain managers. And the language that's spoken, the common tongue of the modern football transfer, is one Brian Clough wouldn't have understood.

The process has its champions: Niall Quinn, for one, who looks back fondly on his time as Sunderland chairman navigating his way around the 'marvellous madness' of deadline day. And it's still not short of critics. *Vice* magazine has described the January window as a 'throbbing, chuntering month of swoops, coups and bullshit', while the football writer Barry Glendenning refers to it as a 'glorified trolley-dash through the supermarket of international football humanity'.

Whether dangerous distraction, necessary evil or irresistible circus, the transfer window continues to spin on its biannual orbit, drawing everyone in the football world into its gravitational pull. We feast on its ugly rumours and its careless whispers. And no one remains nonplussed about it. For player, manager, chairman, fan, agent, scout, broadcaster or journalist alike, the window can't be ignored. It incessantly tugs at your sleeve. You can't avoid having an opinion about it.

It can be a bewitching and baffling place, even for its main protagonists. Peter Crouch calls it the 'one part of our world so weird, so cloak and dagger, that even those of us at the centre of it all aren't really sure what's happening'. Players are still the commodity, sometimes with little say about the direction they're traded in. They can be, in Crouch's eyes, 'flotsam on the tide'.

For all involved, a transfer window can be the best of times, it can be the worst of times. It comes loaded with dread for clubs with little money to spend or for those struggling to keep hold of their best players. But it comes ripe with excitement for anyone connected to clubs with cash to splash. Draw up the shopping list and let's spend some money.

Each window takes a different hue. Some are frantic, others are flat. But at the heart of each one is the hope of an improved life for a football club. No club is immune from this. From the Premier League downwards, the idea that a new signing can single-handedly reverse fortunes, turning despair into joy, is an irresistible one.

While the transfer window provides grist to the cynic's mill, it also empowers football's hopeless romantics, from club chairman to fantasist fan. It offers the promise of better days, of sunlit uplands. It allows everyone to keep dreaming.

Nige Tassell,
May 2019

CHAPTER ONE

FACT FROM FICTION

'I don't want to be wrong. I don't look at it as fish-and-chip paper. I see it as a dent in the reputation'
– Mike McGrath

In the mid-morning hush of the bar of a five-star Knightsbridge hotel – the kind of establishment where top-hatted concierges wouldn't entertain the notion of guests actually pressing a lift button themselves – discretion is the watchword. Here, assignations are unfailingly private; eyes for only whoever's right in front of them, ears for only their companion's words. You can imagine a fair few transfer deals have been struck and shaken on in the bar's darker corners. In short, it's the kind of high-level meeting place that's the natural habitat of big-name footballers and their smooth-talking representatives.

This also makes it the perfect location in which to meet, and get to understand the whispered ways of, one of the UK's most high-profile football newspaper reporters. After stints at the Press Association and Wardles news agency, Mike McGrath has spent more than half a decade decoding and deciphering transfer rumours on behalf of the *Sun* and the *Sun On Sunday*. This is a man charged with separating fact from fiction.

His bullshit detector is turned up to the max.

'It's about trusting your contacts in what they're telling you,' he explains. 'That is the most important part. As newspaper journalists, we can't actually wait for Aaron Ramsey to sign his pre-contract with Juventus. We have to try to find out in advance – how long he's signing for, how much he's signing for, what his squad number's going to be . . .

'You can go onto any website and there'll be a rumour. But my first point of call is always my contacts. I listen to what they're saying and I may then see if anything's been written about that before. You have a level of scepticism that's really healthy and you have to try to find out the veracity of it. You ring round your contacts, but things can shock you. When it's not a story you've been involved in and it just pops up somewhere else, you might disbelieve it to begin with.

'I don't think many people were on to Diego Dalot going to Man United in the summer of 2018 until the club's statement came out. That didn't come with a big build-up. You might say it wasn't one of the biggest transfers in the world, but they did keep it under wraps. Fabinho going to Liverpool from Monaco was another. Nobody had worked on that story until he signed. Or, if they did, it was maybe just a few hours before. That was a surprise, which reflects the discreet way that Liverpool go about their transfers. And, from what I've been told by my contacts, they don't get told by agents who they should be signing. They tell agents who they want to sign. They've got a clear way of working in the market, which meant the Fabinho deal was able to be kept quiet until the very last minute – or even after he'd signed on the dotted line.'

The ability to detect bullshit at twenty paces is crucial to the reporter who wants to create a reputation by only revealing stories of truth and efficacy. 'Everybody has their own way of working and they rely on people who are involved in deals – or are close to these deals. There are a lot more people now involved in transfers. Two clubs are doing the deal and there are employees working at both clubs, and the player has people working for him too. It's down to finding out the best information, however that's possible. You want contacts who know what's going on in a transfer deal. As a journalist, you need to get to know whoever these people are; common sense would tell you that there are more people with information on what might be happening. There are a lot more eyes and ears.'

Idle speculation isn't a currency that the worth-their-salt journalist can dare to trade in. That can be left to Twitter feeds like Indykaila News, an account boasting 280,000 followers and which puts out a hundredweight of transfer gossip every day. But its quantity-over-quality output can't genuinely be enlightening to many of its followers. Some of the rumours it posts are so spurious, illogical or patently ridiculous that they've led plenty of people to regard it as a parody account.

Certainly, no print journalist with a reputation to build or maintain – and a (possibly fragile) circulation to protect – can afford to allow themselves to be hoodwinked by any such tall stories. There's egg on faces if so. And the history books contain some salutary lessons in this respect. The case of Didier Baptiste is one such tale.

In the final year of the last millennium, a struggling Liverpool team was linked to Baptiste, a French under-21 left-back who plied his trade with Monaco. His nationality alone gave the story a veneer of credibility, as it would mean that he'd be linking up with compatriot Gérard Houllier, by then the unilateral boss at Anfield following the departure of joint-manager Roy Evans.

It was the *News of the World* who first made the claim about Baptiste's move, reporting that the Frenchman 'would be an ideal addition to the Liverpool back four'. *The Times* and the *Observer* picked up the story, as did the club's own 60p-a-minute ClubCall phone line. But faces turned as scarlet as the Liverpool home kit when it emerged that Didier Baptiste didn't actually exist; he was merely a character from *Dream Team*, Sky One's football-set soap opera. Experienced journalists had been easily taken in. At three different publications, in three different editorial departments, the filter that sifted fact from fiction hadn't been switched on.

These days, in the age of social media where spurious rumour and idle gossip have no end of outlets, journalists need their stories to be as watertight as possible. To reach that point, due diligence and deep research are required, often well in advance of the trading period. 'It's important you work outside the window,' says McGrath. 'Clubs get a sense of what they want a couple of months before. They don't start looking on January 1st. Prior to the window, you might get a sense of what the market might be doing, so the work you do beforehand is vital. You can't just call someone up and say, "Is this happening?" You need to know who's representing who and you need to make sure you're on the other end of the phone. You can't go into the window completely cold, hoping that news will fall into your lap. It doesn't happen like that.'

Playing a strategic long game is, though, counterweighted by the pressure to break a story, to make that headline before anyone else, to be ahead of your journalistic brethren. During McGrath's five-year spell on the *Sun on Sunday*, this was a particularly tall order, trying to keep a certain story under wraps and away from the grabbing hands of those reporters on the dailies. 'It wasn't uncommon to be working on something from Tuesday until Thursday – and to be quite happy with yourself: "It's fine. I've got the splash on Sunday" – and then pick up the paper on Friday to find you've been scooped by another journalist who's worked on the same thing at the same time but has been published a couple of days before. You're left with nothing.

'There is pressure on everyone working in football media to be first in breaking that story. Not just to be right, but to be quickest too. This is really difficult. And journalists' reputations rest on it. A journalist's following on Twitter can be bigger than the circulation of a national newspaper and this is because of what they deliver on their Twitter feed. That competition is intense to be the first, and to trust your contacts to give you the right information so that you are fast *and* accurate.

'It doesn't get any easier. Holding material is even trickier in the age of social media. It's made the job slightly harder, but journalists thrive on competition. You go up against your rivals to get the better story. That's the essence of any journalism. We all know where we stand. We're going up against rolling news and social media. But it's rare to find a journalist of any age who wouldn't at least go on Twitter to see what's on there. Twitter is actually a traditional outlet. I don't treat it as a source, but it is a media outlet – a feed of news that other people are providing.

'If you have a bone fide story, a bang-on exclusive, and it breaks in a newspaper at seven o'clock in the morning, when people are down the newsagents, that's brilliant. It's still possible and it still happens. And that's what we're striving for. I say seven in the morning, but more realistically that means ten o'clock the night before when the back pages get revealed.

'You have small moments when you think, "I've done all right there." One of my recent stories sticks in my head – Eric Choupo-Moting to Paris Saint-Germain. This guy couldn't kick a ball in the reserves at Stoke. The story was that he was going to PSG and I got loads of stick from people who said I didn't know what I was talking about. And then he signed. I enjoyed that one. But if I get one wrong, I see that as a defeat. Just as a professional footballer doesn't want to lose a match, I don't want to be wrong. I don't look at it as fish-and-chip paper. I see it as a dent in the reputation.'

McGrath orders another coffee, another hit of caffeine. The days as a football reporter on a national paper – and these days for him, after his move from the *Sun on Sunday* to the *Sun*, are now on a daily national paper – can be long, especially during the two windows. Insatiable, even. Unlike the summer, January comes with a full programme of league and cup matches too. The reporter has to be open all hours.

'During the season, I'll do a game on a Saturday and usually one in midweek. The rest of the time, my editor wants news. I don't have a quota, but I want to be on top of new stories. I try to meet my contacts face to face, which obviously involves travel and time. And I'm on the phone all the time. My one-year-old son doesn't talk a lot, but he'll pick up a phone, or anything that vaguely resembles a phone, and start gabbing away, because that's what he sees me doing. I don't switch my phone off, but I will put it on silent when I sleep. But football is twenty-four seven. You can take a really important call at ten thirty at night. Most people generally work nine to five. You would think people wouldn't want to be bothered before nine am or after five thirty pm. But I find that's when the best stuff in football happens. You could take a call at nine pm. and that might be your back-page lead story.

'You're not waiting around for people to call you up. You should be always digging for stories and verifying things by calling as many people as possible. You should be on your phone all the time. The battery should be down to nought midway through the day.'

McGrath's news-gathering will invariably include injury updates and perhaps the odd training-ground bust-up involving teammates or a war of words between uppity player and disciplinarian manager. But the most valuable morsels, the nutritious titbits being fed to the readership, concern those all-important arrivals and departures.

'Whatever readers you listen to – whether it's the cabbie who's taking you to a ground or somebody you meet on the train to a match – they're always interested in "Who are we signing?" The transfer market is the one thing they want to know about above all else. The newspaper has to reflect what the fans want and what they're demanding, so what's going on is the market is the currency we deal in. Is their club spending enough on the team? Is it spending too much? And, obviously, who are they spending it on? Maybe it's more appealing to the reader, to the fan, because it's behind a curtain. They desperately want to know what's going on, who's going to be the next big signing, who's going to be that new number nine …

'I know journalists who don't like the window, but I actually do. It's the fruits of your labour. You're hoping that all the hard work you've done comes good in the window. But it might not. It's an open market: a transfer will happen or it won't happen. You stand and fall by what you write.

'The day before deadline day is the worst. You don't want to miss the one. But I like deadline day itself – the drama and the challenge. There's a finality to it. A player will sign for a particular club or he won't.'

A rare guarantee of certainty in a fluid landscape. 'It all comes out in the wash.'

* * *

Andy Wright was not unlike many other football-obsessed teenage boys anxious to consume – and be consumed by – transfer rumours and gossip. He grew up in a Manchester

United-supporting house and can remember, in pre-internet days, how he and his dad were glued to Ceefax in order to learn of any updates on Alan Shearer's mooted move to Old Trafford. 'Has it updated? "BA stewardess says Shearer's name is on the flight-list for United pre-season tour." Oh my God. This is happening!'

The adult Andy Wright is a little less wide-eyed and gullible than his teenage self. He needs to be. Wright holds the position of trading director for SkyBet, the man with ultimate responsibility for all the bets placed with the online bookmaker, including its football markets, which feature a biannual book on the transfer window. If you think a certain player is going to stick or twist – and if, should he twist, you have a fair inkling of that player's final destination – SkyBet will offer odds. Hazard to Real Madrid? Pogba back to Juventus? Kane to stay put? Its traders are ready and waiting.

SkyBet has been running a book on the transfer window for nearly ten years and was the first bookmaker to do so. 'Going back a few years,' explains Wright, 'it would only have been a handful of players you could bet on. Back then, it would have been only the equivalent of Sanchez, Aubameyang, Mkhitaryan … Just four or five. Now it's around a hundred or so players. It grew out of customer requests. A trading floor – and certainly the one here – will try to facilitate customer requests. We've grown to understand this is an e-commerce arena we're in and the old trader-vs-punter mentality has gone away a bit. Customers can ask us for a particular bet and if we say no, we might then lose that customer's business for ever, as they could ask William Hill who then give them a price on it. Our RequestABet facility is very much about giving control back to the customer. It's a two-way street. If what you want to bet on isn't on our site or on our app, come and ask us and we'll do what we can – within reason.

'You get some truly ridiculous things being asked of us. "Can I have a bet on my next-door neighbour to become a Commonwealth Games gold medallist swimmer in the next twenty years?" "No idea, but here's a price." Customers in this digital age expect to get what they want, rather than what they're allowed. The world has changed a bit and the traders have certainly become a little less protective of margins. It's now more about giving customers an experience. We're an entertainment business. It's fun. No way is this making or breaking our year.

'For the last few years, we've offered "to stay" odds – where a player doesn't move. In a way, this was to counteract a charge that was laid at our door. Previously we just offered "Where are they going?" odds and if the player didn't move, every bet would be a loser. So we now offer "to stay" odds and this obviously gives customers the option to say, "I think that story's nonsense. Four to one for Sanchez to stay at Arsenal? Fantastic." So we just try to offer customers as many options and the things they want as possible. We're definitely right to offer "to stay", but we never make money on it.'

The proximity of Sky to SkyBet (the latter used to be owned by the former, but is now the property of the Canadian company The Stars Group) is manna to the conspiracy theorists, the suggestion being that Sky Sports News could give more credibility to an unlikely transfer rumour than is due in order to drive bets to its one-time sister organisation. The pair, though, are not in cahoots, as Wright is keen to stress.

'Yes, we're a Sky brand and we license the name. But we don't get information from Sky reporters. It just doesn't happen. My answer is the same as the head of trading at Paddy Power or William Hill would say. We have no advantage. That's the honest truth.'

How SkyBet gathers the intelligence that allows them to grade and measure each rumour that comes into their orbit is fascinating. While their traders will religiously read the daily rumour mills that grind into fast-spinning action as the next window approaches, these aren't the material for calculating the odds they'll offer. The most direct source available to them is observing how their customers interpret each fresh rumour. As football fans, the traders will have their own instincts, but it's the punters who sift through the nonsense, who give a story credence or reject it out of hand. Just as the value of, say, a house is determined by the amount that someone is prepared to pay for it, the value of a transfer story is partly ascertained by whether (and by how much) someone is prepared to wager on it. That is, the punters' activity is the primary determinant of the odds of whether they move up or down.

'More than any information we can glean from Sky journalists or the BBC gossip column,' says Wright, 'customers know what's going on. We can't be across everything. One evening we saw a run of bets come in for a player involved in an on–off transfer. The bets, which suggested he was going to Man City, were coming in from the West Midlands, which was where he lived. A bit of investigation into the customers involved showed that they knew the guy personally and were at a house party with him. They had opened an account with us and were, for want of a better expression, filling their boots. It highlights the fact that we're sat in an office in Leeds. We haven't got people out and about at house parties, so we're reliant on using the skill of our traders to understand and interpret the customers' betting patterns.

'A customer might bet on twenty transfers in each window but, for example, everything they bet on concerning Arsenal or Crystal Palace is always right. With data analytics, we can pinpoint a customer and keep an eye on them. They can do whatever they want with anything that's not Palace, but we need to be flagging their Palace bets to the team as quickly as possible and get alerts set up. His or her ten-pound bet is worth far more than my ten-pound bet. They're informed and I'm not.'

A sharp trader – one quick to protect the integrity of the market and its margins – needs to demonstrate the skills of the private investigator to find out more about a certain bet-laying punter. 'There are so many people involved in a transfer. It could be the chauffeur for the family that owns a club. If he's told to go and pick a player up and deliver them to the stadium, he's got a decent idea that they're probably in talks. He can put two and two together. You can do a bit of snooping, but it's hard to know what someone's angle is. The chauffeur might just have texted a random mate who lived the other end of the country – "Guess who's in the back of my car?" He might not have been thinking about it from a betting perspective, but his mate has interpreted it and run with it. You need to understand the cold, hard facts: this guy knows about Leicester City, that customer knows about Crystal Palace. So get them flagged, put them on watch lists and monitor their betting activity.'

The trader needs to second-guess the customer's motivations far more than those of the actual player being transferred. Does the size of stake correlate to the credibility of the bet that's been placed? 'Ultimately it's a customer's choice how much they bet. One man's pound might be another man's ten pounds. But if a customer who usually bets a pound suddenly puts a twenty-five-pound bet on, they're obviously more sure about that one. What is it that they know?

'There's the wisdom of the crowd too. If there was suddenly a flurry of "Mkhitaryan to stay" bets – even if they were just one-pound bets but there were twenty of them – we'd have to consider why twenty people in the last two minutes have come to the same conclusion. And what makes a single trader's opinion stronger than their twenty? Sometimes, though, you can read too much into particular bets. It might be an Arsenal fan who wanted Mkhitaryan to sign, but put a pound on him to stay at United so that if he did, they could at least be happy by having a pint with the proceeds.'

And SkyBet's traders also need to be keeping half an eye on their competitors too, as their rivals have a physical advantage over this team anchored to a third-floor office in Leeds. 'If William Hill or Paddy Power started cutting a player, we need to be aware they've done that. We don't have any retail presence. They've got shops in north London, so if a load of people in a branch near Tottenham's training ground start backing Lucas Moura and they then start cutting the price, we need to be mindful of that. We're not just going to move because they've moved, but it's another factor that builds up the picture of where we should be.'

The successful trader not only has to be a sharp-witted detective, but they also need to have eyes in every direction in order to pay sufficient attention to the multiple screens before them. 'Sky Sports News should be on one TV screen, Tweetdeck with lots of different journalists should be on another. But if the computers suddenly blew up on the desk and only one screen survived, you'd want it to be the bet monitors – just to see what's going on. You almost accept that if Sky say a transfer is done and the yellow bar says "completed", one or two bets will be laid by customers who are a little bit quicker than us to react. That happens. But what we can't do is lay twenty or thirty or fifty bets. But we've learnt enough from the past that "done deals" aren't always done.'

These bet monitors, the constantly updating screens showing as-it-happens betting activity, are the sacred scrolls, the holy texts that demand the greatest level of worship and scrutiny. For within them, the gospel truth can be found – albeit a truth defined by the wave of trigger-happy customers whose boot-filling progress needs to be swiftly nipped in the bud.

Out on the trading floor, Zach Amin is that eagle-eyed trader. As football risk manager, he's sharply attuned to sudden bursts of activity. With four screens in front of him, his eyes dart between each one. And if the system flags up a bet that requires deeper scrutiny (one of the alerts is his computer making the sound of a mooing cow), Amin will examine the bets placed so far on that particular player and look for discernible patterns, whether these be in the evolution of this particular transfer story or in the betting histories of particular punters. He'll also look to see what's being said on social media about this player, along with a quick consideration of how credible the source is.

Close scrutiny is required so that nothing significant is missed. This is not a charitable enterprise. As much as Andy insists it's an entertainment business, the book always has to balance. The bottom line of a trader's day is to protect the bottom line of the business. Four years into his time on the SkyBet trading floor, Amin's brain now works instinctively and instantly, effortlessly calculating 'to stay' odds that act as the counterweight to the 'to move' prices. His economics degree has provided him with a full and unswerving appreciation of how markets move and behave. An A level in maths allows those speedy calculations.

A bet on Islam Slimani leaving Leicester to go to Beşiktaş has just been flagged up for further scrutiny. 'There's little-to-no information to go on here,' he explains, going into detective mode. 'It's just a twenty-pound bet. These odds have been as short as four to one, but have been pushed back out. And Slimani played last night against Fleetwood, which would suggest he was less likely to leave.'

Nonetheless, Amin trims the odds on the Algerian leaving for Beşiktaş from 20/1 to 14/1, balancing the book by extending what's being offered on him joining another club. Over the course of the previous week, only 50p has been taken on him moving to Watford, so those odds get lengthened from 12/1 to 16/1. A few seconds later, Sky Sports News announces that 'Beşiktaş are interested in Leicester City striker Islam Slimani.' Amin is quick to respond. 'That would justify a bigger move then. We've not really taken any business on him going to Newcastle, so let's push them out.'

Amin continues to reduce the odds on a Slimani move to Beşiktaş, this time down to 8/1. In the process, he extends the price on the striker heading north to Newcastle, a move that's seen little business bet-wise over the previous two weeks. The relative silence is presumably a response (or non-response) to the ongoing confusion over the extent of Rafa Benitez's transfer budget.

The odds on Slimani staying at the King Power Stadium are then increased; again, only a few bets have been taken on this to date. Altering Slimani's 'to stay' odds from 5/1-on to 3/1-on allows Amin to further reduce the Beşiktaş odds down to 6/1. Three minutes ago, this was a 20/1 bet. The odds are now less than a third of what was originally being offered.

Amin justifies the cuts based both on the Sky Sports News story and on the fact that no significant bets have been taken over the past five days on any other outcome for Slimani in this window. 'The weight of the money is coming down on Beşiktaş at the minute.' More bets are placed on the move to Turkey. The odds continue to tumble. 3/1 now.

The accelerating activity – with punters presumably interpreting the confluence of breaking news and slashed odds as a deal with a strong chance of progressing – is irrespective of the fact that Amin has taken this action in reaction to what the market itself was doing. It's not down to any intelligence he's been privy to. 'That phone isn't a direct line to Jim White at Sky Sports News.'

Furthermore, the reported story only said Beşiktaş 'are interested in', not 'are having talks with'. It's a fragile house of cards, often with little or no foundation. The basis of the story might even be no more sophisticated than someone sat at home in their pyjamas, entertaining themselves on Twitter. If Beşiktaş are in need of a striker and Slimani isn't getting much first-team football at Leicester, the crude equation drawn up in the mind of the rumour-monger gets legitimised by appearing on social media – even if it's an equation where two and two are unlikely to make four.

Within the space of ten minutes, Slimani to Beşiktaş has gone from 20/1 to 3/1 based on very little firm intelligence; this huge reduction only fuels the activity more. It's circular and self-fulfilling. From this office block in Leeds, and without any tangible intelligence on what's actually occurring, the agenda is being changed. The snowball gathers both size and momentum, when it was barely a snowflake in the first place.

The previous week, the odds on Antoine Griezmann swapping Atlético Madrid for Liverpool were reduced spectacularly and swiftly – from 33/1 to 7/2 – when there was a flurry of bets and a run of money. 'It wasn't because we knew he was going to go. It was just the weight of money being put on. We can't just sit on that and accumulate huge amounts of liability. It would be bad bookmaking practice. We reacted purely down to the business we've seen. We had a few smaller bets the following day but since then it's fizzled out and he's back to 16/1. Often we'll see a flurry of money and the selection's odds go really short. But then the next day there's nothing. The story's out of the news.

'All you need for a run of money is a couple of whispers from a few dodgy Twitter accounts. We've seen false information put up by somebody as a bit of a wind-up and then Sky have picked up on it and it blows up on Twitter for about a day. It does happen.' Amin notes that one of those who've made a bet is 'a very prominent transfer punter, so he's probably got Tweetdeck set up and is following reputable feeds for any snippet of information.'

'We use some customers as marks. There's one customer who's very, very strong on his Chelsea business. If he comes on and backs something Chelsea-related, we're happy to use it as a pretty significant marker and completely carve the price up.' There are a lot of W's against this customer's name; W means 'win'. In the past, he's backed N'Golo Kanté to go to Chelsea, Nathan Aké to leave Stamford Bridge for Bournemouth, and José Mourinho to be unveiled as the next Man Utd manager. 'He certainly knows people in certain positions to get that information. He has a value to us. He's making money off us but he's saving us money at the same time.' This particular punter has effectively taken the twin roles of both scout and research assistant. He probably remains totally oblivious.

There are the more official soothsayers, too. 'As a Liverpool fan, if I see information on Twitter, the only people I'll really pay attention to are a handful of journalists who I know have information. Like James Pearce who works for the *Liverpool Echo*, or Paul Joyce from *The Times* or Chris Bascombe from the *Telegraph*. I really pay attention to their information and I'm then more aggressive with the price cuts. You see murmurs from other people who are less reputable. But really it's the money that dictates what you'll do with the market.'

The flurry of activity around Slimani aside, this morning – halfway through the window – remains relatively quiet. It's certainly in direct contrast to deadline day when the seven-strong football trading team is pulled in all directions. 'It just goes absolutely crazy. We have no idea what's going on behind the scenes. Moussa Sissoko is a good example from a couple of transfer windows ago. He was going to Everton, then he was going to Tottenham. Then he was going to Everton, then he was on a chopper to Tottenham. It was an absolute nightmare. Is he staying? Is he going? We didn't have a clue.'

'It's all hands to the pump on deadline day,' agrees Andy Wright. 'The scrollers just go crazy. It's business, business, business. And if it looks like it's going to be relatively flat transfer-wise, we'll offer things like 'Which clubs have signed the most players?' or 'How many deals will be confirmed on Sky Sports News between ten o'clock and midnight?'. These things help to keep the excitement ticking over.'

On the final day of the window, the all-seeing-eyes of the traders have to be even more focused. 'Where it's different for the desk itself on deadline day is the sheer weight of business. This makes it a little harder to see signal and noise. You could suddenly have twenty twenty-five-pound bets on Sanchez going to United and not have the time to digest them as we'd normally do. "Who's putting the bets on? Are they someone we should respect? Have they got some information?" If the bets are flooding in, though, we haven't got time to have a dig around. There's a bet coming in every two or three seconds. But it's fascinating to watch.'

Quiet day or not, this morning has been fascinating to watch, too. I take one last glance at the Slimani book. With still no more bets placed on Watford or Newcastle being the next destination in his career, Zach Amin has dropped the Beşiktaş odds still further. The player is now 7/4 to be heading out east. Going by the numbers alone, and the swiftness with which the situation has been redrawn, the casual observer wouldn't be blamed for believing that Slimani's destiny has been signed, sealed and almost delivered.

In the end, though, like the vast majority of rumours, the Beşiktaş link vanished into dust. Of course, it was never much more than that. Rather than the Turkish capital, Islam Slimani confounded today's odds. He chose to pack his bags for St James's Park instead.

* * *

In the eighties Cold War movie *WarGames*, a teenager, sat at his computer in his bedroom in Seattle, poses as an artificial intelligence researcher in order to have a little fun. Having inadvertently hacked into a high-level government computer system, he starts to play a game called Global Thermonuclear War, not realising that doing so meant he was in danger of triggering an actual conflict between the US and the USSR.

Thirty years later, a teenager, sat at his computer in his bedroom in High Barnet, poses as a football journalist in order to have a little fun. He didn't need an intricate knowledge of computer programming to do so; he was a child of the social media age. And he wasn't in danger of accidentally starting World War III. His ambitions were a little more modest.

As a sixteen-year-old schoolboy, Sam Gardiner was frustrated about how his youth seemed to disqualify him from respect from the adult world. A died-in-the-wool Arsenal fan, he became exasperated that his opinion on the club – on tactics, player selection, recruitment – counted for nothing, either in the stand at the Emirates or within the Gunners-supporting online community. 'I went to most of the home games and quite a few of the away games. I engaged with my friends over Arsenal, but I wanted to voice my opinions in a broader environment. So I'd get involved in conversations with Arsenal fans. The fans who'd gained popularity would be the ones who'd say, "I've been going to Arsenal for fifty years." They had this cloak of authority due to their seniority. They'd tell me that, as they were going to Arsenal well before I was born, my opinion was invalid.'

Gardiner had a plan. From the family home in north London, and having looked into the legalities, he set up a fake Twitter account. He invented an alter ego whom he'd pose as online: he was now Dominic Jones, a former football scout who wrote for *Goal!* magazine. Gardiner began posting identical observations from both his personal account and that of the fictional Jones. His intention was to prove a point: that, as a sixteen-year-old, his analysis of football wasn't being taken as seriously, and regarded as being as valid, as those of an industry insider. 'I was trying to defy the stereotype of sixteen-year-olds having zero knowledge or articulation about football. I sought to establish a moral imperative that one should listen to someone for their opinions, not their age.'

Pricking that balloon of pomposity was the over-riding objective, the principal principle. It wasn't about having a little mischievous sport by delivering outlandish opinions and gaining follower numbers by laying traps lined with tasty-looking clickbait. In his bedroom, he was deconstructing the methods of, and the authority invested in, respected reporters. 'As a kid, you get told to respect your elders. But that assumes that age equates to wisdom, and it's an assumption that often isn't true. I was a different kid and I always saw the world in a different way.'

His cover was blown when a genuine *Goal!* writer challenged his credentials. But Gardiner didn't panic. He simply slipped out of view and set up another Twitter account. This time, having downloaded a portrait of a businessman found on the thirteenth page of Google Images and uploaded it as his alter ego's avatar, Dominic Jones had morphed into Samuel Rhodes, a fictional freelance football writer for the *Telegraph* and the *Financial*

Times. He had covered his tracks and was again open for business.

What happened next vindicated Gardiner's original thinking. As the Samuel Rhodes Twitter account gained followers at a rate of knots, his personal feed was becalmed. 'The difference in engagement was quite remarkable. In the space of about nine or ten months, the journalist account had reached 30,000 followers, while the sixteen-year-old's account stayed on 200 followers. The same tweets would get 2,000 retweets and two retweets. On the sixteen-year-old's account, the response was, "I've been going to Arsenal longer than you've been alive." But on the journalist's account, his words were followed religiously.'

In order to sound like a credible broadsheet sportswriter, Gardiner liberally dotted crumbs of transfer talk among his wider opinions; 'they validated my appearance as a journalist'. He was gaining a reputation as a pretty dependable source of transfer stories, and Premier League players began to follow him on Twitter. And his reputation was built because he proved rather adept at second-guessing the transfer market.

'No one's an expert in the market, but I was somewhat good at being able to predict it. It is pretty formulaic. Certain clubs were always looking for certain types of players, like Chelsea always looking for the next Drogba. Arsène Wenger had a very predictable recruitment philosophy. He neglected the positions which they needed to address the most – such as a combative defensive midfielder and an experienced centre-back – and went for creative playmakers instead. It was pretty easy to put two and two together and say, "Arsenal are going to go for this guy." There are always six or seven players they'd been linked with and they were almost certain to get one or two.

'I just saw the raw facets of the transfer window as something that was very easy to interpret. I could see it, I could understand it and I could predict it, which gave credibility to my tweets and my predictions. I understood the transfer market in a holistic perspective – who was going for who, how they were going to get him – rather than simply wanting to believe transfers would happen. Most people want to believe and they convince themselves, but you have to detach yourself to understand the actual elements behind a transfer.

'Every fan thinks "I'd definitely go for this player" or "I would one hundred per cent spend money on this guy", but the number of factors which influence a transfer is infinite. For instance, I can't quantify how much a player likes to be in a sunny country and therefore would choose to play in Spain, but that's a factor. Another is whether a player's kids have just started school and therefore will stay put and sign a new contract. It's very easy for a fan to simply say, "Yeah, I'd get him." You need to understand the process.'

Even when the rumours weren't made flesh, Gardiner's instinct for matching club and player got him – or, at least, Samuel Rhodes – noticed. His prediction that Mo Salah was on his way to Anfield, made a full five years before the Egyptian did actually relocate to Liverpool, was picked up right across the internet, most notably by Al Jazeera. The story went global, even though the source was merely the imagination of a schoolboy.

'It wasn't a constant machine of fake news, but reliable journalists and news outlets would quote me. Twitter accounts dedicated to transfers would quote the *Telegraph* or whoever I was supposedly working for without even Googling whether I existed or not. All you had to do was Google 'Samuel Rhodes journalist'. It was literally that simple. But the transfer window is a feeding frenzy. Everyone feeds off everyone else's tweets and opinions, and opinion is disguised as fact.

'You can convince yourself about almost any transfer, within limits – not "Messi to Barnet", obviously. You see a club linked to a player and you think, "That makes sense. I believe it. He'd fit in well with this manager." I don't know whether football fanhood exists because of our intrinsic tribal nature but, as football fans, we're obsessed and highly supportive of our team. If they lose, we're upset. If they win, we're happy. And this unexplainable passion will lead you to convince yourself of various things, including transfers that might happen. It's fundamental, basic hope. What is support about? It's about positive emotions, such as hope and jubilation. And you want to share that among fellow tribe members, and then it spirals out of control.'

Plenty of Gardiner's stories didn't pan out how he'd suggested they would, but he enjoyed a not-dissimilar strike-rate to some life-hardened journalists who were paid handsomely to come up with daily stories to feed the insatiable rumour beast. One of his big successes was a tweet announcing that Roberto di Matteo would be sacked as Chelsea boss the following day. While the conditions for the Italian's removal were apparent ('It was a clear formula. Abramovich sacks a lot of managers and never really had confidence in di Matteo'), Gardiner lucked out with the exact timing. Cue much credibility and many new followers.

He became quite brazen in his posts, suggesting that he'd had personal one-to-ones with players and managers, when in fact he'd been sitting in double geography. Tweeting as Samuel Rhodes, his tweets would offer snippets of conversations his fictional alter ego had supposedly had with high-profile football people. One suggested a private assignation with José Mourinho.

All the time, though, he wasn't employing the techniques and diligence of a trained journalist. He obviously didn't have a list of reliable contacts within the industry. He didn't need to; his main source was his imagination. But real journalism did ultimately catch up with him. 'I was planning to finish the job and reveal the story and the imperative. I set myself a target of a hundred thousand followers before I did so, which I would have probably got to in another year. But it got shut down. The *Telegraph* said, "He doesn't write for us. He doesn't represent us." And at that point, I'd got so big that I couldn't swap identities again.'

But Gardiner had made his point, to call out the hypocrisy of the rumour-mongering around the transfer window, what Sir Alex Ferguson calls the 'farce of half-truths'. And, over the course of a handful of media interviews, the teenage hoaxer, the faceless speculator, made himself visible.

This visibility bore fruit. Now in his early twenties, he works as part of the team behind the football app Krowd9. He was headhunted after the man who would become his boss read about his adventures in the press. There are definite shared objectives between Gardiner's bedroom tweeting and his employer's business. 'We're providing a platform for fans to banter and articulate their opinions. We're trying to incite the flow of conversation about football.' He's a man still on largely the same mission: elevating the opinions of normal football fans, while showing their inherent value.

Gardiner – his teenage precociousness having transferred into easy self-confidence as an adult – feels no shame about his morally suspect teenage activities. 'I don't regret the idea of doing a transfer rumour. But the one regret I have is that people may have bet on it, that they may have lost money based on a fake rumour – although betting on transfers was much less common when I did it. Ironically, I did tend to get plenty of rumours right, so maybe I did make money for some people.'

Ultimately, he feels vindicated about his actions – even if he got busted for it before he could enact his great reveal. No one died. No fraud was committed. 'There wasn't a downside to it,' he shrugs. 'It was nothing illegal.' Gardiner might also argue that he was merely feeding a hungry audience, that he was simply supplying a demand. If punters were too blinkered to question the veracity of what was being put in front of them, to do anything other than blindly believe, that was their choice.

And if this hunger did render the end user unable to sift fact from fiction, it proved that the appetite for transfer titbits – irrespective of the source's credibility – was nothing short of ravenous.

CHAPTER TWO

SCOUTS' HONOUR

'If I were to advertise my job, there'd be a queue from Land's End to John o'Groats'

– Alfie Apps

Scouts are the espionage kings of football. While they're available and accessible when needing to answer to the beck and call of clubs and ambitious parents alike, the cut-throat and competitive nature of their work also requires the highest level of discretion and possible subterfuge. Their methods need to be invisible, leaving no footprints behind, no trace of tracks that offer a scent to their bitter rivals.

For someone with such an impressive track record for unearthing future diamonds, those uncut gems that still carry a little dirt, Alfie Apps is astonishingly invisible. This is the man who uncovered the likes of successful future pros like Gareth Barry, Jlloyd Samuel and Liam Ridgewell, the man who brought Thomas Hitzelberger and Andreas Christensen to English football. But he's also someone who flies at speed under the radar, retaining his mystery. A Google search for a picture of him will draw a complete blank.

Today, though, the scout has come in from the cold.

Being available on a Sunday lunchtime in January represents something of a rarity for Apps. Now working exclusively with players in the Spanish leagues, he's abroad every weekend during the season. Every weekend bar this one, that is. While he relaxes with a bowl of tom yum soup in a Thai restaurant on a Brighton back street, Spain is currently celebrating Three Kings Day, the time at which patient Spanish children finally get to excitedly open their Christmas presents. Nursing the tail-end of a bout of flu, Apps has opted to stay in East Sussex for the weekend.

He can't be accused of not putting the effort in, of not racking up the air miles. He holds his phone up to me and scrolls through dozens and dozens of airline reservations and receipts. In the last 365 days, Apps has boarded an astonishing 128 flights. You don't need to be a mathematician to calculate that that's the equivalent of one every three days.

Employed over the years by Aston Villa, West Ham and Chelsea, Apps originally entered the scouting trade by accident, by the back door. Once upon a time, while on holiday, he bumped into the former Villa striker Gary Shaw, a man whose goals propelled the club to the First Division title and the European Cup in the early eighties. A friendship ensued. Several years later, Shaw invited Apps to a game at Villa Park. It was the famous 3–1 win over Manchester United, the 1995 match that led Alan Hansen to offer his infamous sneer at Alex Ferguson's youthful line-up: 'You can't win anything with kids.'

After the game, Shaw's old strike partner Peter Withe, by then chief scout at Villa Park, had a proposal for Apps.

'He said to me, "Alfie, you can work down south for me if you want. But I'm not paying you." So I started at the bottom level. I didn't earn a penny. No mileage. No nothing. At the time, I was a property developer, so scouting was just a hobby.

'But I became quite successful. I got three or four decent players, and then I got three or four top players. Gareth Barry was mine, Jlloyd Samuel was mine, Thomas Hitzelberger was mine, Liam Ridgewell was mine. I also took players like Jerome Thomas and Gary O'Neil to Villa, who they didn't sign.

'So I moved up the ladder. I stayed part-time because I was still doing property development, but a few years later I left and went to West Ham for a year. I didn't enjoy it there. Villa came back in for me and I became the full-time European scout for their academy. I was there for four years. Then I got headhunted by Chelsea six years ago to be European scout for both the academy and the first team, covering Holland, Germany and Belgium. I stayed for roughly another four years.'

We meet four days after Chelsea have made their first signing of the recently opened transfer window, the United States winger Christian Pulisic, a £58m capture from Borussia Dortmund and thus the second-most expensive outfield player in the club's history. Several days of inquest later, many continue to question the reasoning behind the deal for a player who, albeit still only twenty, has found his performances in the Bundesliga plateauing of late. While Pulisic was putting his pen to a five-and-a-half-year contract, Bayern Munich were rapping loudly on Chelsea's door with a succession of bids for another winger, the Englishman Callum Hudson-Odoi. Munich's initial offer was reportedly to be in the region of £30m, a sizeable amount for the then largely untried eighteen-year-old. The Germans were presumably emboldened by the knowledge that, with the arrival of the American at Stamford Bridge, the Blues now had a surplus of wide players.

While the amount offered for Hudson-Odoi was half of that coughed up for Pulisic, he was far from half the player. Indeed, many thought that the Englishman offered the greater range of creativity of the two. Cue another potential academy departure, indirectly pointed towards the exit door by the impatient regime occupying the club's upper floors. There was no indication that Pulisic could do anything that Hudson-Odoi couldn't – and he was quite possibly capable of less. One thing Pulisic could achieve, though, was to turn many Americans into overnight Chelsea fans – overnight Chelsea fans who believed that the purchase of a top-dollar, box-fresh replica shirt was the first and best way to confirm their affiliation to their new denomination.

A natural conclusion to draw from this episode – and from plenty of others involving Chelsea's academy gradu-ates – would be that there must be an ongoing, unsolvable tension at the club between those running the academy and those charged with bringing in high-price, established stars from overseas, the presence of which would fracture, if not obliterate, home-grown dreams. Apps shakes his head. 'No, Chelsea just wanted the best players and that was it. If there was a better foreign player than an English player, they wanted him. The frustrating thing with the academy was that they didn't get the players through. They did all the hard work but weren't getting them through. And to this day they're not.'

When he swapped Villa Park to Stamford Bridge, Apps made an immediate mark with a certain young defender from Denmark. 'Andreas Christensen was one of mine. I found him at fourteen. That was about the time I was changing clubs and I actually took him to Villa first. Villa could have had him but they took too long to decide. I watched him playing in an under-fifteen tournament in Holland, an annual tournament called the Marveld. I noticed him there and then, a few weeks later, I watched him in Denmark with a guy called David Wilson, who still works for Chelsea but was with me at Villa at the time. "Just go and watch him, will you?" He came back to me. "Alfie, he's a Rolls Royce. The only thing is his dad is the goalkeeping coach at the club he's at." But it wasn't tricky at all. The Scandinavians always want to come to England.

'So we got him across to Villa with the permission of his club, Brøndy. He came across three times and on the first occasion, his dad said, "Where do I sign?" The brand-new training ground was fantastic. Christensen loved it. He didn't realise how good he was then. Then the next year he found out how good. Virtually the whole of England were breaking records trying to sign him.

'When I first went to Chelsea, I had to put together a list of players that I'd bring to the club. Christensen was one of them. Charly Musonda was another. Marc Albrighton was on that list too. As soon as I joined the club, I said, "Here's Christensen's number." He was signed within six months. Chelsea won the race financially. He didn't have an agent, but his dad was very shrewd.' A pause. 'To say the least.'

To suggest that the more successful scouts are well organised would be a crude understatement. Their processes and procedures need to be unbreachable, their net tightly drawn. Nothing can slip through. No one can get away.

'When I was at Chelsea, I watched every player in every team in the Bundesliga on video. Video scouting is massive now. On top of travelling, scouts are doing three or four video matches every week and doing the reports on top. The days of going to a game and ringing up to say, "Yeah, he's a good player" are gone. Now it's a case of writing full reports. And when you're at home, you're writing reports from the telly. It's a full-on, full-time job.

'I was at Chelsea at the time of the *Moneyball* book. That changed scouting as we knew it. Before then, it was a case of writing things down on bits of paper which would then get filed in a typical filing system. *Moneyball* changed everything about stats, but unfortunately it went too far to that side. Now it's somewhere in the middle. Some clubs, like Fulham or Brentford, are more on the stats. They might have six or seven interns doing all the stats on every player. Other clubs want to use the eye – but they still use stats to a certain extent. That for me is the perfect set-up.'

To some observers, the battle between old-fashioned scouting and new-era analytics is a fundamental struggle of art versus science. It can also be seen as a generational one.

'There are a lot of interns at every club now who, because they're good with numbers, think they're instant scouts at twenty-two or twenty-three. But it doesn't work like that.

'Stats can tell you how far and how fast a player has run, but they can't say whether a player had thrown in the towel or whether he'd fallen out with another player on the pitch or whether he was ill. There are lots of variables that stats don't cover. Stats work more with first-team players than they do with kids up to the age of nineteen or so. There's physical development to factor in. If you've got a kid who's five foot nothing, the figures on him are going to be terrible. But in three years' time, when he's grown to six foot four, his figures are going to be great. But in that time, if you go by the stats alone, he'd have been got rid of because he's not good enough.

'When you've got a young player coming out of the youth system, you don't know how he's going to react in front of the crowds, whether he's going to freeze. You're not going to see the best of him for a few years, so you need that "eye" element. And that's where the value is. The value is finding those young ones at seventeen or eighteen, who are on the cusp of getting into the first team. They're the ones you want. They're the ones you've got to find.

'We say "jam tomorrow". You don't want the jam today. You've got to leave a bit of fat on it. They're the ones you want – the ones who are going to grow. They've got the technical ability and the awareness. Awareness is everything. Someone who looks over their shoulder fifty or a hundred times a game. You watch Iniesta. He looks over his shoulder every four or five seconds. Why? So he knows what's around him. He knows where the ball's going before he's even got it.

'And I'll look for hairs on their legs. If they've got hairs on their legs, it means they've reached puberty. It means they're developed. And if they're developed at thirteen or fourteen, they ain't growing no more. It's silly little things like that. Not many scouts look for these.

'Now, at a lot of the big clubs, scouts are only required to do reports. You're just a report writer. Do the report, put it in. Although you're giving an opinion, it's all about the number, the total score given to a player. If they're looking at a left-back, they'll probably want twenty or thirty reports on him and they'll give him a score each time. At Chelsea, it's between one and four. An average score that's more than 2.75 means he's a decent player. If, over twenty or thirty games, if he's in the threes, that means he's a very good player. He's a target.

'There's a guy in Spain, and I won't tell you the club, who does fifteen hundred reports a month. *Fifteen hundred.* But the art of being a scout isn't doing reports. The art of being a scout is two things. One: standing on the side of a pitch, listening, getting information. Two: having a good eye and seeing the physical development and technical ability of a player. Liam Ridgewell's a good example. I first saw him play for Kent at under-fourteen level. I was stood next to these two guys.

'"Oh, I like him."

'"That's my son."

'"Got any brothers?"

'"Yeah."

"'Where?'"

"'Standing next to you.'"

"'Oh, right. You've answered my question then. He's going to grow ... '"

Apps is no longer aligned to one particular club. He now works for the Wasserman Media Group, one of the world's largest sports agencies, scouting players in Spain for them to represent and to offer to clubs. 'I'm on the opposite side of the fence now. And I prefer it. There's no politics.

'My job now is to find players for English teams and Spanish teams. Clubs come to me. I've had Man United on the phone this morning, ringing me for players. You see, clubs can't cover Spain in the way we can. We've got eleven full-time guys working for us out there, whereas a club might have just one guy covering Spain. We've got a database of seventeen hundred to eighteen hundred players in Spain, from the age of twelve up to eighteen, and then another database of first-team players above that.'

Apps holds up his phone again. This time he's not showing me innumerable flight reservations. His phone is currently displaying the database his team have put together of players from a single Spanish club picked at random. It's Celta de Vigo. His finger keeps scrolling down the screen. The information keeps flowing. 'There's six pages of that,' he says. 'And that's for every club.' His finger stops scrolling and investigates the player shown – the left-back, David Junca Reñé. 'Hmmm, he hasn't had many reports on him, so he can't be all that good ...

'But there's lots of value in Spain in the second tier. There isn't the money in Spain that there is in England.

A lot of them won't even be on the same money as those in League One. And they're not coached as much as in England. It's more about individual flair, so when you do get a gem, you get a real gem. A lot of Spanish players couldn't have developed in England. Take David Silva at Man City. He couldn't have developed in England. Too small.'

To make the endeavour work, Apps and his team need to create a conveyor belt that will deliver an endless stream of Spanish talent over their threshold. But there's an obstacle to this; Spanish players are very loyal to their agents and rarely defect. To build their portfolio, WMG need to find players and take them under their wing at a young age. Fortunately, that's exactly how and where Apps initially made his mark.

'A lot of clubs are coming to us saying, "We need a right-back" or "We need a striker – what have you got?" Because they know I've got a good reputation for finding players, they trust my judgement. And I won't give them a bad player. I won't do it. I'd rather say that I haven't got one.'

Like everyone I talk to, regardless of their role within the transfer process, Apps isn't happy with the status quo and keenly offers his alternative. 'I don't believe in the transfer window. If you need a player, you should be able to just go out and buy him whenever. The transfer window creates both a rush at the wrong time and artificially high prices. But no one's ever come up with my idea. This is it. A Premier League club should be able to buy players from the Championship and below throughout the year.

A Championship club should be able to buy players from League One and below throughout the year. A League One club should be able to buy players from League Two and below throughout the year. And so on. That would put money back into the system, wouldn't it?'

His proposal shows that, while working within the here and now, Apps' gaze is often to the far horizon. He thinks strategically, which puts him in the best position to forecast the changing landscape. 'Historically, the best players in the world come from deprived areas. End of. So you've got to go and find them. For me, the emerging countries in the next few years will be Germany and the Scandinavian countries. Why? Refugees. They've got nothing, so what do they do? They go and play football in the street.'

While showing that instinct to second-guess the direction of the market, Apps no longer has to play the same game of espionage that he once did. The sense of competition is less now for him. His job is to uncover the best players for WMG and, once they become WMG clients, attract the attention of those scouts among whom he used to work. 'Once I've got the player,' he reasons, 'I want them all to know about him.'

Despite the intense competition between scouts – a landscape where duplicitousness and double-dealing aren't uncommon – there is a sense of brethren and fellowship among their number. 'When I first started years ago, in the four corners of a pitch you'd have West Ham over here, Man United over there, Chelsea over here and Villa over there. All of them would be saying, "Look at that prick over there. What's he doing? What's he saying?" With the advent of scouts travelling to Europe more often, you're watching the same games and staying in the same hotels. So you become close friends. Some of my best friends work for Man United, Liverpool, Man City, Chelsea, Arsenal ...'

But, fundamentally, the scout is a lonely hunter. 'I'm in a hotel on my own most of the time,' he sighs, 'but there's no substitute for covering the ground. The first thing a club will ask is, "Alfie, have you seen him?"

'If I was to advertise my job, there'd be a queue from Land's End to John o'Groats. Unquestionably. But it's hard work. Tremendously hard work. The knowledge has been accumulated over years and years. You can't give people that knowledge. Where to go. When to go. The contacts. The type of player the clubs want. You can't replace it. A lot of people think they can just turn up and do it, but they can't.

'This Wednesday, I'm flying to Alicante and driving to La Manga to watch Valencia versus Germany under-sixteens. On Thursday I drive back to Valencia where I've got meetings with players. On Friday, there are more meetings with players. On Saturday, off to Zaragoza for more meetings and watch a game. On Sunday, I'm watching Zaragoza play Malaga, then driving to Barcelona, which is a three-and-a-half-hour drive.

'I'll fly home on Monday morning, but I've got a meeting in London in the office in the afternoon and will finally get home late Monday night. I'm home for one day before I fly to Turkey where England and Spain under-sixteens are playing in a tournament. I'm there Thursday, Friday,

Saturday before flying home. Then it starts again the week after. That's hard work, that is. It's intense.'

A grin across the restaurant table. 'But it's not a job, is it?'

* * *

Among the endless parade of jewellers in London's Hatton Garden – the scene of heist and hijack over the years – a new, high-value commodity is now cherished and protected. This is the home turf of 21st Club, caretakers of this new asset. If its name conjures up a mental image of a mysterious cabal of shady, morally suspect characters, 21st Club's line of business is the polar opposite. Its employees are disseminators of information, intelligence and analysis – that is, information, intelligence and analysis exclusively pertaining to the business of football, in particular the transfer market. And their working ways are anything but mysterious and shady; they will happily share this commodity with any football club that calls upon their help.

In a cafe round the corner on Leather Lane, the eatery-heavy street that's now quietening down after the flurry of a weekday lunchtime, Omar Chaudhuri sits across a high wooden table. For the next hour, he will disseminate information, intelligence and analysis about 21st Club itself. As the organisation's head of football intelligence, he is charged with presenting new ways of thinking to a sport that doesn't necessarily welcome fresh insight. Just an hour in his company, though, can reboot the entire way you perceive the recruitment of footballers.

An economics graduate, Chaudhuri shunned the well-worn path his contemporaries were taking, along streets paved with gold that took them to the City where they'd soon be pocketing fat pay cheques. Instead, Chaudhuri focused on sport and began a blog where he 'railed against some of the myths you hear about. And I discovered you can use data to find new truths.'

His blog brought him to the attention of Prozone, the pioneering Leeds-based company who had been collating football data since the mid-to-late nineties. They swiftly hired him. 'They had analysts who provided support for clubs' basic data and video requests, but my job was to dig into the data in a way they hadn't really done before, despite them sitting on years and years of really valuable information. There was a fair tradition in football by this stage of people counting passes, tackles, shots and goals. A scout would go and see a player and like him, then the numbers would be used to support that view, cherry-picking the best stuff. But part of my job was to find new truths, as I had been doing on my blog.'

After a couple of years, Chaudhuri followed his boss, Blake Wooster, to London where he had set up 21st Club. The new company was offering something different to what the existing data providers had been supplying up until that point. 'Prozone was very much a performance-analysis firm, helping analysts and coaches with tactics, sport science, all that sort of stuff in terms of their game-to-game preparation. 21st Club is very much more focused on a strategic point of view. We predominantly work with boardrooms, sporting directors and owners, trying to help rationalise mid-to-long-term decision-making. So we're less involved in tactical analysis, and more about adding some long-term thinking to what's a very short-term sport.

'As head of football intelligence, I oversee the analysis side of the business. In all the work that we do with clubs, my role is to take all the smart stuff that our guys are doing in the office and try to make it applicable and easily communicated to clubs. Football doesn't have a great data heritage, so there's this gap between football and the data side. That's where I step in.'

Where a club's recruitment policy might have a possibly blurred outlook that's too close to its subject to focus properly, 21st Club pan out to take in a wider view that benefits from more context. 'Clubs can only scout a finite number of players,' says Chaudhuri, sounding not unlike Alfie Apps. 'They can only see so many players in a year. They can only watch them so many times. While that can give you a detailed view on a player, there might be thousands of players out there that you're missing. And that's what data allows you to do. If you know what correlates to success in transfers, then you can apply those factors to a much bigger pool of players. If, for instance, you know that the age of the player and how much they're playing and how much experience they have is important, then you can do a blanket search on a database, see who comes up and pull those players out.

'One of the challenges, though, is that there's so much data. Companies like Opta and Prozone have been collecting it for fifteen to twenty years now, and at an increasing level. Say you wanted to sign a player who'd been playing in La Liga for a couple of years, there'll be information available about every single match he's played, all the touches he's had, all the movements he's made. That's a lot of data to analyse. And you can't analyse it in isolation. You've got to analyse it in the context of all the other players. How is it affected by who he was playing against? How is it affected by who he was playing with?

'That takes a lot of skill and finding those people who can analyse that data is quite difficult. A lot of people with those skills are going to be attracted by big salaries in the City or in engineering or whatever. Football clubs aren't, at this point in time, paying the kind of salaries that will attract those kind of people into the game. So there's some tension there to an extent. Even though all clubs use data to a greater or lesser degree, there are vast differences in the quality of analysis that exists within the clubs. It's going to be some time before all clubs are up to speed with using that data.' And that's where 21st Club come in.

As willing as Chaudhuri is to explain the purpose and process underpinning the company, he declines the twin invitations to name which top-flight clubs they work with and the most high-profile player they've recommended to a club who then signed him. He does, though, explain that they have around a dozen Premier League clubs as clients, a similar number in the Championship, and more overseas.

Some of these clubs might simply be provided with off-the-shelf software that can help recruitment departments identify basic inefficiencies. For instance, a director of football may have been approached by an agent or scout about a certain player. Tapping that player's name into the software can illuminate what the key risks with that player might be, along with his estimated market value and salary expectation. For mid-level clubs, whose pockets are less than deep, the results can help to ensure that they're not spending too much of their precious transfer budget on just one player.

Other clubs might engage 21st Club's services more fully. 'We have retained relationships with clubs where they'll buy anywhere between five and fifteen days a month with us. Not all of that will be spent on recruitment, but recruitment decisions are some of the most important made in a club, so we will spend a fair bit of time on that. That's where we'll do some of the more bespoke work, really digging into what that club requires. For example, a club might ask us to do some research, perhaps to understand what type of strikers translate well to the Premier League or to the Championship. We'll go away, do our research and then present it. This might be to a scouts' meeting or to the chief exec or the head coach might even be involved.

'Other times, the work might be on an individual player basis. A club might say, "We've got these five players on our shortlist. Can you give us a second opinion on them through the data?" By and large, we try to make it as bespoke as we can. Every club's got a different circumstance, whether it's the size of the club, the type of staff they have, the coach they have, whether it's the owner's backing or not. All that type of stuff makes a difference as to how you approach a club.'

I ask Chaudhuri whether traditional scouting and data analytics are in innate opposition with each other, fundamentally different approaches that share little common ground. 'A lot of people see it as art vs science, but we don't see it like that at all. It's about science *complementing* the art. They aren't necessarily in conflict with each other. It's about providing the right tools to give the scouts: "This is where you should be looking and this is what you should be looking out for."' To Chaudhuri's eyes, one feeds the other.

Explaining the value of data, and 21st Club's particular use of it, might not be the easiest task in a sport known for its entrenched views and decades-old received wisdom. The upper tiers of football clubs are populated by hardy, weather-worn souls who might not be the most receptive when a bunch of young guns arrive, ready to subvert the thinking the older men have held all their careers. They can easily – voluntarily, possibly – be blinded by science and spreadsheets.

Inevitably, though, there will be kindred spirits within a club, progressive individuals who will have issued the initial invitation and who share some philosophical alignment with 21st Club. Those from more old-school footballing backgrounds are unlikely to be making that first call. And once Chaudhuri and his colleagues are through the front door, not everybody will be automatically on-side and open to persuasion.

'I've sat in a number of scouts' meetings and you often get quoted the outliers. For instance, clubs often tell us that the age that strikers peak is around twenty-seven or twenty-eight, but when you look at the data, it's actually between twenty-four and twenty-six. So clubs end up overpaying for older players and not recognising that they need to sign them a bit younger. I was in a meeting at a club once and the manager at the time said, "The research is all well and good, but everyone in this room will tell you that Michael Owen peaked at twenty-one and Teddy Sheringham carried on playing until he was forty." That's undeniably true, but if you want to play the odds, if you want to give yourself the best sporting chance, you don't look at the outlier. You look at what history tells you. If you go for the one in two thousand, you'll get one in two thousand.'

When working with a club on its recruitment, Chaudhuri will first determine what the size and strength of their squad needs to be. Most managers will plump for the full twenty-five-man squad – and twenty-five senior players at that. In the choppy waters of football management, such an approach represents an understandable insurance policy, maximising the insulation between a manager's ongoing employment and the issuing of a P45. Straightaway, though, this would sound alarm bells for Chaudhuri. A clear financial inefficiency has made itself known right from the off.

'The twentieth player within a Premier League squad tends to play less than ten per cent of the minutes, tops – the equivalent of three or four games a season. And one player – one eleventh of a team – across three or four games a season isn't going to have an enormous bearing on a club's final finishing position. So we try to encourage them to look within their academy. The risk of playing a young player isn't as big as what clubs think. When you look at results when clubs play young players, they don't do any worse. Sometimes they do better. You offer clubs that perspective because it's a more sustainable approach to squad-building. Understandably, there's a lot of pressure on head coaches. They've got a short time in the job and don't want to feel as though they're taking a risk, which young players can seem to be. But if you're a club and you're thinking about the future and sustainability, then you absolutely have to be looking inside first.'

Chaudhuri and his team would then look at the individual players. 'Sometimes our evaluation of the current squad will be different to the club's own, and there's where we can identify weaknesses and areas for improvement. Clubs are obviously watching their own players week in week out, but things can get missed. A classic stat that's evolved over the past five or six years is that of "expected goals". It's a metric that allows clubs to quantify whether their strikers are consistently getting into good-quality positions to score. Actually, if a striker is getting into good positions to score, it's a better predictor of how many goals he's going to score in the future than the goals he's actually scored. If a player's pinged five in from long distance, he's not necessarily going to do that in the long run, whereas someone who's got into the box and had the chances – even though he might have headed it wide or scuffed his shot – is probably going to do better long-term. So sometimes you get discrepancies like that, where clubs think they have a wasteful striker when actually he might just have been a bit unlucky in front of goal and his performance will improve over time anyway.'

Sometimes the clubs that 21st Club get invited into aren't the obvious ones, particularly overseas. 'Red Star Belgrade came to us last summer. That was a surprise. You don't often think of clubs out in Eastern Europe using data, because their budgets are so small. You need to be able to buy data and get people in who can analyse it. Clubs like that rely a lot on agents, but agents feed them a narrow view of the world. Data, on the other hand, should be an unbiased view on the players out there. Red Star came to us with a shortlist of attacking midfielders, but asked if we could provide another list of suggestions from our database of players they could look at. And they ended up signing one of the players we recommended. It's very satisfying when that happens.

'Even if a club doesn't end up signing a player based on our suggestions, it's nice that they acknowledge there's some value to be had by using data. We also work in the recruitment of head coaches. That's where you really do find value. Head coaches are very much on a merry-go-round and so suggesting ones who aren't on that merry-go-round is quite rewarding.'

In plenty of quarters, the commissioning of data analysis could be seen as a luxury, a plaything of the cash-rich clubs eternally dining out at football's top table. Chaudhuri is at pains to explain how the 21st Club database – which contains around 140,000 players and between 3,000 and 4,000 clubs – is of great use to Premier League club or Finnish third-division outfit alike.

'The right data can apply to anyone. In fact, data is generally of more benefit to a smaller club than to a Real Madrid or a Barcelona. There's actually a perverse inverse correlation. The more money you have, the smaller the pool of talent you can scout. If you're at the top end – if you're Barcelona or Real Madrid or Bayern Munich – there are probably only a few dozen players in world football who are actually going to improve your team. Yet you have all this money to analyse these players. As you go down the leagues, there are thousands and thousands and thousands of players who can improve your team, but you have a tiny amount of money to analyse these players. And this is where data can be powerful. If you cast your net out wide, data allows you to analyse a thousand players at your fingertips. Real Madrid or Barcelona can get ten of the best scouts in the world to watch one player every single week and get a real detailed view on him to decide if he's good enough or not. But this isn't possible for a Swindon or a Southend.

'Constraints can actually stimulate innovation. If you run out of money, you have to find new ways of signing players, right? So you give young players a go, a bit like Southampton did when they went into administration all those years ago. Or you try to find those inefficiencies in the market, you try to find where really cheap players are in new markets.'

There is, of course, an inherent difficulty when scouting overseas markets as opposed to a domestic one. How does a club gauge the level and quality of play in other countries relative to its own league?

'If I'm a Premier League club and I'm watching a game in the Netherlands, it's quite hard to determine if a player is playing quite well. It could be to do with the quality of the opposition, or the quality of his teammates. How does it translate to my league? You see this time and time again.'

Chaudhuri illustrates his point by using the example of The Netherlands. Over the years, the Eredivisie has supplied the Premier League with some really successful players, such as Luis Suárez swapping Ajax for Anfield. But there have also been some duds. Afonso Alves fits this bill, the archetypal big-money flop. Signed by Middlesbrough for an eight-figure fee on the back of his better-than-a-goal-a-game career at Heerenveen, the Brazilian striker failed to enjoy anything like the same impact made by his fellow South American Suárez in the red of Liverpool.

Comparing performances across different leagues is key to successfully evaluating a player's future success in another country. 'We do this in part by using what we called our World Super League, where we try to imagine all the teams in the world in one big league table, playing each other week in, week out. That gives us a sense of where Manchester United sit relative to Ajax, sit relative to Ipswich Town, sit relative to Vitesse and teams all over the world. And if you look at our World Super League and correlate that historically with transfers, you can see that when a Premier League team signs a player from a bottom-half Premier League-level team overseas, the players tend to do as well as players from bottom-half Premier League teams. That's an inefficiency that exists, because when you watch other leagues, it's very hard to determine that.'

Along with gauging the relative strengths of each league and its teams, inefficiencies can be reduced if a stream of talent emerges from a largely untapped – and thus value-for-money – market. 'A great example is France. The French leagues have become really popular places to sign players from for the Premier League in recent years, because of successes like N'Golo Kanté and Riyad Mahrez. That means that every club in the Premier League has a scout, or multiple scouts, out in France. That drives up demand, which drives up prices. Even though there are plenty of players in France good enough to play in the Premier League, you're going to pay a premium for them. So can you find other markets where players tend to cost less?

'Perhaps Premier League clubs have tended to undervalue a certain market. Maybe they've seen one or two players from there fail, so they think the five hundred or six hundred other players there must be rubbish too. Again, by using those team qualities, we can help identify targets. Yes, there might have been a couple of failures from a particular country, but actually, if you look at these three teams here, they're all Premier League mid-table quality and their best players are contributing huge amounts to their team and so could easily improve a Premier League side. Identifying those markets will then help allocate scouting resources, which will then help a club identify talent in more detail than other clubs.'

Chaudhuri and 21st Club acknowledge that, no matter how sharp the application of science, the human element dictates that player recruitment will always have its vagaries and unpredictability. It's not an exact science. But, as they say, it need not be a crapshoot, either.

The nature of football's restricted trading period, however, means that as the days go by, the guns are increasingly reached for in advance of the crapshoot. It's both inevitable and inexplicable – and it's where a club's inefficiencies are most conspicuous, most pronounced.

'Prices do go up as the window progresses,' confirms Chaudhuri, 'usually in the region of one or two per cent a week. This doesn't sound like much, but when you're talking about paying millions of pounds on transfer fees, that escalates quite quickly. You can certainly save by buying early rather than late. And if you can buy early and sell late, you're onto a winner.'

There are certainly optimum times for a club to cash in on an asset, points at which reactivity and opportunism artificially redefine the market. 'If a player scores a goal at a World Cup, the amount he will be sold for that summer goes up fifteen per cent. And that is totally nonsensical. One goal in a tournament that has nothing to do with club football should have absolutely no bearing on his ability to perform in your team. But clubs pay a ten-to-fifteen per cent premium on that.'

Such illogical human impulses ensure it's far from a pure science. There are plenty of other vagaries within the game that affect outcomes. 'People working in data always talk about sample size. Any random thing can happen in a match, so you need a greater volume of games. But football doesn't allow the kind of sample size that statisticians prefer. If a player has had an injury, you might only be evaluating them over fifteen or twenty games in a season. You have to evaluate everything in that context. Even though it's still a small sample size, you're still providing information and evidence that a club can base their decision on, rather than going, "He's had a great couple of games and he's bound to improve our team."'

Any degree of improved rationality has to benefit the game's recruitment philosophies, but the day-to-day, hour-by-hour pressures on managers often sees them reacting without the full weight of reason behind their decisions. The application of a little science – particularly at the mid-season point – would be welcome and beneficial, as Chaudhuri observes.

'I remember looking at spending during the January window, because that's when a lot of the panic arises. Clubs towards the bottom of the league table tend to spend big. I tried to quantify how much you would need to spend to improve in January. I found that in order to improve by 0.1 points per game over the remainder of the season – so effectively earn one or two more points over the second half of the season – you have to spend about thirty million pounds. To have a tiny improvement, it's *thirty million pounds*. That's because there's so much variation around that. Some teams have spent thirty million pounds and have got worse by three or four points, and some have got better by three or four points. So, on average, the actual increase is tiny.

'That's not to say you should be spending one hundred million, because there's such high uncertainty around that, but it just goes to show there are better ways of earning an extra 0.1 points per game. It could be doing smarter recruitment rather than just spending all that money and assuming that the price is associated with quality. But it's also about utilising data around opposition analysis, it's about sports science, it's about understanding about the quality in your own academy. There's a lot of work that can be done there and it comes at a fraction of the cost of a transfer fee and wages for that new signing.'

Again, though, the ever-tightening short-termism steering football, and the self-preservation guiding a manager's dealings, will all too often result in knee-jerk, panicked recruitment. It's human nature, after all. If something's not working, you strip out the deadwood and get some fresh timber in. If it is human nature, some clubs are resolute in working beyond it.

Chaudhuri cites Liverpool as the Premier League club that's operated most efficiently in the transfer market in recent seasons, historically buying early in the window and not succumbing to the temptation of an inflated, eleventh-hour signing. Southampton, too, have earned his respect, a club that hasn't overpaid on players, that's looked in under-exposed markets, and that have promoted from within by giving youth a chance in the first team.

The respect and regard in which Chaudhuri holds such clubs as Liverpool and Southampton suggests there must be frustration with others who don't employ such a reasoned recruitment strategy. It's not difficult to picture him – in the closing minutes of the deadline-day crapshoot as clubs' guns blaze in all directions – shedding his calm demeanour and hurling objects at the TV screen when the latest overpriced, panicked purchase is announced.

'There is an element of that. We'll have Sky Sports News on in the office on deadline day and will be thinking, "Football is crazy. In what other industry would you be behaving like that?" But the flipside is that, as long as clubs are doing that, there's an opportunity for smart clubs. And that's how we like to see it – an opportunity to win by spending far less than what's being spent and doing it in a far smarter way, so that clubs on a budget can achieve. We like an underdog in this country and if an underdog can be smart, it's quite an exciting story. There's probably less of this chaos in American sports. In the NBA and in Major League Baseball, all the teams have really sophisticated analysis now, so everyone really knows who the good players are through the combination of traditional and data scouting.'

The increasingly quiet deadline days suggests that reason and rationality are coming to bear much more on the market. Chaudhuri agrees. 'You're going to see that more business-like approach to things. German clubs historically haven't panic-bought either and if you look at the way those clubs are run, they take a much more corporate view. Sustainability is a boring word, but it's important. Clubs going out of business is no fun for anyone – and it certainly isn't for fans of that club. When I see mismanagement, it really annoys me. There's a better way of doing things. You can win without all that ridiculous way of going about it.'

If the science of data was ever at war with the art of scouting, the white flag of truce has been waved. The two approaches can co-exist; more so, they can operate as some kind of partnership. Neither is perfect, but each can improve the other.

'We often say recruitment is a fifty-fifty game,' concludes Chaudhuri. 'If you look at signings historically, by a couple of different measures, you tend to see that about fifty per cent of signings succeed and about fifty per cent of signings fail. So it's a little like a coin flip. But if you can give your-self a fifty-five or sixty per cent chance, you're saving yourself millions. And that's the perspective we take. No matter what level of data or smart scouting you do, nothing's going to make every single signing correct.

'But you can nudge the odds in your favour. You can do a bit of card-counting.'

CHAPTER THREE

BARGAIN BASEMENT

*'It's not the fear of the unknown. It's the excitement of
the unknown'*

– Alan Hardy

Richard Scudamore hadn't meant to make the room laugh. On 13 June 2012, the Premier League chief executive addressed the assembled media to reveal the new contracts for the right to televise live top-flight matches – how many games each broadcaster would be showing and how much they'd be paying for the privilege. When Scudamore announced the overall value of the new packages, he described it as 'a decent commercial increase'. That was underplaying it somewhat. The chuckles rippled across the room.

For that day was a hugely significant one for the balance sheets of current and future Premier League clubs, one that would for ever change each club's income and thus its spending power in the transfer window. The 'decent commercial increase' was instant proof that BT, the new player on the pitch, meant business. It wasn't so much dipping a toe into live football broadcasting as plunging both feet straight in. The new deals highlighted the financial commitment willingly undertaken by both BT and Sky, and were staggeringly more valuable than previously. The combined agreement was now worth £3bn over three seasons, a 70 per cent increase on the previous three-year deal. The league's twenty clubs would have been salivating at the windfall. Those just promoted from the Championship – QPR, Norwich and Swansea – must have believed they'd landed in wonderland. It didn't peak there. By 2018, the figure for live TV rights for the period 2019–2022 had swollen to £4.46bn.

The amount that a Premier League club receives from this overflowing pot of TV revenue reflects both their final league position and how often their matches appear live on TV. It's a payday for each and every Premier League club, regardless of their place in the table at season's end. West Brom know this. When they finished rock-bottom at the end of the 2017–18 season, the Baggies' hurt was softened to the tune of £94m (along with the awarding of additional parachute payments over subsequent seasons). The top earners – champions Manchester City – weren't exactly pleading poverty either, taking home just shy of £150m, an amount three times the GDP of the Polynesian island of Tuvalu.

A by-product of this sharp rise in income is that Premier League clubs no longer feel the pressure to make sure their transfer budgets tally and balance. Those days are over. Transfer-specific sustainability is now neither priority nor necessity. And UEFA's Financial Fair Play regulations, aimed at guaranteeing that clubs don't over-reach themselves by spending beyond their means, become less relevant when it comes to transfers – even when a pile of cash has been spent on new players – thanks to the TV money making the other side of a club's balance sheet look unnaturally plump and healthy. As the *Guardian*'s investigative football journalist David Conn adroitly indicates, 'the fees being paid now are eye-watering, the wages are unthinkable, the top agents' fees often payable to their bases in tax havens – difficult to accept, but most clubs are in fact living within their outsized means'.

This allows top-flight clubs to spend if not recklessly, then certainly with largely unchecked generosity. The quickest study of the figures for Premier League clubs' expenditure on, and income from, transfers for the 2018–19 season shows that just two made a surplus. The other eighteen were in the red when it came to recruitment. The worst culprits were Chelsea who had a net spend of £139.7m, followed by Liverpool's £129.3m. Surprisingly, Man City's net spend was just a little over £20m, a figure kept low by the sale of a number of fringe players for decent money. Both midfielder Brahim Diaz and goalkeeper Angus Gunn commanded eight-figure fees, despite making minimal first-team appearances. In fact, Gunn hadn't made any.

How the two clubs who did make a surplus had done so was easily explained. With the distraction and, more importantly, the expense of building a new stadium dominating thoughts and finances, Spurs didn't spend a single penny on transfer fees in either of that season's two windows. Watford were the other club without a deficit; their surplus of £19.57m was due to the sale of a single player – Richarlison to Everton for £35m. Without it, they'd have been comfortably in the red on their transfer budget too.

The numbers continue to boggle the deeper you drill down. A total of £1.49bn was spent by the twenty Premier League clubs across the 2018–19 season, with the average deficit on transfer activity being £50m per club. Or, rather, these numbers *should* boggle. But with all but the three relegated clubs receiving in excess of £100m from the Premier League the previous season, the spending doesn't look too rash or impetuous. Logical, in fact. Maybe even sensible. Speculate to accumulate. Speculate to stay in the league. Speculate to keep receiving that bumper pay-out.

That's the story of the Premier League, at least. To pretty much all other levels of the English game, this would be a wholly unheard tale, an alien landscape, a scene from another planet. Theirs is a different reality, one with its own perspectives, its own contexts.

On the first day of February 2018, a palpable sense of relief – euphoria, even – flavours the corridors of Meadow Lane, home ground of Notts County, the oldest club in the Football League and the current occupants of second place in League Two. There's an easy bonhomie among staff, and a spring in the collective step, suggesting that life is currently good on the north bank of the River Trent. The only measurable tension is between veteran right-back Nicky Hunt and the former Leeds and Manchester United striker Alan Smith, who are absorbed in an ultra-competitive game of table tennis across the corridor.

Hunt and Smith are not the only Premier League alumni around the place. The man who has guided County to the kind of lofty heights the club could only have dreamt of eight months earlier was a stalwart of the top flight for many years, stirring up things in midfield for Bolton, Newcastle and West Ham. For the uninitiated, the letters written in marker pen on the toe band of his flip-flops offer a big clue. They spell 'Kevin N'.

Kevin Nolan has brought a great deal of nous, knowledge and experience to Meadow Lane during the twelve months he's been in charge. And it hasn't just been his own. Early on in the job, he persuaded former Newcastle teammate Shola Ameobi to sign for these other Magpies. A few months later, his old Bolton pal Hunt had been enlisted to the cause. But cajoling those in the twilight of their careers to drop down the leagues to play for him is one thing. Recruiting the remainder of the squad on the kind of budget that the average Premier League player spends on haircuts and tattoos over a year is another. But Nolan seems to be managing it. He's just successfully negotiated his first full January transfer window as a manager. That's why relief is the over-riding emotion this afternoon. Deadline day was a successful, if slightly dramatic, one.

The experience of the previous twenty-four hours – in fact, of the previous thirty-one days – was in marked contrast to the way Nolan regarded the transfer window as a player. 'The window would open on January 1st and, because you have so many games coming up at that point in the season, you can't do as much as normal and so you'd sit on the sofa and put the transfer news on the TV. The yellow flash – "This player is moving", say Sky sources. All that sort of stuff. You'd sit there and be fascinated. And when you got to the final few days, you'd be glued to it once you'd finished training. I remember sitting there with the lads a few times at Newcastle, avidly watching everything go on. When I went to Newcastle in 2009, I was part of it. I was a deadline-day move. It was crazy. But now I'm on this side, it isn't half tiring.

'The amount of work that goes into signing just one player is unbelievable. That was a big surprise. I thought they just turned up. One player could take two minutes. I ring the club – "Yup, fine." I ring the player up. No problem. He's not got an agent. Next minute, he's coming through the door and it's done. Or, you ring up and it's, "Well, he might not be available. But speak to the lad." So you speak to the lad. Then you speak to the agent. Now you're trying to agree a contract with the agent. The club then say they want more money for him. They have all the demands and you've got to match them if you really want the player. Is this kid really worth spending fifty grand on? Is it right for us to do that? There are so many obstacles that can get in the way. The list goes on and on and on.

'Agents want to be paid, players want to get the money they want, and the club want to be happy with what they're giving. These are all things that our decision is based on. We can't afford to throw money away. We're a club trying to get as high as possible so that we can be sustainable. We don't want to be chucking money at it. We've got to do it the right way. We've been sensible. And we've got to remain being sensible and not get carried away with what we're doing.'

The intensity of the January window, with its in-built, mid-season panic that can destabilise even the least insecure manager, makes it a different beast to July and August.

'The summer window's not so bad,' says Nolan, propping his legs up on an adjacent chair. 'You can get plenty of deals done because it's open so long. It's more comfortable. You know exactly what your targets are. "This is the squad. This is who I want to keep. I'm looking for this, this, this and this. These are our main targets." You'll normally have your A, your B, your C and your D. This is your top target. If you can't get him, you go somewhere else. And if you can't get him, you go for him.

'But in the January window just gone, I've talked more about players who aren't at this club than I have about my own players. That's the most time-consuming and disappointing thing. You've got to juggle transfers and matches. That's not a complaint. That's just the way it's got to be. You've got to look at players, you've got to discuss them. You get a name from an agent. "What's the lad like, first and foremost? Is he a good lad? Does he want to work?" The majority of lads you get in are going to be good enough ability-wise, but it's about getting the right kind of person. We don't want bad eggs in the group.

'You've got to keep on the ball with everything, but not get distracted away from what you want. We've been quite good in that respect here. We knew exactly what we wanted and were prepared. We lost Ryan Yates in the window, which was a big blow for us, but we had people in mind who we wanted if he ended up leaving. And we got them in. You've got to prepare for that. Someone might come in with a bid that you can't refuse, especially at our level. If a million-pound bid comes in for one of our boys, very rarely are we going to be able to turn that down. But if we get someone in to replace him, it's going to be for a small fee. You're not going to be getting a million pounds back to spend. But other clubs know that we've just got a million pounds, so hold out for more. It's just a merry-go-round.

'It then gets down to the last couple of days and that's when everything starts going completely crazy. It might be because they've had a few bad results and they need to get three players in. So they get those players in and then there's the domino effect. So if a Championship club gets three players in, that affects League One and League Two. A player who might not have been available at the start of the window might now be available. So you ring up that club again. You revisit that player. You constantly revisit and revisit and revisit. A player might now be available on loan. Or perhaps a new manager's come in during the window and that player's dropped down the pecking order.'

Nolan and County had done some of their business early in this window but, coming into yesterday, two clear targets were still outstanding. One of them – a loan deal for the young Brighton defender Ben Hall – was straightforward and hitch-free. 'The agent wanted him to come here, the kid wanted to come here, and Brighton wanted him to go out on loan. This was the preferred destination, so everything connected.' Hall's paperwork was approved before midday, by which time the obligatory photos showing him holding up his new black-and-white-striped shirt were already being circulated. The other target – the Derby striker Mason Bennett – was somewhat more protracted, despite the two clubs only being separated by a fifteen-mile stretch of the A52. His loan move was approved only five minutes before the 11pm deadline.

'We were all sitting here just hoping. Mason was already over here – he'd signed his stuff and done his medical. So it would have been a big blow, a massive disaster, a big old kick in the whatsits if it didn't go through. But thankfully Derby made it possible.

Our chief executive nearly had a breakdown. But I was very, very confident that it was going to happen. They wanted it to happen and wanted Mason to have the best opportunity to flourish in the next four or five months.

'He's very highly regarded at Derby and they didn't want to release him in case they didn't get the people in who they wanted. They thought the best thing for Mason would be to go out on loan, but they couldn't allow it because they didn't have enough back-up for the first team. And if they didn't get anyone in, Mason would have been the back-up. If the first choice got injured, he would be in and might have played ten games. But getting someone in allowed Mason to go out on loan and be involved week in, week out, playing football away from Derby where it's been such a high-pressured place for him. It's his next bid for his development. Go out, play games, get that sort of consistency and go back to Derby a different player.'

Loan deals are the salvation of clubs in League One and League Two, the oxygen that helps them breathe, the lifebelt that keeps them afloat. Only one of the five players who joined the Magpies during this window commanded a fee, with the Afghan midfielder Noor Husin moving from Crystal Palace for an undisclosed amount. Matty Virtue, a box-to-box midfielder, came on loan from Liverpool, while Liam Noble returned to Meadow Lane on a free, following an eventful eighteen months at Forest Green Rovers where he captained the Gloucestershire side into the Football League for the first-ever time before being released five months later.

The loan system is a two-way street. At the end of the arrangement, a lower-league club like County isn't giving back what they were given. A younger player who's been persuaded that a drop down the pyramid will enhance his career isn't expendable cannon fodder. This is a player of quality and high future potential who's been invested in and imbedded at one of the top academies in the land. And, after swallowing his pride and agreeing to a loan spell, he'll return to his parent club a more experienced, more rounded player. Not only has he been handed an opportunity to finally play first-team football, but he'll also have been mentored by his battle-hardened, short-term teammates. This is especially true at Meadow Lane where Ameobi, Smith, Hunt and others like the veteran striker Jon Stead can help shape and mould these malleable young players.

'The lads who get sent here are going to get exposed to really good professionals. Parent clubs want them to learn from the positive and professional environment. And that's what we've created here, which helps us trying to build relationships with all the clubs in the Midlands. We want people to come here and say, "I got treated really well there. I really enjoyed my time. And I'd love to go back if I can't get anywhere else. But if I do, I've only got good things to say."'

Attracting loanees from Premier League and Championship clubs is made infinitely easier when the lower-league club is riding high in their particular division. Last year, with County languishing second from bottom of League Two, almost the *lanterne rouge* of the Football League, recruiting players to drag them out of the mire was akin to scaling a twenty-foot wall without ladder or rope. Unsurprisingly, the very real spectre of non-league football wasn't a point of attraction.

'Last year we had to sell the club more. We were trying to sell a vision which, over the phone, was difficult – "We're not going down" etc. They only had to go on Google to see we'd lost ten of the previous eleven or twelve games. "Oh, hang on a minute …" And you can't blame people for that. But pretty much everyone who said "no" last January has been in contact over the summer to tell us they think they've made a mistake and they should have come here. They had an opportunity to play and they wished they'd taken that.

'What we've found now is that – compared to last year – when we phone clubs, everyone's gone "Yeah, that's a possibility." That's great – it shows how far we've come in a year. We're definitely getting treated differently. Most definitely. I spoke to numerous players last year, but they were talking about relegation. This year, we've not had that. They just want to come because we're looking at promotion. They see a great pitch, they see the changing rooms are brand new, they see everything's going in the right direction. We were a club that was struggling, that was in intensive care. And seeing where we are now, it's been an unbelievable turnaround.'

Nolan stifles a yawn; yesterday was a long day. Although, despite the late finish, it could have been longer. 'I knew we were going to be here late, so I spent the previous night at home in London with my family and didn't get to the club until about three o'clock in the afternoon. We knew we were really looking for only two lads. Now if this had been this time last year, I'd have been in at seven am until eleven pm and beyond. So this year wasn't as stressful as it normally is, but I still took a large amount of calls in those eight hours. Is there that special one? If a Championship club has just signed five players, will someone now become available who will suit us? You look at these things to make sure you don't miss out on someone who might be there. You've still got to keep on your toes.'

The excitement of the previous night continues to energise Alan Hardy. This was his third transfer window as the club's owner; he installed Nolan as manager the day after his takeover was rubber-stamped twelve months ago. For a man who's made his money in interior design, the football world represents a different challenge altogether. Every day brings a new lesson.

'Each window has been really different. We were ninety-first in the league during the first one and we struggled to get any players in who we really wanted. We had a list that the gaffer would have liked, but we couldn't even get through to several of those players' agents because of our league position. There were twenty games left in the season and we were staring relegation in the face. They would have been telling their clients not to go to Notts County because if they got relegated, they'd be playing non-league football next season. But thankfully we got some loan players in and we avoided relegation.

'The summer window was better. We started again with a clean sheet. However, there was still a feeling of reluctance and reticence to come to us because we'd only just got away with it. What had changed? What would be different next season? So as much as we tried to paint a picture of this beautiful, bright future, it was much harder to get rid of a bad reputation than create a new one.

'But this last window has been like bees round a honeypot. Now that we're second in the league and are drawn against a Premier League team in the Fourth Round of the FA Cup, all of a sudden it's different. The tables have been turned. Those agents who were advising their players not to come to us a year ago are suddenly getting in touch. The gaffer was absolutely clinical with them: "No, you've had your chance. We needed your help but you didn't want to join the party. Don't get on the bandwagon now." He was clear. Anyone who declined us in our moment of need needn't come to us when we're doing well. And we were inundated by agents whose players actually wanted to come to us.

'But the players we really wanted were still tough to get. Our aspirations have changed. It's no longer about survival. It's now about cementing our place in the automatic promotion places and building a team that's fit for purpose for League One next year. It's a completely different dynamic to where we were twelve months ago.'

For a proven deal-maker (the high-performance sports car parked outside could be seen as a measure of Alan

Hardy's commercial acumen), the slow progress of the Mason Bennett transfer clearly fascinated him. He's keen to disclose the details of the whole saga, to recount and relive the anxiety.

'The whole day went in waves of excitement, frustration, excitement, stress, excitement ... As each hour passed, the emotion changed. But what was really interesting to me was to see that we are just a link in a chain. It was like moving house. Derby wouldn't release Mason until the player they were looking to bring in had signed. And we were looking to release a player, but not until Mason was ours. At one point, there was a further complication involving an international player going to the club that Derby was taking a player from. We were in a four-link chain. Everything else had to happen for the transfer to work. That was completely new to me. Normally they're free agents or clubs just let them go.

'Come one o'clock yesterday lunchtime, we were told that it had accelerated. Things were falling into place and it might be as quickly as three o'clock. Three o'clock came and went in the blink of an eye. As did four o'clock. As did five o'clock. At eight pm, it was still fifty-fifty.

'We were talking to Derby, who were brilliant throughout the whole of the day, and they were respectful of the fact that, come half-past eight, we'd have to go into Plan B. So they said they'd send Mason over to us to show they were serious and so he was at least in the building, could be put through his medical and could sign the paperwork. If they hadn't said that and it had got to quarter to nine, we would have probably parked Mason and resorted to the back-up. Two hours is about the amount of time it can take eighty per cent of the population to get to Nottingham. If we were in Exeter, we'd be in trouble.

'So Mason arrived here at quarter past nine. He had his medical, he'd signed on the dotted line, and we'd emailed the forms back to Derby by five to ten. But Kasey Palmer, the player going to Derby, hadn't even arrived there by then. He was driving up from Chelsea, but Chelsea hadn't let him do so until his replacement had arrived there. As soon as the replacement showed up, they released Palmer to drive to Derby. The chain went on.

'He arrived at half past ten, with the window closing at eleven o'clock and him yet to do a medical. He did that – which, I'm sure, wouldn't have been as thorough as Derby would have liked – then signed on the dotted line. The papers were emailed to us at ten fifty-five pm. When quickly checking them, we thought there was a page missing, but it was there at the back. So we ended up emailing it over with three and a half minutes to spare before the window closed. By that time, though, we'd missed the chance to loan out our player, so he didn't go. The chain had been four links, and three of them got done. But the player leaving us didn't because we simply ran out of time.

'We also really fancied a player from Everton U23s, but they had a game last night so both [Everton U23s' boss] David Unsworth and the player were wrapped up in that. By the time he'd have come off the pitch and we'd have got speaking to him at half past nine, he'd never have got here for eleven o'clock. But it's a great position for us where we are talking to Everton and Brighton and Derby – Premier League and Championship sides.'

Space had emerged in the County squad because one of their two loanees from neighbours Forest had been recalled to the City Ground. While Jorge Grant remained at Meadow Lane, Ryan Yates headed back over the river.

'Some clubs understand the value of the loan system and some don't. Some you should be eternally grateful for them allowing you access to their players. Sometimes they lose sight of the fact that, while they're on loan, their players get hugely developed as footballers and as people. Ryan is a prime example. The gaffer used to spend hours with him. I was often here until eight o'clock at night and I'd pop my head around the door. "Night, gaffer. See you tomorrow." And he'd be there with Ryan and the whiteboard, showing him clips of his last game. He'd be showing him what his last run was and comparing it to a Premier League player's run. "That's the run that Fàbregas made. Look at his shape, look at his pace. Now look at your shape, at your pace."

'There's a lot of that that goes on behind the scenes. It's not just a case of bringing in a loan player, putting him on the training pitch with twenty other players, and playing him on Saturday. We feel we have a duty of care to that player, to develop them, to bring them on. We did that with Marc Bola last year. I think Arsenal will accept he was a better player when he returned to them than when he arrived. That's not just through playing games. That's through coaching and analysis and helping him develop.'

Then there's the benefit of the squad's older statesmen, the wise elders. 'The golden oldies show them how to behave as professionals. Some of these loan players will be running out tomorrow in front of eighteen thousand people. They wouldn't have played in front of eighteen *hundred* people at U23 level. That'll be a new experience for someone like Ben Hall. If he plays on Saturday, he will grow as a person, just in the space of a game. That's the sort of experience that we can give.'

Being a forward-facing kind of owner, Hardy allows himself one last contemplation of arguably one of the most topsy-turvy days he's ever experienced in business. 'I'm optimistic as a person so I saw yesterday as an opportunity. We didn't know what was going to come in. We could have ended up with a player who wasn't on our radar who an agent presented us with. And there was one of these, who we just missed out on. He went to another London club instead because the geography suited him. When we woke up in the morning, we had no idea we could be talking to him and attempting to get him in. And that's really exciting.

'It's not the fear of the unknown. It's the *excitement* of the unknown. The excitement of "Are we going to get him?" is overlaid with "But what happens if we don't? Is that back-up plan going to come off?" And then you're working on pure adrenalin.

'But I don't see the point in a thirty-one-day window. Absolutely pointless. I don't know what the stats are, but it wouldn't surprise me if 97.3% of transfers were done yester-day. You don't need a month. Let's just have seven days. I'd say twenty-four hours, but the club secretaries would pull their hair out. So come back from Christmas, first of January it opens and seventh of January it closes.'

Before I vacate the back corridors of Meadow Lane, I ask Kevin Nolan about how content he feels about the window as a concept. 'I haven't got all the answers, but it definitely needs a revamp. I don't think the mid-season window should be crammed into one month. It could be done over a more prolonged period – maybe opening at the beginning of December and closing at the end of February. In December, you learn more about your squad, but in January you don't get to focus on them because there are so many games, especially in the lower leagues. Today is February 1st and we've already played thirty-five games this season. And we have Premier League managers moaning about occasionally playing two games in four days. We do that all the time. We've got Saturday, Tuesday, Saturday, Tuesday. Saturday, Tuesday for the next three weeks. But in March and April, we've got no midweek games at all. We've got to get that right. And the window has to work with the fixtures. I could have six players getting injured in the next three weeks and no replacements. But if the window was open for the busy December to February period, you'd get three months. It doesn't have to be madness, madness, madness.'

I let Nolan know which plan his boss considers would make a better transfer process – that narrow seven-day window. He looks genuinely incredulous, in the same manner that he used to during his playing days whenever a free-kick went against him.

'You're joking, aren't you?' A shrug of the shoulders and a shake of the head. 'Me and him would have well fallen out by day two …'

*　*　*

Deep in the bowels of Swindon Town's County Ground is the Lou Macari Suite, a windowless room as diminutive as the former Manchester United striker it's named after. Macari is commemorated here as, during a spell as manager in the mid-eighties, he led the club to successive promotions. On the wall, there's a framed team line-up from before the start of the 1987–88 season. Optimism is shot across the squad's faces. The old Division One trophy, set out on the immaculate pitch before the team, sparkles in the August sun. And judging by the deep tan of Macari's legs, he looks to have enjoyed his summer.

The current occupant of the managerial hot seat is also partly known for his healthy tan. Phil Brown strides into the room – black training top with his initials on the chest and black shorts showcasing those mahogany legs. He has never looked remotely pale or wan. This is a man who's kept his tan topped up in whichever sunshine spot he's been billeted to – Bolton, Hull, Derby, Preston, Southend and now Swindon, a town suffocating in damp, misty gloom on this particular October afternoon.

Unlike Kevin Nolan, Brown has considerable experience of navigating the twists and turns of the transfer window. He's an old hand at it. At each of the clubs he's managed – even the two seasons he steered Hull City on the Premier League adventure – Brown has had to demonstrate great parsimony. This wasn't voluntary at any of them. These were his constraints. Very tight they were too, especially at his last employer in Essex and now at this current one in Wiltshire.

But short purse strings aren't a problem for this versatile, imaginative boss. Over the course of eight years as an assistant manager (two at Blackpool, six at Bolton), he learned from another how to duck and dive, how to dodge and weave. He learned from Sam Allardyce.

'At Bolton, we were competing with some of the big boys in the transfer market, but we knew that we couldn't. We just didn't have that kind of money. We had to be frugal, so we investigated a different way. And that different way was the loan with a view to a permanent. We were probably one of the first ones to pay a loan fee. We brought in the likes of Jay-Jay Okocha, Youri Djorkaeff and Ivan Campo. People were going, "How? How did you manage to do that?" We brought in a UEFA Cup winner in Bruno N'Gotty. Stelios Giannako-poulos had won seven titles in a row at Olympiakos, but he was looking for a fresh challenge. They were attached to big clubs. Okocha was at PSG. His was a loan with a view to permanent, and then a free transfer. Why no one else took him I don't know. It was a piece of genius from Sam.'

Striking out as a manager in his own right, he applied Allardyce's teachings to his own deals. And he needed to. 'I don't think I've ever been with a club that was competitive in the transfer market. It's either been free transfers or finding a way to get the player in, whether that was chairman to chairman, manager to manager, owner to owner.'

But when Brown took Hull into the top flight in 2008, the rules of the game suddenly changed. 'I think the plan was to get to the Premier League within three years, but we did it in one, so the financial reward came flooding in earlier than expected. We were now sitting at the top table and were in competition with the big boys. But they were off the map as regards their budgets. We were bottom when it came to money. My budget for that first Premier League season was between twelve and thirteen million pounds. In the second year, it went to nineteen million.

'We were still getting those year-long loans that Sam had taught me about. Jozy Altidore was one, a player who'd gone from US football into Spanish football for ten million dollars, which was a lot of money, and I was getting him out of Villarreal for a million-pound loan fee. So we competed in the way that I knew. We survived that first season to get another year in the Premier League – and to get another thirty-five, forty million quid, whatever it was back then. It was competitive, but you still had to maximise resources.'

But with this money, however comparatively low it was in Premier League terms, came the chance to spend some proper money for the first time in Brown's managerial career. Anthony Gardner joined from Spurs for £2.5m, while Jimmy Bullard's move from Fulham cost double that. 'Bullard was the pinnacle for me,' says Brown, with no small amount of satisfaction in his voice. But he couldn't afford to reconstruct an entire team of that kind of value. 'Cherry-picking some players from big clubs was key. We'd get them on a free and give them better wages. All of a sudden, people in my changing-room were getting twenty thousand, twenty-five thousand, thirty thousand pounds a week, rather than the single-figure thousands they were getting before as a bottom-end Championship team.

'One of the transfer coups for me was bringing Dean Windass back to the club. He had been released at the age of eighteen by my assistant manager Brian Horton, when he had managed Hull. Brian had told him he'd never make it. That was hilarious for me. He'd not only made it in football, but he'd come back to Hull.

'"Brian, I'm thinking of bringing Dean Windass back here."

'"What's it going to cost?"

'"It's a free. Bradford can't wait to get rid of him. But we've got the baggage of dealing with Dean Windass. And you've got more baggage than me. You told him he'd never make it at eighteen. Now he's twice that age."'

Since those comparatively flush times at Hull, when Brown had plenty of options to sign quality players, the purse strings have been ever tightening. 'We're in League Two trying to get promoted,' he says of his current position. 'There aren't an awful lot of finances down here. There's not an awful lot of the cherry pie. I'm not at that big table now.'

During his near-five years at Southend, he only paid a transfer fee on two occasions, bringing in Rob Kiernan from Rangers for £125,000 and Cian Bolger from Bolton for £25,000 ('but then sold him to Fleetwood for the same amount, so drew even on that'). The remainder were free transfers or loans. The balance sheet looked even healthier, thanks to Brown making £3m from selling a trio of players to clubs higher up the ladder.

If his spending at Southend appeared frugal, it's been non-existent at Swindon, despite the sizeable intake that arrived at the County Ground during the close season. In his last five and a half years of management, Brown has paid hard cash for a player on just two occasions. In considering this, though, don't read a lack of spending to be an indicator of a lack of activity.

'We had a very active transfer window here at Swindon this last summer. Sixteen players went out and eleven players came in. That's a twenty-seven-man turnover in one changing room in one month. That is hard work off the field of play. *On* the field of play, it becomes even harder because you're trying to mould it together and it's really difficult. You're learning on the job. But if the owner is willing to do that, then he's backing me one hundred per cent. And if he's backing me one hundred per cent, I've got to commit to the project – and the project can't be a one-month period or a six-month period. It's got to be long term. You've got to allow these players to bed in. So give us a two-year plan that can get us out of this division and maybe up to the top end of League One.

'My job at this football club is to win promotion. That's my remit. The chairman's given me a budget and when he says I'm up to budget, that's it. End of story. So then it becomes a trade. When the January transfer window opens, I might have to get three players out before I get one particular player in. I've got to balance the books. But if the chairman then says, "We've got half a chance of promotion here. There's that

player. Forget about the three out. If you can move, we will."
And that's the relationship I've then got with the owner.

'What I've got here at Swindon is an ex-player and ex-agent who owns the football club, who chairs the football club, who has a hands-on running of the football club from a financial perspective. He knows how the game works and how to get the deals done. That's the kind of relationship I want. I can have a football conversation with him. So if I needed a player, I could say, "You saw the performance on Saturday. I'm desperate to get a left-winger", and this ex-player and ex-agent, who's watched a million games like I have, would say, "Leave it with me." A businessman wouldn't necessarily see it. "Leave it with me" is music to my ears. I'm then dealing with football, he's dealing with finances.

'If it were purely a financial one, it would be "Your budget's three million pounds and you've reached it. You might still want that player, but it ain't going to happen." But I've got to understand that as well. So if I can say, "He's out and he's out and he's out. I'm now down to two point seven million", there's three hundred grand to spend. But we can all do the maths, can't we?

'Paul Duffen at Hull didn't have football experience, but he learned very, very quickly on the job. He once praised an interview where I called him – my chairman – one of the backroom staff. Paul was delighted with that. Whenever there was a staff meeting, he wanted to come. And he added to them, he gave them value. Whenever we went on a night out, he was there, picking our brains when we were half-cut. That for me was ideal. But his only claim to football was that he supported Spurs. That was it.'

While actual transactions are restricted by the calendar, the process rolls on throughout the year. No club stops thinking about new blood. Even the most successful team needs a transfusion once in a while. But finding the right players takes time. It's a never-ending process, one that's usually far from linear, and thus far from swift.

'I've got a new chief scout who's watched one player in non-league five times already. I got a phone call on Wednesday night. He'd watched him again. The process is normally then, "You need to see him." If I then see him and I agree that he's better than what we've got, the first bid goes in on January first. But if the scout goes to see him five times and the fifth time he comes back and says, "He ain't good enough", I then wouldn't go. But going to see a player five times is pretty much five weeks. Then the assistant manager and I – or the goalkeeping coach if he's a goalkeeper – will go to see him play.'

The wish list of players is never short on candidates. It's self-renewing. Interest in one player will drift away, but that interest will always be reinvested in a new potential target. Names are rubbed off the board; new ones added. But that relentless search has to be watertight. No stone unturned, everyone watched – if only for reasons of self-preservation.

His eyes light up as a memory pops into his head. 'I'll tell you a genuine story here. I was manager of Preston North End and Jamie Vardy was playing for Halifax Town. My chief scout had seen him twice, the assistant manager then went to see him, then the first-team coach, then me and the assistant manager. Every one of those reports came back with an A star. "Sign him, sign him, sign him." Each was a match report about one player – not a line on each of the eleven players, or the ones that catch your eye. Just him.

'Fleetwood, who were just down the road from Preston, bought Vardy for around a hundred and fifty thousand pounds and then sold him to Leicester for one point two million. My chairman came into me and threw the paper on the table. "Why can't we sign players like this?" I went to my drawer and I brought out all four reports we had on him. "That's why we can't. Because you told me we had no money to spend." We had done our job one million per cent. And that proof actually shocked the chairman.

'I still do that now. I still do a full match report if I see someone that I like the look of. My three coaches do that too, plus I've got a chief scout on top. You've got to try to do that because if my chairman comes in and says, "What about him?" and I've not got the answers for him, then I'm a bad manager. But if I say, "Chairman, have we got any money for him?" and we've not, then the decision's up to him.'

The transfer window represents an additional pressure on the manager, already one of the most publicly pressured career choices there are. He can be judged – by the board, the local press, the fans – on the basis of several transfer-related criteria: whether he managed to retain their star player, whether he caved into the pressure of selling him, or whether a new marque signing, one closely allied to that manager who may have paid over the odds for, has failed to come up with the goods.

'That's where your sharing on the pressure should come in. Why should it fall on one man? A manager picks the team and decides on the tactics. I get that part. From a financial perspective, the performance of a football club used to be wholly down to the manager or to the guy at the top signing the cheques. Now it's not. Now it's shared. These days, you have chief executives and directors of football and directors of finance. You name it. They're at every level. I've got a director of finance here and a chief executive, and this is fourth-tier football.'

This collective burden-sharing rarely strays beyond the boundary of theory. The job security of a chief executive, for instance, is notably more robust than that of the managers he or she will appoint. Several first-team bosses will come and go before any rumbles of discontent will threaten the position of the man or woman at the very top. In marked contrast, it'll invariably be the manager who'll be the recipient of the ultimate blame, regardless of the forces beyond his control that have created, or at least fostered, artificial expectations. The manager is always the first in the cross hairs.

It's no surprise, then, to hear that Brown doesn't relish the clamour of an on-rushing transfer window. 'I hate them. Here's an example why. I sent Mick McCarthy a text message on June 18th about Luke Woolfenden, an Ipswich player who was on loan at Bromley the previous season. Then Mick left the club, so I phoned up the new guy, Paul Hurst.

'"Congratulations on getting the job. I'm just putting down a marker for Luke Woolfenden."

'"Browny, I'm desperate for centre-halves myself. I'll be looking at him in pre-season."

'That first marker was on June 18th. On August 31st, seven minutes before the window closed, we signed Luke

Woolfenden on loan. It cost me two and a half months of my life. The system's farcical. Absolutely farcical. I can't give you a better example of how poor the window is for a manager.

'The window is for the media. It's not for managers. The game of football's not benefitting from it. Don't get me wrong – when Kylian Mbappé goes for two hundred million pounds, the game's doing brilliant, isn't it? So I'm not slagging the game off there. But it's not doing *us* any favours. That two hundred million will be divvied up left, right and centre. Money will be going all over the place. Being able to monitor it, police it and be legitimate with it all is very important. It's one of the vital cogs in the wheel. But if you can't because you've lost control of it, then just open the window. Let us trade.'

Brown's tune is in harmony with those of so many other managers. 'Having a window is a restriction on trade. I don't think any other business is like it. We've got to look at a different system. I'm never one for standing still in football. I'm all for new ideas, for innovative thought processes, for investigating how we can improve our wonderful game. You name it. But have I come up with a better way? The answer's no. But that's not my job. My job is to deal with what's put in front of me.

'But, if someone stops you from trading, that by definition squeezes the sausage-making machine into multi-million-pound deals that should only be a million. When some outside force squeezes you to do that, the economy is wrong. It's false. It's artificial. We know the economy is going to go up. It's not going to go south, it's going to go north. But this false economy covers crazy north. It's off the map. It's out of the universe.

'I don't know why we're frightened of an open transfer market. What's against you trading? Surely that's the way the world works. I'll give you an example. The World Cup gives football a false economy. It accentuates the false prices that already exist. The World Cup inflated prices to a crazy level. But one club, one man – Daniel Levy at Spurs – said after the World Cup, "I'm not paying those prices." He'll pay *his* price, Spurs' price. I'm not saying that everyone's got their heads unscrewed, but he's got his head screwed on with regards to the false economy of the world of football. I don't know Daniel Levy. I've never had a coffee with him or anything. But what he says is absolutely bang-on.'

Despite his hands-up protestations that he doesn't have the answer to a more efficient, more logical transfer process – and that it's not his job to come up with the solutions – Brown does offer one suggestion to lessen some of the chaos: allow clubs to trade throughout an extended, three-month, mid-season window, but in return would be their guarantee not to jettison their manager for the following nine months. Brown's managerial brethren, forever riding out or tossed about by football's choppy waters, would surely approve on both counts.

One year, though, Brown did manage to avoid the chaos of late January, when those choppy waters were momentarily becalmed for him. 'There was one window at Southend where, because I didn't have enormous funds, I got two or three free transfers in early and I actually went home on deadline day and had a meal and just enjoyed myself that night. People were coming up to me and saying, "But it's transfer deadline day. What's wrong with you?" It was as if I'd done something wrong. But I'd handed my homework in early!'

Whether completed in advance or right down to the wire, a manager's signings define his tenure. If favourable results aren't forthcoming, if those new arrivals haven't performed, the boss is vulnerable. And this is what Brown encountered. Those eleven players who signed for Swindon during the summer weren't given what he would have regarded as sufficient time to bed in – at least, insufficient time under his command. A month to the day after we met, and a day shy of nine months in the job, Brown and his assistant Neil McDonald were, in the well-worn euphemistic parlance of football, relieved of their duties at the County Ground. Five wins in the first seventeen league matches of the season was deemed an unsatisfactory foundation from which the project could grow. Despite Brown's caution, better results appeared to have been expected in the corridors of power, regardless of that huge churn of personnel over the summer.

If a been-around-the-block boss of Brown's profile and vintage can find himself the victim of impatience, younger managers of comparatively tender age and experience are certainly not immune to football's ever-shifting sands when the squad they've assembled fails to deliver on perceived promises. Less than four months before Brown's departure, Kevin Nolan had already exited stage left at Meadow Lane.

His replacement, Harry Kewell, was hailed as Notts County's 'long-term solution'. The Australian occupied the manager's office for just ten weeks.

* * *

If the lower leagues clip the wings of managers, especially those managers with backgrounds in more cash-rich environments, they can also send certain players on a steep trajectory to heights never experienced before.

Dayle Grubb is one such upwardly mobile player.

At the start of December 2017, Grubb was the star midfielder for Vanarama National South side Weston-super-Mare, putting in the latest in a string of eye-catching, extraordinarily consistent performances over several seasons with the Seagulls. It was business as usual: playing semi-pro for his hometown club on Saturday afternoons and Tuesdays evenings, while being gainfully employed by day as a PE teacher at the local primary school half a mile down the road.

One month later, though, part-time became full-time. Grubb's transfer to Forest Green Rovers of League Two became official that day, a belated crossing of the threshold into the world of the professional footballer. Despite spending nine years at his hometown club, and despite reaching the comparatively pensionable age of twenty-six without kicking a single ball in the Football League, his departure from the Woodspring Stadium was almost inevitable. Over the course of almost three hundred games for the Seagulls, Grubb notched a handsome eighty-six goals from central midfield. Indeed, his twenty-nine goals in the calendar year of 2017 alone were only matched in the top six tiers of English football by his soon-to-be Forest Green teammate Christian Doidge and some bloke called Harry Kane. Dayle Grubb was a fish that had clearly outgrown the pond.

Already into the latter half of his twenties, his impressive stats suggest either a modest level of personal ambition, or a stunning dereliction of duty on the part of a significant number of Football League scouts.

Three weeks after the Forest Green deal went through, Grubb makes his first return to Weston's Woodspring Stadium since he left for Gloucestershire. Tonight, he's merely a spectator as his old team take on local(ish) rivals Bath City. We arrange to meet between the dugouts once the game's kicked off, but so constant has been the stream of well-wishers wanting to know how one of their own is now faring in the Football League that it's not until half-way through the second-half that Grubb manages to reach our rendezvous point on the far side of the pitch. The prodigal son is in demand.

Having signed a pre-agreement with Forest Green Rovers the previous month, Grubb's transfer took effect on the first day of January, joining his almost exact contemporary Virgil van Dijk (the pair were born a fortnight apart) as one of the first confirmed transfers of the window. But while they found their names next to each other on that day's list of transfers – 'a bit surreal, yeah. Pinch yourself' – it was the £75m Dutchman who obviously made the biggest headlines (headlines justified when he was named PFA Player Of The Year fewer than eighteen months later). As van Dijk busied himself with hunting for a Cheshire mansion that reflected a six-year contract yielding a reported £180,000-a-week salary, the most significant by-product of Grubb's eighteen-month deal was being able to – or being forced to – quit his teaching job. The keys to the school's sports equipment cupboard were surrendered in return for his first full-time salary in football and a daily commute up the M5.

'Over the last few years, I got to the stage where I thought if a move to the Football League hasn't happened yet, it'll never happen. Luckily, I had a really good start to the season and Forest Green made their interest concrete. There were a few other interested clubs – both Football League and Conference – but I've always said that Forest Green is an attractive team. It's quite local to me, which is important, and their style of football interests me. Once they put their offer in, that was where I wanted to play my football.

'A lot of people at Conference South level have agents, and I had a few agents speak to me to see if they could help me, but luckily I had good people around me. I didn't want anything to hamper my move and wanted to do it myself. The money wasn't the be-all and end-all. Maybe I could have got more money somewhere else, but I just wanted to make the move happen and didn't feel the need for anyone else to be involved. It didn't take long for it to be agreed.'

In contrast, van Dijk's transfer was a protracted saga that began the previous summer, a courtship that included an apology from Liverpool for an illegal approach for the player. That wasn't the only contrast between the pair's respective moves. Their personal circumstances differed somewhat, too. At football's high end, a transfer means a top-level player swapping one luxury house for another luxury house in a different part of the country. Grubb's switch, though, has been genuinely transformative.

'I was working at the primary school, which I really enjoyed and they were really good to me. But full-time football is what I have always passionately wanted. I'm training every day, getting fitter, getting sharper, getting better. I'm lucky to be leading the life I am now. I'm in the privileged position of playing football for a living and I'm not going to waste it. My life has changed for the better.'

Before, Grubb had to fit football around his day job. Now that the game is his main focus, it obviously doesn't fill eight hours a day. 'It's crazy. Sometimes I finish training at two o'clock and I've got the rest of the day free. If we've got a midweek game, I don't have to get up early for work the next day. But it's not taken too much to get used to it. It's what I always wanted to do. I'm not going to complain about being bored or anything like that.'

That hasn't been the only culture shock. Previously, playing regional football in the Vanarama National South meant travel to away games wasn't too onerous; Gloucester City were the most northerly club in the division during Grubb's final season. Last weekend, though, Forest Green were away to Carlisle – a 500-mile round-trip from Rovers' base in Nailsworth – and all for a 1–0 defeat. 'It's a bit different than I'm used to. We go up the day before, train on the way, stay at a nice hotel and have nice food. The long trips aren't so bad. Maybe the journey back after the game is a bit more of a chore, getting home late. But I want to do it. I want to play at these grounds.

'Some of the lads here at Weston are ambitious and hope to push on to that next stage. Maybe, now they've seen me do it, it's a more realistic aim. For them, it's natural to think about transfers. In football, you want to do as well as you can. You want to play at the highest level. It's still in the back of your mind. You're still hopeful that a transfer might arise.'

Behind us, Weston are awarded a penalty. Up until the end of last month, it would have been Grubb putting the ball on the spot. Our conversation pauses while the kick is taken. His successor is as unerring from twelve yards as he himself was in the white of Weston. Three-one to the home side.

Not that Grubb has been remotely shy himself when it comes to finding the net in the Football League. Two goals on his home debut for Forest Green against Cambridge United – a pair of net-busting drives, at that – provided confirmation that moving up two tiers was a comfortable career upgrade, while also hinting that it was an unnecessarily belated one.

Dayle Grubb's time hadn't gone. But it could certainly have arrived a little earlier.

CHAPTER FOUR

HOPE IN YOUR HEART

'Fans need their drug – and that drug is transfer rumours'

– Matt Ladson

Day 31, the final hours of the January 2018 transfer window.

Today, players and agents and clubs will hurl themselves out of the trenches and go over the top, committing themselves to glorious futures or ignominious failure. This is the day on which reason and rationality take a break. Transfer deadline day. D-Day.

London wakes early and excited. Phones on bedside tables are reached for, small screens squinted at through pinhole eyes. The first thought of the day isn't provided by the moralising tones of some man of the cloth on the *Today* programme – not unless he's delivering an overnight update on whether a chosen club is any closer to filling that desperately needed defensive-midfielder vacancy.

London shuffles off to work, scanning the transfer gossip columns of the morning papers on the Tube and on the buses, looking for clues, looking for signs. But the capital knows that it will be several hours before today's headlines are made, before the whispers turn into audible, legally binding declarations.

Not all of London shuffles off to work, though. Some are so locked into the day, so obsessed by what might happen and their need to hear/see/read about it at the moment it happens, that they've shown foresight and booked time off. Or they've not shown foresight and have decided to sag off work nonetheless. It's a pivotal day, after all. It may well be the twenty-four hours around which their dearly beloved club's season pivots. It's a day to spend at home pressing the refresh button on their phone's sports news apps and Twitter feeds with all the dedication and delusion of an obsessed ex-boyfriend. Or it's a day to be out and about, in the bone-shaking chill of January, doing exactly the same.

Not many appear to have shown foresight in London Colney. It's safe to say that the welcoming party here at Arsenal's training ground, ready to embrace the just-signed Pierre-Emerick Aubameyang, is a modest one. At the end of the lane from which the high-performance cars of the club's stars emerge after training, it's a mere scattering of diehards. There's a single press agency photographer waiting to get the first unofficial snap of the new striker, along with just half a dozen Gunners fanatics, likewise wanting to get the first autograph of the man from Gabon.

In fact, not all appear to be fanatics. One of them is an unimpressed girlfriend clearly press-ganged into spending several hours in the cold in the hope of catching a fleeting sight of the superstar signing through the tinted windows of a speeding car. She stomps her booted feet on the ground, trying to improve their circulation. Two more of the faithful are schoolboys who've bunked off lessons, all cheeky grins and nervous looks over the shoulders. The sole security guard, charged with keeping the frantic, possibly unruly hordes at bay, is far from overworked.

This is how it's increasingly been at training grounds on deadline day over the past few years. No baying masses, no raucous reception. There was one particular incident in 2014 outside Finch Farm, Everton's training ground, that contributed to the changing nature of the party. As dusk fell, Sky Sports News reporter Alan Irwin addressed the camera to update the football nation on a potential move to Merseyside by Manchester United midfielder Tom Cleverley. Suddenly, lurking out of the gloom, came a purple dildo, brandished by a mischievous fan who promptly tried to insert it into Irwin's ear as he delivered his live report.

That qualified as high jinks. A more sinister incident happened during the same transfer window when protesting, firework-wielding Crystal Palace fans forced the channel's reporter to abandon his post at Selhurst Park ('We fucking hate Sky Sports' went the chant, articulating frustration about the changing nature of top-flight football since the broadcaster got on board). A colleague of the reporter was also advised, for his own safety, to remove himself from outside the Emirates where he was relaying the story of Danny Welbeck's switch from Old Trafford. In both cases, the threat to personal safety outweighed any spectacle that such an outside broadcast could offer.

That was the last window in which Sky allowed a potentially unruly crowd to make their presence felt on a live report. No more do the channel's reporters share the pavement with the fans. They now broadcast from the safe harbour of inside the training-ground compound or behind the stadium's firmly closed gates. While they might not be invited into the innermost sanctum on deadline day, at least taking position in the car park is infinitely more dignifying than being battered by a sex toy in front of the nation. Or worse.

The numbers of fans devotedly hanging around on pavements, verges and street corners has now, understandably, somewhat diminished come January 31st. The entertainment value is, it has to be admitted, low. Indeed, the highlight of the last hour was when a white Transit van slowed down as it approached the training-ground junction, just for its driver to bellow 'SWANSEA!' at the small gathering. Last night, Arsenal capitulated 3–1 to the Premier League's bottom club.

Every five minutes or so, the security guard's walkie-talkie crackles into life, a sign that a car is about to leave the compound at the other end of the lane. The fans take their positions on either side, unsure whether the new club-record signing will be in either the passenger or driver's seat. Phones are raised, ready to document his first public sighting, the rapid uploading of which to social media will earn modest bragging rights to justify the day off. Flash settings are switched on, hopeful that their glare will penetrate those blacked-out windows.

This is the day when a club's existing stars play second fiddle. When Jack Wilshere's car drives up to the junction, the attention given to it and him is largely polite, perfunctory. There's a bigger prize to be had today. The next car – still not that containing Aubameyang – stops and winds its window down, revealing its driver to be a listener of Radio 4. Club captain Per Mertesacker, who didn't play the previous evening, indulges the truant schoolboys, in direct contravention of the warnings of a nearby sign: 'Please note – players are not allowed to sign autographs. This is not their decision.' To be fair, he's posing for pictures, rather than scribbling his name. So too, a couple of minutes later, is the youth team hotshot Eddie Nketiah. The iPad is the new autograph book.

The traffic continues to emerge from the training ground, but still no Aubameyang. A cherry-red vintage Rolls Royce glides up the lane, its progress documented by those raised phones.

'Who was that?' asks one bystander as the car heads off to the nearby junction with the adjacent M25.

'No idea,' replies his mate. 'Someone important though, I reckon.'

A brown UPS van comes next, the perfect, windowless vehicle in which to smuggle a new player out in an attempt to avoid the gaze of the faithful. Not that, indeed, we're in possession of any firm evidence that Aubameyang is actually at the training-ground right now – and that single security guard isn't in a hurry to confirm either way. The robes of high-vis safety-wear bequeath a curious power on their holder.

The whipping winter wind eventually proves too much for the cheesed-off girlfriend who, after several hours of tolerance and patience, finally persuades her boyfriend that enough is enough. In the absence of the cabaret provided by Sky's cameras and reporters, it's not been the most thrilling of experiences.

The schoolkids make a move too. After all, they need to be back home for tea at the allotted hour in order to convincingly carry off their day of deceit. There's no selfie of them with Aubameyang on their iPad to keep hidden from their parents, but they're content enough. An actual sighting of the future darling of the terraces is, ultimately, of secondary importance to his inky squiggle on a three-year contract. And his signature isn't the only one to warm Arsenal hearts today. Mesut Özil has ended a year of speculation by finally putting pen to paper to extend his stay at the Emirates for three further years. His reward for the stand-off? A reported doubling of his wages, making him the highest-paid player in the club's history. For Gooners, that's mere details. In the final year of his contract, and looking like a departure from north London was all but inevitable, this is as important a piece of news as that of a new marquee acquisition.

While Arsenal delivered two thick slabs of good tidings to their fans during daylight hours, the devotees of the capital's other clubs still only had hope to feed their sharp appetites as dusk descended on deadline day. The nourishment provided by confirmed signings had yet to be served. Over at the London Stadium, things were even quieter than at London Colney. It could still go either way.

* * *

After being sworn in as vice-president of the United States in 1961, Lyndon Johnson astutely observed the simultaneous limitations and possibilities of his new position: 'In this, I am nothing, but I could be everything.' And so it is on deadline day for a fan of a club that's yet to declare its hand. Optimistic souls remain steadfast in the belief that the lack of an announcement is merely down to slight kinks in the deal being ironed out. A quiet day could yet, and very quickly, turn into a glorious day. They ignore the fact that, as the hands of the clock turn unstoppably towards the eleventh hour, no news is increasingly bad news.

I make a circumnavigation of the London Stadium's outer perimeter, that winter wind in my face in one direction and at my back in the other. I encounter just a single Hammers fan as I orbit the ground. Admittedly, he's an optimistic soul, one with the metaphorical wind permanently at his back. Jake is a twenty-something postal worker who's diligently booked a day's holiday to chase his side's final-day recruitment drive. He spent the morning outside the training ground and has been hanging around the stadium since lunchtime. He's changed locations for a reason; he has a specific goal in mind this afternoon. Jake wants to be the very first West Ham fan to buy and wear a replica shirt with 'Schneiderlin' across the shoulders. He then plans to march up and down the interior of nearby Westfield shopping centre in an attempt to earn admiring nods for his devotion to the claret-and-blue cause.

But there's a flaw in the plan. There has been no further news about the Everton midfielder Morgan Schneiderlin heading to the capital, and the club shop here at the stadium – where Jake hopes to order his shirt from – closes its doors at 5pm. That's in half an hour's time. He remains optimistic, having had his hopes buoyed by the news that another Evertonian, the Dutchman Davy Klaassen, is, contrary to earlier rumours, staying put at Goodison. With one less midfield berth available, Jake surmises that east London will now, to Schneiderlin's eyes, resemble an attractive and juicy carrot.

He could gamble: get the shirt done before the shop shuts, before confirmation of any deal. Be prepared. Show foresight. It might be a shrewd move, or it could backfire, seventy-five quid down the drain. There are plenty of embarrassed examples to be found online of those in a similar boat to Jake, professing love for a player before pen has acquainted itself with contract – an Arsenal fan who jumped the gun to get a Mahrez shirt printed, or a Man City supporter whose chest, to this day, still bears a hastily tattooed name: Kaka.

While Jake elects not to undertake the gamble, both the ongoing inactivity and the bone-numbing cold of the day haven't dented his enthusiasm, even though he's had to charge his phone twice in cafes over the last few hours to combat the battery-draining effects of constantly refreshing various Twitter feeds. 'I couldn't sleep last night. Deadline day is your birthday and Christmas wrapped up in one, isn't it? But Santa seems to have forgotten us so far. Maybe he's just overslept. I've got faith.'

If Schneiderlin does sign in time, Jake will definitely be the first to pay tribute via the medium of a replica shirt.

He's got no competition. Down in the basement of the club shop, there's not a single other customer around. The members of staff at the desk where names are added to the blank canvas of first-team shirts have no orders to fulfil. With their shifts ending in fewer than fifteen minutes, they're now in tidy-up mode. A casual observer wouldn't be able to tell this day from any other non-match day, such has been the deadening silence round these parts. Perhaps a clue could be found in the fact that the club hadn't arranged ad-hoc late-night opening hours to deal with the flurry of new arrivals and the clamour for box-fresh kits bearing their names. Perhaps, deep down, the hierarchy knew the headlines would be made elsewhere.

As the store's doors are locked behind me, I head back out to reconvene with Jake, but reality appears to have made his acquaintance and there's no sign of him. He's gone home, that optimism finally dented. Love proved blind. Santa never came. And neither did Morgan Schneiderlin.

As quiet as West Ham's club shop has been this afternoon, it's a wholly different state of affairs a dozen-odd miles to the west. Admittedly, the fact that tonight Chelsea have a home game against Bournemouth ensures that business is brisk here in the Stamford Bridge store, but there's another reason. Deadline day has been more fruitful here than it has over in Stratford, thanks to a who's-going-to-blink-first transfer triangle that saw Michy Batshuayi leave Chelsea for a loan deal at Borussia Dortmund and Aubameyang swap Dortmund for Arsenal, allowing Olivier Giroud to complete the triangle and become the latest in a lengthening line of big-money strikers to don west London blue during the Abramovich era.

But before the Frenchman himself has had a chance to try on a Chelsea shirt with his name on, several fans have already done so. Unlike their counterparts over at West Ham, those employees in the Chelsea club shop tasked with adding names to shirts have had a busy couple of hours. The racks are bulging with tops embossed with 'Giroud 18' on the reverse. Fans are forming an orderly queue to snap pictures of the racks before excitedly sending them to Arsenal-supporting pals. 'Personally, I've not sold one of them yet,' explains a member of staff manning one of the many tills. 'But I'm an Arsenal fan, so I'm still trying to get my head around it.' This public admission of his true allegiance causes mild concern among both his colleagues and the snaking queue of customers.

There are some fans who've not been content with just a snap of the new shirt and who've signalled their approval of Giroud's signing by digging deep into their pockets. Simon is a futures trader in the City who, after all the conjecture over the previous twenty-four hours about the Aubameyang/Giroud/Batshuayi triangle, has found it difficult to keep his mind on his work today. 'Don't tell my boss, but my eye was off the ball a little today. Distracted is what I was. But when confirmation came through that we'd got Giroud, I did do a little fist-pump under my desk. No one spotted it, though. At least I think they didn't ...

'I usually take both deadline days off work, but I'm off skiing next week so didn't have any annual leave left this time around. I just love it. It's a weird addiction. It's mostly ninety per cent bollocks – just spurious gossip or wishful thinking. We shouldn't be drawn in by it all, but every time we are.

'I'm happy with Chelsea's business. We've had a good window, although I'm not completely convinced by Ross Barkley. He's no Frank Lampard. Not yet, anyway. But Giroud is absolute quality. I can't believe Arsenal let us have him, especially after Alexis Sanchez went to Old Trafford. That's two direct rivals who now have stronger squads. And to think, going by the rumours, we might have settled for Andy Carroll or Peter Crouch. Giroud's in another league.'

Giroud was playing for Arsenal in that defeat to Swansea the night before, his latest and last appearance in that super-sub role that Arsène Wenger chose to reserve for him during his time at the Emirates. This evening, though, he's swapped the blue of Arsenal's away kit for the blue that instantly identifies his new club the world over. The switch was quick and absolute. A transfer can turn the tables, warping existing realities, recalibrating allegiances. Yesterday, Giroud belonged to one of Chelsea's biggest rivals. Less than twenty-four hours later, he's already halfway to becoming the new darling of the Shed End.

Outside the club shop, Simon sheds his powder-pink Ralph Lauren work shirt and slips on his new purchase. 'How do I look?' He looks convincing; with his build and his beard, he could pass himself off as the Frenchman's brother, were it not for his Thames Valley accent. A couple of Simon's pals express their approval, before all three burst into song.

'One of our own! One of our own! Olivier Giroud, he's one of our own ...'

* * *

'At the end of the day, fans know what a game was like. They watched it. They know the score. They formed their own opinions. The only thing they don't know about football is who their club is about to sign. So the thing that they are very, very interested in – and that they're more likely to click on – is transfer rumours.'

Matt Ladson knows what football fans like and, largely, how football fans think. Well, those who support Liverpool, at least. For nearly twenty years now, he and his old schoolfriend Max Munton have been running the This Is Anfield website; he proudly confides that they started it a full two years before the club itself launched its own.

This Is Anfield actually started life as a school project. 'It just sort of developed from there. It was a geeky hobby that grew and grew. We kept it going while we were both at university, while we were living abroad, and when we came back to Liverpool. It's now a full-time job for four of us and there are a dozen or so regular freelance writers and contributors. We have almost three million followers across social media platforms. On an average month, we have around two million unique visitors, which goes up significantly during transfer windows.' A pause of modest self-satisfaction. 'It's quite a big operation.

'The aim of the website back then was very different. It was more about opinion pieces written by ourselves and our friends, and was very much in a hobbyist manner. Then I came back from living in the US about five years ago and decided that the nine-to-five job was not going to be for me. So I gave it a crack at going full-time and, a year later, Max quit his job. We've both been full-time since then and are reaping the rewards. You've got to gamble and hopefully it pays off. So far it has, touch wood.'

What began life giving a platform to fans' voices has since grown to be much more. It's now a one-stop shop for all matters LFC, but which doesn't have a layer of PR veneer of an official site. 'We want people to come to us and whether they agree with the opinions isn't the point. It's more that this is the only place they need to visit to get opinions, videos, news ...'

And, when it comes to transfer talk, it aims to be the voice of reason among the deluge of hype and scurrilous rumour. For Ladson, the January 2019 window has been no different from any other. 'When newspapers produce a transfer story, all the other papers reproduce and regurgitate it. What we try to do is add a slant, to provide context. Fans might be seeing a particular news story, but the reality is that it's not going to happen, or it's very unlikely to happen – and we'll provide the good reason why. For instance, the likelihood of Jürgen Klopp signing a centre-back in this current window is very, very slim. He has consistently said he doesn't need to sign one, that he doesn't need to panic, that he's never panicked. He's not going to sign a player for one or two weeks to cover injuries. And he has a history of not throwing new signings straight in at the deep end, anyway.

'Fans need their drug, and that drug is transfer rumours. So many sites now publish so many misleading stories because they know supporters will still click on it, even if they don't necessarily believe what they're about to read. They still want to see what's being said about their club.' And, each and every time that a false rumour is repeated – or reshaped or exaggerated – elsewhere, it receives a little more credibility. The falsehood gathers momentum.

'We've seen it regularly in the last few years when a journalist has maybe made a quick passing comment on a news item on a TV show or a podcast and that's been turned into an article somewhere, then twisted and regurgitated.' Ladson and his team have an intimate knowledge and understanding of the kind of transfer talk that floats Liverpool fans' boat, but refuse to run a story on a potential signing if there's nothing new to say. There has to be substance to everything they write, not mere rumour-mongering to draw more visitors to the site.

'Last summer, every article that we published which related to Nabil Fekir got a huge amount of interest because people were so eager for Liverpool to sign him from Lyon. He was a player who the club had clearly identified and who fans felt would be a good signing. But it just didn't get over the line. To this day, there are still media outlets that play on that. They know Liverpool fans have an interest in him coming to Anfield, even though it's quite clear that he's not actually going to come now. The interest from the club has ended. It's a non-story. But there are outlets that have certain traffic targets and they know that a story about Nabil Fekir going to Liverpool gives them the traffic that they need.

'We have no target in terms of site traffic or revenue. It will be what it will be. It's as simple as that, really. The *Liverpool Echo*, for instance, have certain traffic targets from their ownership, from Trinity Mirror or whatever they're called nowadays. But we are still fans. We won't put anything out there that's misleading just to hit a certain traffic target. We will report as we see fit. And we are more likely to explain why a move isn't going to happen rather than claim that they're on the verge of signing that player.'

Launching the website a year before the window was introduced has allowed Ladson to see, from close quarters, the escalation in interest in transfer matters over the years since. 'As writers, we weren't really covering transfer talk on the site in the early days, but the forums were quite heavily dominated by it. And whenever we got problems with the server, it was invariably because of transfer deadline day. I remember the day when Liverpool were meant to have signed Clint Dempsey from Fulham, but it didn't happen. We were very short upfront and it was clear as day that a striker was needed. We had the whole hysteria of Liverpool not signing a player and our server was sent offline because so many fans were up in arms that we hadn't signed anyone.

'It's happened on a couple of other occasions since then. One of them was the time that we signed Luis Suárez on the same day that we sold Fernando Torres. That was a massive deadline-day story that everybody wanted to read about and share their opinions with fellow fans, especially those not based in the UK.'

As impressive as the site's year-round stats are, two months mark the high-water mark of traffic: August and January, the biannual climaxes of the window. August is particularly popular. 'People like things that are new,' reasons Ladson. 'A new season, new ideas, new optimism. It's sunny outside. We might be signing this player. We might have finally sold that player. It gets people happy. And when they're online, people want to read good, happy things. We receive better traffic when Liverpool win rather than when Liverpool lose. We print the same kind of content after a game no matter whether it's win, lose or draw. But after a win, that content will drive higher levels of traffic and after a defeat it will drive less. People don't want to read about it. They don't want to go over a Liverpool loss.'

This preference for good-news stories extends to transfer talk. 'Stories about incoming players definitely receive greater response than those about departing players. If it's a player who's not a mainstream signing, it's "Who is this guy? Is he actually any good? Tell me more." Even Naby Keïta, who Liverpool signed a year before he came to the club, created a lot of debate. A lot of people weren't entirely sure of him. Some people were massive fans of his having seen him in the Bundesliga. Some people asked "Why have we got him in now?", while others thought it was great business, signing and securing him ready for the following year.

'It's just the thought of the player arriving, his potential. Where's he going to line up? And then there's the knock-on effect. What does it mean for the player already in that position?'

Supporter speculation – whether it be about a new player, the future of the manager, plans for a new stadium – is as old as the game itself. Opinions have always been aired, whether on the terraces or in the tap-room. Online forums are merely the twenty-first-century equivalent of the saloon bar, albeit with a far larger potential audience than a gaggle of mates enjoying a post-match pint.

'A hundred per cent,' agrees Ladson, 'I've used that analogy many a time. It's basically what a football fan was doing ten or twenty years ago, but back then it was in the pub with his friends, whether right after the game or a couple of days later. Now people see the internet as a way of putting their voice out to a much wider audience. Now, I think that's a fantastic thing, but the problem I have is when mainstream media take half a dozen tweets from supposed Liverpool fans and then say, "Liverpool fans rant about new signings" or whatever it may be. The reality is that they picked out a very, very small number of supporters and this leads and informs the opinions for the rest. That's a real bugbear of mine. After each match, we produce a "Fans React To …" and try to gather at least twenty people's opinions, rather than just picking out a handful on Twitter and claiming it to be what all Liverpool fans are saying. The reality is that most logical and sensible fans are not saying anything remotely of that nature.'

The main source for Liverpool fans to swap transfer gossip and tittle-tattle on This Is Anfield is through the forum's Unreliable Rumours thread. This, though, isn't a free-for-all; Ladson and team are ever-protective of the site's integrity and a list of prohibited sources is in place. Both the *Sun* and the controversial website/podcast/YouTube channel KopTalk are on the list; transfer rumours from either aren't published on the site (although the former's ban relates to their reporting of Hillsborough three decades previously, rather than being a reaction to the reliability of their transfer stories). There is a further list of 'very unreliable and unwanted sources', which comes with the warning that 'posters are strongly discouraged from posting their almost comical, sensationalist transfer rumours'. These include the *Daily Star, Metro* and the Spanish website Don Balón. The Spaniards actually appear on the list twice because, as the This Is Anfield moderators explain so poetically, 'they're SO fucking shite, they need to be repeated'.

Sources regarded as reliable – the *Liverpool Echo, The Times*, the *Guardian*, the *Telegraph*, the BBC – get a hat-tip, as do certain journalists whose day-to-day work concentrates on matters Anfield. That is, people who know what they're talking, and typing, about.

On the day Ladson and I talk, Liverpool are four points clear of Manchester City at the top of the Premier League. With much of this success down to one of the most watertight recruitment policies in English football, has the level of transfer discussion on the site decreased as a result? Does having the most settled squad at Anfield since the start of the 1990s shrink the transfer agenda, both in terms of arrivals and departures? It's certainly a contradiction Ladson is aware of.

'Liverpool have got an absolutely fantastic transfer strategy at the moment. For me, their recruitment is a benchmark that other clubs should be looking at. But, yes, its success certainly affects things on the site. This current window is likely to be our quietest yet as Liverpool are highly unlikely to sign a single player. And if someone leaves, it's not going to be a high-profile player. Other Liverpool media, who have those traffic targets, are running stories that aren't really news. In the media today, there's a story about Lazar Markovic and how Liverpool still want to get rid of him this month. Talk about writing something because you need a Liverpool transfer story! We all know this is the case. It's the most obvious thing in the world. He's been training with the youth team for the last five months. He hasn't played for the club for almost four years. It's not exactly Fernando Torres going to Chelsea for fifty million ...'

Whether the This Is Anfield forums have contributed, in their own small way, to Liverpool's near-flawless activity in the transfer market is an interesting thought to chew on. After all, it would be rather myopic of the club to ignore the opinions of three million fans, creating what is in effect a ready-made, large-sample focus group.

'I couldn't say,' says Ladson diplomatically, but with a smile. 'But I can say that John W Henry followed us just before he purchased the club ...'

* * *

'Are you ready to have your say in the UK's biggest football debate? Your teams, your views. Get ready – *this* is 606 on BBC 5 Live, with Alistair Bruce-Ball and Chris Sutton ...'

It's a Sunday evening in late January in central London – specifically in Portland Place, where Broadcasting House, the BBC's mothership, is docked. It's the quietest time of the week here in the newsroom and its immediate environs, the slightest skeleton staff haunting each floor's open-plan office. But one particular corner is a scene of hustle, bustle and no small amount of banter.

It's an hour before 606 – the evergreen outlet that encourages, enables and empowers football fans to rant and rave to the nation – goes live. Tonight the show will be kicking off much later than the 6:06pm transmission time that gives it its name. The red 'on air' light won't illuminate until a few minutes before eight o'clock, on account of squeezing in all of this weekend's FA Cup Fourth Round commentaries.

In theory, this should give the youthful production team a little more time to hone tonight's content. A new feature is being introduced this evening, though. 'The Simulation Game' aims to call out the worst examples of diving during the weekend's matches and is still in the process of being chiselled and honed. While the team keep half an eye on the TV screen showing Chelsea's perfunctory despatch of Sheffield Wednesday, the main point of discussion right now is what music should accompany the new feature. Tom Petty's 'Free Fallin'' ultimately gets the nod, despite it being a song older than most of the production crew.

At the hub of all this preparation is Alistair Bruce-Ball, the 5 Live commentator who, alongside sparring partner Chris Sutton, took over presenting duties for the Sunday edition of 606 a few months back. This means that tonight's show will be the first in their tenure to cover the closing days of a transfer window. The expectation is that the phone lines will be busy with fans wanting to either praise their club's judicious early business or decry how lethargic progress has been. And with deadline day less than a week away, some speculation over which players might be on the move in the next few days wouldn't go amiss.

While tonight should produce more transfer-related discussion than usual, Bruce-Ball is keen to stress how interest isn't reserved for the windows. 'It's always there. It's always bubbling away. Fans are always talking about who their team needs and if they signed these two players, they'd be world-beaters. After all, we've never seen the perfect football team, have we? That's the ideal but you'll never get there. Manchester City are probably getting pretty close, but the argument that everyone brought up this year was there being no replacement for Fernandinho when he was injured. When he's been missing, they've struggled. For all their world superstars, this little bald-headed Brazilian fella in the middle of the park is the man who makes it all tick. So Pep Guardiola will still be looking. Managers never rest. He'll have this summer's targets in mind and then the window after that and then the summer after that. It's never-ending.

'But we don't necessarily stir things up, unless there's a big story in the offing. For example, if a team suffers a heavy defeat, this could lead on to us asking what will happen to Player X if the team continues playing like that, which then leads to the question of who'll come in in Player X's place if he leaves.'

The hustle, bustle and banter increases when Chris Sutton arrives. With his son Ollie acting as his chauffeur, he's hotfooted it from Selhurst Park where he was co-commentating on the Palace/Spurs tie for BT Sport. The office is getting busier now. Jonathan Overend has also just arrived from SE25, from where he was anchoring *Sport On 5* this afternoon. He's here – along with former West Ham and Villa captain Nigel Reo-Coker – to record the Football Daily podcast. Theirs promises to be a less boisterous, more reserved affair than 606.

Other than the sideshows – such as the new 'Simulation Game', and 'Sutton Death', the ongoing quiz between the two presenters which this week takes the world's biggest transfers as its theme – 606 is shaped by the themes and subjects its listeners want to talk about. While Matt Ladson sees more activity on the This Is Anfield site when the news is positive, is the opposite true on the radio? Are callers more likely to phone up to moan about a signing they disapprove of rather praise one that fits the bill?

'My automatic response to that,' says Bruce-Ball, 'would be what I would have said when I was just a listener, not the presenter. My feeling then would have been that they were negative and that there was usually something wrong. But actually, from hosting the show, I've found that that's not the case so much. As a presenter, you listen more. When you're listening in the car, you're not completely concentrating. The calls that then stick in your mind are the fans who are grumbling, despite their clubs having won fifteen trophies in the last twenty years.

'I can't think of a call we've had this season when it's been, "Oh God. Why have we signed him? What a waste of money." No one has given up on someone before they've even started. In the early stages of new signings, people are willing to give them a bit of leeway. A new player is allowed a bit of time to find their feet and, if they get off to a flier, all well and good. If a player quickly scores a couple of goals, it's "That was obviously what we needed. Hurrah."

'But the Chelsea fans gave Álvaro Morata a go, before deciding they'd had enough. It's then difficult to turn that opinion the other way, for them to come good again. I think our listeners will give a player a chance until it's showing that it's not working and then they pile in. When Christian Benteke arrived at Palace, the Palace fans were going, "Let's see what he's got. Let's give him a go." But now they've decided he's never going to score again.

'Although I watch a lot of football, these fans who are calling in watch their team week in, week out. They know more than we do, which is why you've got to let them have their say – unless they're talking absolute rubbish, when you've got to pick them up because you've seen enough of their team to know that's nonsense. Most of the time, though, you've got to let these fans talk and guide you. It's then up to you to ask the questions that any journalist would. You get the ranters and the ravers calling in, but there's no denying the callers love their football clubs and have been going to watch them for years and years and years. They're deeply passionate and that's why they bother to pick up the phone. You've got to respect that.'

There is, of course, the danger that those who call the show aren't necessarily a representative sample of a particular club's wider support. If a caller is a gregarious type, he or she is more likely to vent their spleen in such a public manner than someone meeker and milder. As Bruce-Ball himself admits, '606 is for people whose blood is boiling, fans who've walked out at half-time'. The quiet fan isn't the one to reach for the phone. The noisier ones are the dominant ones.

'True, although I would say that when someone comes on who's like that, I would always punt for callers who felt the other way. "OK, that's one opinion. If you're a Tottenham fan who thinks completely the opposite, give us a call." In a two-hour programme, you can't be totally representative. That's just the way it works sometimes. And I do enjoy listening to the articulate caller who argues an interesting point. But, on a show like 606, you do want strident opinions, you do want people to sit up and listen.'

At nine minutes to eight o'clock, that red light gets illuminated as presenter, grumpy sidekick and a couple of dozen callers go live to the nation. As well as asking for reaction to this weekend's cup ties, Bruce-Ball – excitable Tigger to Sutton's world-weary Eeyore – opens the floor to the listeners. 'That transfer window is closing on Thursday, so your thoughts please on what you want and who you need at your club.'

Watching from the studio gallery is like watching from among an orchestra. Steve the producer is the conductor, eyes and ears in all directions, issuing continuous prompts to both broadcasters and backroom team alike. Everything is fast and furious. To his right is Peter, the knob-twiddling studio manager; to his left is Matt, who's putting together audio clips as the programme progresses, and Joel, the assistant producer who's vetting potential callers.

Joel's role is particularly fascinating. Outside the gallery, two researchers, Lucy and Jack, field the phone calls and then rate their suitability for going on air, determined by both the subject that's vexing them and how well they're expressing their opinion. Based on the researchers' ratings and notes, Joel then selects the next potential contributor and calls them back. If they sound good to him, he'll ask them to hold on the line before they go live in a few minutes. While Joel gets to shape the direction of tonight's debates to some extent, he also shoulders plenty of burden. The quality control is down to him.

One of tonight's more erudite callers is Karen, a West Ham fan who wants to pass comment on the saga revolving around Marko Arnautović, the collapse of his proposed move to China and the subsequent signing of a new contract at the London Stadium. 'I personally think he'll go in the summer anyway. He's just got some more money for a few more months. He doesn't want to stay at West Ham. He's got an extension, but I think his ambition is to leave. He's kissed the badge and all that, but we've been there a few times with lots of players. You can say I'm a cynic, but I've seen it so much over the years.'

Karen's comments are reasoned and grounded in history, as well as being calmly communicated. Her blood is more simmering than boiling, and neither Bruce-Ball nor Sutton can find much in her words to take umbrage with. It's the same with John, a Manchester City supporter who's complaining about how the club is losing its youngsters because of a recruitment policy based more on big-money signings, rather than allowing youth to breathe and flourish. Citing

Jadon Sancho's success at Borussia Dortmund and Brahim Diaz's departure to Real Madrid during the current transfer window, John is concerned that Phil Foden will be next out of the door at the Etihad.

'We're losing them all the time because they're not getting a chance at City. I think Mahrez was a bad buy. It may sound stupid, but I don't think we needed him. I thought we could have strengthened in better positions. We should have given Diaz and Foden a chance.'

John is a constructive caller. He's not irrationally tilting at windmills, like some of the more extreme listeners spurred into picking up the phone. He offers an alternative system, positing the notion of having, in every first-team starting line-up, a mandatory three players who've come through the academy, along with two more on the bench. 'It would stop chequebook management, as well as helping the national team,' he observes. As much as he clearly loves butting horns with callers, Sutton also appreciates a well-argued observation. He believes John's concern over Foden is well founded, that the midfielder will have had his head turned by Sancho leaving the Etihad and subsequently breaking into the England squad. But the question is raised over whether promoting youngsters into the first-team would mean a drop-off in quality. John doesn't agree it would, but Sutton points to the pressure on Pep Guardiola. 'Man City want to win things.'

The deep-pocketed Man City quandary is one that Newcastle fan Jake would love his manager to be vexed by. 'He has got four days to make some signings or I do believe, and it pains me to say so, if Rafa doesn't get two or three men over the line, that'll be it for Rafa Benitez and New-castle.' Bruce-Ball and Sutton, unable to read Mike Ashley's mind, can't offer much solace.

A couple of hours of discussion and debate flash by, with the two presenters acting as sounding-boards – therapists, even – for both the listeners' invective and their dreams. Occasionally, though, a caller might simply be ringing to invert the process, to call on the twin-barrelled expertise of one of 5 Live's most senior commentators and a highly dec-orated, highly opinionated former player, to ask them what *they* think.

'We had a good call the other week,' concludes Bruce-Ball, 'from a Manchester City fan about this Fernandinho thing. "Chris, who should we get? I want to know who we should get." And it stumped us. We both thought, "Blimey, I've not actually thought about that." You're trying to think of someone who's available and realistic. There's no point in just chucking out Real Madrid's midfield because they're not going to come. Chris actually came up with Declan Rice, which I thought was quite a good shout – not neces-sarily saying he's ready to play at the base of Manchester City's midfield, but that was the kind of idea that fan was looking for. Again, fans are more knowledgeable than we sometimes give them credit for. They've got their ear to the ground and won't just put forward things they've picked up in the paper. They might have good contacts at their chosen club and will suggest certain players.

'But you also get the outlandish ones. We had a Totten-ham fan on earlier in the season and we were talking about them not having made any signings. He was going off on one. But in the same sentence, he said, "Basically, this summer we should have got Ronaldo and we should have got Jack Grealish." He was comparing the two, which amused us. Slightly different ballparks …'

CHAPTER FIVE

FIRST CASUALTIES

'I said to my dad, "I can't go back to League One. Everyone will laugh at me. I'm from Arsenal, I've played for England Under 21s. I can't go to League One. No chance"'

– Benik Afobe

A football club isn't a cooperative. No one is created equal. There's a clear hierarchy among its players, one that shifts and recalibrates itself with each contract renewal, each pay rise, each purple patch of form, each new arrival.

Those out on the fringes seldom move upwards. They tread water or they sink and slide. This is especially true in the Premier League where the odds remain stacked against academy graduates making the highest grade, climbing to the upper reaches of that hierarchy. The short-termism of a manager's tenure, plus the gush of cash flowing through each of the twenty clubs' coffers, means that proven, ready-made options remain the preferred way to populate a squad. A quick deal is done, with that incoming player taking his place near the top of his new club's ladder. Everyone below moves down a rung.

If upward mobility seems impossible for home-grown talent, the best that one such player can hope for is to tread water. In football, this means going out on loan. Sometimes there's a developmental advantage to this: the chance to gain experience elsewhere, to improve as a player. But there are plenty of examples where, says ESPN's Nick Ames, 'players hop from club to club in a state of arrested development, landing back where they began with little obvious benefit'. The *Telegraph*'s Adam Hurrey would agree. 'Quite how much thought and planning goes into where these battery-farmed young (or old) players are sent each summer isn't entirely clear.'

There's a multitude of players, currently contracted to Premier League clubs, who fit this profile. Chelsea appear to have a monopoly on them. Take Michael Hector, for instance. While he was at Reading, he went on loan no fewer than eleven times. Since he joined Chelsea, he's added four further temporary secondments to his CV. Todd Kane is another. Still contracted to the Blues, he's currently at Hull City, his eighth loan spell of a nomadic career largely spent in both the Championship and the Netherlands.

Lewis Baker is another Chelsea serial loanee who's also done time in the Eredivisie, with Vitesse among his numerous loan placements. Tammy Abraham still ultimately calls Stamford Bridge home, despite spending each new season scoring goals for fun for a different club. The Brazilian striker Lucas Piazon has been farmed out across Europe several times; what stands him out from his loanee contemporaries, though, is that he's spoken out against his treatment rather than blithely accepted his lot.

'It makes no sense to go on loan,' Piazon moaned to the *Daily Mail* near the beginning of the 2016–17 season, having just joined Fulham on a one-year loan. 'It's not good for any player in my experience – or the experience of the other boys. I don't see it as a positive thing any more. To be in a different place every year is not good for me at twenty-two.' Having served time in Spain, the Netherlands and Germany, remaining in west London for his latest secondment should have pleased, or at least placated, him. It appeared not. 'One, two, three loans – maybe that's enough. It's time for me to stay somewhere more than one year.'

Twelve months after his mini-rant, Piazon got his wish. Sort of. He signed for Fulham on a second successive season-long loan.

Piazon's grumbles aside, perhaps these players are appeased by the fact that, as a few other serial loanees have historically made the transition to the big time, going out on loan doesn't necessarily mean being shunted into the sidings. A loan spell could be an alternative route, perhaps even a fast track, to success; they could be following in the boot prints of internationals like Jesse Lingard (loaned to four different Championship clubs), Ryan Bertrand (nine loan spells while a Chelsea player) and, of course, Harry Kane, who temporarily pulled on the shirts of Leyton Orient, Millwall, Norwich and Leicester before establishing himself at Spurs.

Some of those Chelsea academy graduates, though, have tired of being sent from pillar to post. Acknowledging they're never going to break through at Stamford Bridge, they've cut their losses and sought permanent moves. They realised their best long-term prospects lie elsewhere.

Nathaniel Chalobah and Nathan Aké both reached this junction in their careers, taking the turns marked 'Watford' and 'Bournemouth' respectively. Their former youth teammate Patrick Bamford also flew the west London nest, his goalscoring exploits at MK Dons, Derby, Middlesbrough, Crystal Palace, Norwich and Burnley finally securing him a permanent contract with Marcelo Bielsa's Leeds.

While Chelsea famously have dozens of players on loan at any given time, they haven't had a complete monopoly on serial loanees. Any club with easy access to sizeable funds will have accrued at least a modest stockpile of young footballers. Both Manchester City and Arsenal will have a chunk of players out on loan at any one time, many of whom turn out for several clubs before being welcomed, if they're among the fortunate few, back into the fold at their parent club.

Benik Afobe was once one of those Arsenal serial loanees. Now the permanent incumbent of the number nine shirt at Stoke City, his path to the Potteries has been far from a linear one. This is a man who, at the age of twenty-two, had already played for nine clubs. Here at Stoke's training ground, after a lunchtime session in the gym, he sits ready to give chapter and verse about his nomadic career to date. But such is his convoluted, complicated past footballing life that he's pulled out his phone as a reference tool, just to make sure he gets the chronology correct.

There was a time when Afobe's career looked like it would only trace a linear route, a destiny to be fulfilled by an arrow-straight journey to glory. He signed his first professional contract in February 2010, as he hit the age of seventeen. There was already a weight of expectation on the shoulders of the young striker from Dagenham who'd joined Arsenal as a six-year-old. The talk around the Emirates was that this was the academy product most likely to not only succeed but conquer. He'd represented England through the age groups and scored goals without breaking a sweat throughout his youth. Barcelona were reportedly keeping tabs on the teenager, interested in him coming to Catalonia.

Having been part of the England under-17 team that won the European Championships three months after going pro, Afobe had a decision to make that November when a certain Arsenal legend had a quiet word.

'I was training with the reserves and had hit good form for them. Liam Brady, who was the academy manager at the time, pulled me out of training. "I've got a friend called Terry McDermott." As a seventeen-year-old kid from east London, I was thinking, "Who's this Terry McDermott fella?" Forgive me. It turned out he was assistant manager to Lee Clark at Huddersfield and was looking for a centre-forward. He asked Liam Brady if he knew any good ones who wanted to make a name for themselves in the lower leagues.

'Huddersfield were second in League One at the time and wanted me to go there as an emergency loan until January. I spoke to my family. My dad said, "You know what? You're going to play first-team football and it's going to be the best thing for you. Go on, have a go. What's the worst that can happen? You're only playing reserve football at Arsenal. Go and see what happens."

'So I swallowed my pride and decided to sign. I signed in the morning on the Tuesday. We had a game against Sheffield Wednesday that evening. I met my teammates for the first time at four o'clock that afternoon. I'd been around the likes of Fàbregas and Nasri, but I didn't know any of my new teammates' names. We were winning 2–0 and I was brought on with twenty minutes to go. Not knowing their names, I was looking at their shirts. "Ah, that's Pilkington. That's Peltier." But, to this day, it's probably one of my best sub cameos I ever made. I didn't score, but we won and I played really well, upfront with Jordan Rhodes. The next day, there was a story in the *Examiner*, the local Huddersfield paper, saying, "We've got a wonder-kid here."

'Moving to Huddersfield and being by myself, I had to grow up really quickly – from living the London life as a kid and then moving to Yorkshire. I had ups and downs there. I got injured. I think I scored eight goals and had ten assists in eighteen or so starts. From the start of January until the end of the season, we didn't lose a single league match. But, after going twenty-five games unbeaten, we lost in the play-off final. I was gutted that we didn't go up, as I'd enjoyed it so much at Huddersfield that I wanted to play in the Championship for them. But we didn't make it and I knew League One wasn't for me any more. I had conquered it as an eighteen-year-old, so I went back to Arsenal.

'That summer, I went away with the Arsenal first team and, personally, I thought I was one of the best players on the trip. I was confident from playing week in, week out. I know it had been League One, but I had no fear. I played in the Emirates Cup against New York Red Bulls – and against my idol Thierry Henry – and I got man of the match. Everyone was saying it was going to be my year. To this day, that's when I think I was at my best. I was in peak condition. I was unstoppable. My best mate, Jack Wilshere, had got into the team a couple of years before and I thought I was going to follow him.'

Disaster then struck when Afobe injured his hip in training, keeping him on the sidelines for six months ('rehab, rehab, rehab'). Once recovered, the following March he joined Reading as an emergency loan. 'It was only for a month. I started one match, came on in two others, and spent another three on the bench. But it was the Championship and it still meant progression for me. They won the title too, so I was part of a league-winning team. Being around players who were Championship winners was a good experience, so that was a successful loan even though I didn't really play.'

Another good pre-season with Arsenal failed to result in elevation to the first team and a third loan spell beckoned, this time a season-long affair to Bolton. While there had been positives to take from the first two, a sighing Afobe struggles to find too much about that particular experience that benefitted him. 'That was tough. The manager who brought me in, Owen Coyle, got sacked early doors. Dougie Freedman came in and wanted to play a different type of football. I had probably been advised wrongly to go there. Not only had they gone down from the Premier League, but their captain was Kevin Davies. We play in the same position and he was always going to play ahead of me.

There was fierce competition for places there – from the likes of David N'Gog and Marvin Sordell. I was playing out wide, just ten minutes here, ten minutes there.

'So I cut the loan short in January and went to Millwall instead, where Kenny Jackett wanted me. While it was still in the Championship, they were lower in the league and I would have got more minutes there. I played four games for them and got man of the match in three of them. I didn't score, but I was playing more like a number ten then – more tricks, more flair. I've changed my game since then. I try to score goals now.

'I was flying at Millwall. I was confident. But in my fifth game, I did my knee. That was the first time my girlfriend, who is now my wife, watched me play. It kept me out for nine months. I was still only twenty but, with the injuries, it was just stop and start.'

Each time injury struck, Afobe would return to his parent club to undertake his rehab. Everywhere he looked were reminders of what he had chosen – temporarily, admittedly – to set aside in seeking regular, meaningful football. His teammates from Arsenal reserves were still exactly where he left them, all dreaming of being granted that chance, while not doing anything especially proactive to make it happen. Being willing to play that waiting game wasn't in Afobe's DNA. 'They might have been training there, having lunch with Fàbregas or texting van Persie, but I ended up getting a hundred appearances in professional football and they only had two or three Carling Cup appearances for Arsenal. They weren't going to learn from a couple of twenty-minute cameos.'

Afobe was putting in the full nine yards to advance his career, while his contemporaries were content to be cocooned and cossetted. He preferred to get out and get dirty, to forge a reputation for himself, even if it meant continually dropping a division or two. He could have taken the easy life, after all. It wasn't unappealing. 'At sixteen, you have kit men cleaning your boots, you have a hundred thousand followers on Twitter, you've got a verified tick, but you've not played a single professional game.'

Afobe uses an effective boxing metaphor when describing these differing approaches, likening a player forever on the training pitches as 'more like a sparring partner'. He himself, battle-hardened by time served in the Championship and League One (and with the scars to show for it), was more 'a boxer who went professional early and who's got the experience, who's been to war'.

Once fit, the striker's next tour of duty was a January 2014 secondment to Sheffield Wednesday. A breeze in the park it wasn't. 'I wasn't the same player. I'd had my two injuries. But I still wanted to conquer the Championship. It was tough at Wednesday. That was the one loan that I didn't like. We weren't winning and I wasn't the player I could be – and I knew it.'

Three months' worth of Stoke's matches are set out on a whiteboard on the wall behind Afobe's head. It just so happens that Sheffield Wednesday are the next visitors to the bet365 Stadium, a chance for him to face his one-time club. In fact, the last visitors were Reading, another team Afobe is an alumnus of. Mathematicians wouldn't find that so remarkable. For a man with such a lengthy CV, the probability of facing a former club is pretty high.

The experience at Hillsborough took its toll. 'I hated football for about six months and needed to get back to my old self. That summer, I said, "No holidays." My friends said, "Relax, the season's over," but instead I decided to work hard. My brother-in-law is a performance coach, so he got my sharpness and speed back. I lost three kilos and my knee work was all good.

'I went back that pre-season with Arsenal and I was the best player in first-team training, every single day. They were probably thinking of loaning me out, but I thought that when they saw me, it would be, "No, he needs to stay here." Two weeks before the season started, the manager said, "Listen, you're going to have to go out on loan." That was when I was really heartbroken, probably more so than when I got injured. I sat there with my mum and dad, and said to myself, "Where am I going to go in the Championship?" Charlton wanted me, and so did Millwall, but by this time Kenny Jackett had gone to Wolves. He wanted me as well and had faith in me, but because I'd been injured, he couldn't say if I'd be his number-one striker.

'Then I spoke to Mark Randall, who had been at Arsenal with me and who was now in League One with MK Dons. I said to my dad, "I can't go back to League One. Everyone will laugh at me. I'm twenty-one. I conquered League One when I was seventeen. I've been on all these loans in the Championship, I'm from Arsenal, I've played for England U21s. I can't go to League One. No chance."

'Somehow, though, after thinking about it, I ended up at League One ...

'I thought I'd give it six months. But it was a risk. It was the make-or-break of my career – more than anything. I said to myself, "I'm going to focus. I'm going to live like a monk for the year and see where it takes me." Karl Robinson convinced me. He wanted me to be his number-one striker and I wanted to score goals. At reserve level, I'd score fifty or sixty a season, but I hadn't really scored goals during any of my loans. I had about thirty assists by the age of twenty-one, but as a centre-forward I was too nice. Karl Robinson taught me to be ruthless. I used to see a psychologist three times a week, who got me being the player I could be. I ended up scoring nineteen goals in half a season for MK Dons. I went from someone who scored two or three goals a season to being the top goalscorer in all four divisions of English football.

'I had played against MK Dons in League One when I was seventeen at Huddersfield and Karl Robinson remembered me. When you play against other managers, it's always good to play well because you never know. You never know the future.' This was Afobe's *Sliding Doors* moment. Without that first spell in League One, he wouldn't have had a second spell in League One, and he wouldn't have subsequently been catapulted into the Wolves team. Most, if not all, of those loan spells contributed to determining his fate. It was an accumulative progression, with Afobe extracting the positives from each loan spell. One step back, two steps forward. Or three steps forward, in the case of his time at MK Dons.

His half-season at Stadium MK was an undeniable vindication of his decision to learn his trade, and earn his stripes, lower down the leagues. 'By that time, I was twenty-one and all the players I'd grown up with had left Arsenal or were still playing in the reserves. Fast-forward to me now at twenty-six and only one of those players – Nico Yennaris, who's just gone to China from Brentford – has been playing at Championship level. Everyone else from my age group is either out of the game or, no disrespect, playing in League Two. They might have made one or two appearances for Arsenal, but at twenty-five or twenty-six, they're nowhere to be seen.

'Suddenly, every team in the Championship, bar two, wanted me during the January window. And Sunderland wanted me in the Premier League. For the first time since I was seventeen, I had options. It was either go back to Arsenal that January to try to break into the first team, or move on. So I cut my ties with Arsenal.

'I went in and said, "Will I be in the first team?"

'"We'll see at the end of the season."

'"No, sell me now. Let me go. I just want to cut my ties."

'I could have waited until the summer and gone on a free. It wasn't sad. It wasn't emotional.'

While Afobe was plying his trade across the country, he – and his striker contemporaries in Arsenal's reserves – were slipping down the hierarchy at the Emirates. Between that first loan at Huddersfield and that sixth one at MK Dons, Arsène Wenger had signed a serious number of strikers. Afobe was a realist who understood that, each time the entrance door opened at the club's London Colney training ground and a high-price new signing stepped through, another nail was being thundered into the coffin of his Arsenal ambitions. The stream of new strikers who flowed in at that time seemed endless – Chamakh, Gervinho, Podolski, Giroud, Campbell, Sanogo, Sanchez, Welbeck … Even Thierry Henry popped back for a couple of months. Out of sight and out of mind while on these loans, Afobe was now at the margins of Wenger's plans. Or even further out. Beyond the fringes.

After fifteen years at the club, his departure was a strangely unsentimental affair. 'I didn't go in and say goodbye. I just didn't want anything to do with Arsenal. I was so confident at the time. I was twenty-one and had scored nineteen goals. On Sky Sports News, they showed it. The top goalscorer in all four divisions: Benik Afobe. I was someone who everyone wanted.

'I sat down with my agent and my family. It was a no-brainer to go to Wolves. My old manager Kenny Jackett was there and he loved me from my time at Millwall. And I was a better player now than I was then. That first spell at Wolves was probably the best time of my career. I was confident on the back of what I'd done at MK Dons. That loan was probably what made me. Loan number six. Without it, I would have never played in the Premier League.

That year-long spell at Molineux, from January 2015 to January 2016, bore rich fruit. He continued to score for fun; the accumulation of his goals that first season for both MK Dons and Wolves came to thirty-two. He was the top goalscorer in English football, drawing the attention of Bournemouth. Ten million pounds later (five times what Wolves had paid for him twelve months earlier) and Benik Tunani Afobe was finally a Premier League player.

But, of course, the story couldn't possibly end there. There were yet more twists and turns in this serpentine career. Having started well on the south coast, a few injuries saw him lose his place in the team. Where others might have been content to be warming a Premier League bench, Afobe preferred to be gracing a Championship pitch and found himself back on loan and back at Molineux. He was perfectly happy to drop back down a division; his career might have becalmed otherwise.

'I could have gone to Watford, I could have gone to Palace, but again I might not have played. So I decided to go back to Wolves where I'd had the best time in my career. I knew the area, I knew the people. Plus, Wolves were top of the table, so I knew I was going to the best team in the league. But it wasn't easy at first. They were winning every week, so I couldn't get in the team. Then they lost a match, I came in and scored, and stayed in the team.'

As Wolves romped to the Championship title, Afobe contributed thirteen goals in twenty-one games, a return that also earned him a permanent contract at season's end. He was back in the Premier League, having only been away from the top flight for a few months. But then came his most curious move yet. Within four days of signing, he was off to Stoke City, now of the Championship. (Officially, the move was – another – loan at first, as Afobe couldn't be registered with three clubs in a twelve-month period. A £12m transfer come the following January.) His second chance of establishing himself as a Premier League marksman had been dashed.

At first, he wasn't best pleased by the unexpected turn of events, reportedly calling Wolves 'disrespectful' for the *volte-face* and moaning about how they'd 'caused embarrassment' to him. Nine months on, his take on the affair has somewhat cooled. 'Everybody always thinks it was obligatory for Wolves to sign me after playing a certain amount of minutes last season, but it wasn't. It was an option, not an obligation. But then the manager had different ideas and wanted to bring in his own players. It was more that the club brought me in than the manager. He wanted to do his own thing and the board wanted to do their own thing. It happens. I wasn't the only one. Barry Douglas also left, to go to Leeds.' (Douglas's departure was equally curious. The previous season, he had finished joint-top, with Leeds' Robert Snodgrass, when it came to assists in the Championship.)

'I didn't have to leave,' concludes Afobe, rising from his chair and stretching his post-training legs. 'I was under contract. But then I spoke to Gary Rowett here at Stoke. It was ideal. I knew I'd be playing. I didn't have to move house and I was happy in this area. And why would you not want to go somewhere where you're going to be playing more and getting more money? So it was another case of swallowing my pride – play a year in the Championship with Stoke and we'll go back up. That's what the idea was, at least …'

With no imminent return to the Premier League in sight, thanks to Stoke's current indifferent form, Afobe seems strangely – and commendably – sanguine about his treatment at Molineux. Having made a not-insignificant contribution to the promotion push, he retains little bitterness about being jettisoned in such a manner. Other players might still bear a grudge. After all, there are greater marks of gratitude than having the drawbridge pulled up on you and being dumped back in the Championship. Access denied.

Benik Afobe isn't alone in watching his former team-mates prosper in the top flight. This story is old, but it goes on. In the summer of 2017, despite appearing thirty-three times in the Championship for Brighton the previous season as they finished runners-up to Newcastle, Ollie Norwood was farmed out on a season-long loan to Fulham. Back to the Championship and no entry to the Premier League for the Northern Ireland midfielder.

Jonny Williams suffered a similar fate, despite also being an international player. The Welshman played in twenty-nine league matches for Crystal Palace during their 2012–13 promotion-winning season, including starting in the play-off final against Watford. Over the course of the following four seasons, though, he turned out just twelve times in the Premier League for the Eagles, instead going out on loan to a quartet of Championship clubs. He ended up in League One with Charlton.

Many players can tell the same tale of how they were released just as they were about to cross the border into the promised land. Another is Harry Bunn.

* * *

As Christopher Schindler's penalty hit the bottom corner and one half of Wembley exploded, Harry Bunn – along with the Huddersfield Town subs and backroom staff – was off like a whippet, out of his seat and streaking across the turf. It was a penalty that meant so much to the Terriers.

Here at the 2017 Championship play-off final against Reading, the final kick of the penalty shoot-out had just secured their return to the top flight of English football for the first time since 1972. The jubilant staff and players piling onto the pitch were now employees of a Premier League club.

It was a status that Harry Bunn would enjoy for sixty-three days.

Bunn – a tall, rangy left-winger – hadn't been a guaranteed first-choice pick that season, his fourth in West Yorkshire, and didn't feature in the play-off final. Nonetheless, he had contributed to the club's success, appearing sixteen times in the league during an injury-affected campaign, as well as scoring the opening goal against Manchester City in their FA Cup Fifth Round replay.

Bunn enjoyed the most settled period of his career while at Huddersfield. He had prospered too; the previous season, he was second in the Championship rankings when it came to providing assists. But then a pre-season hamstring injury at the start of what would become that promotion season ruled him out for a month. With the team hitting strong form early on, he was now playing catch-up.

'When the team's winning, you can't really go to speak to the manager and demand that you should be playing. If I were the manager, I wouldn't expect players to come and see me, saying that. But I managed to make around nineteen appearances in all competitions that season. Obviously I'd have liked to have made more, but it was great to be involved. And we had that good cup run.'

As the season progressed, promotion to the Premier League looked increasingly credible for a club that had been written off back in August as favourites for relegation. This scenario, for a player who's no longer a bolted-on first-team regular, can be somewhat bittersweet. While the gathering excitement of their club's season of success is infectious and difficult to resist, a brake is applied when personal circumstances are then considered. Should promotion be achieved, there will inevitably be new faces arriving to cope with the more vigorous, more professional demands of the Premier League. You might not make the cut. If promotion is missed, the current squad will largely be retained, including yourself. This was Bunn's conundrum.

'I did know that if the club went up, they'd definitely bring in some players. But it was only when I went back in pre-season, maybe the first day or the second day, that the manager came up to see me. "I think it's best that you're up for another club. I don't see you playing." That was the first time I got a definite answer. I'd made sure that I went back as fit as could be and it was a kick in the teeth. But you pick yourself up and get on with it. There are a lot worse things happening in life for other people.'

Having had a few sun-blessed weeks to consider the club's elevation to the footballing heavens, the harsh reality had been delivered rather bluntly on his return to the club post-holiday. Were there feelings of betrayal after years of service, even if his contribution to the promotion campaign wasn't as extensive as he would have hoped?

'I think so. I was surprised I never got a thank you from anyone. That was disappointing. Something as simple as a thank you would have been nice. The manager wished me luck, but the director of football and the chairman were there too. I'd worked under the chairman for three or four seasons. I'd done well for the club and was part of the squad that had won promotion to the Premier League. I'd have taken a thank you from someone at Huddersfield. It wasn't asking too much.'

Were Bunn a less stoic figure, someone prone to ranting and raving, he might have been more vocal about his treatment. Also, even if he was naturally predicated towards this kind of bitter behaviour, an outburst might have made life awkward for his father, the former Oldham striker Frankie Bunn who was, at that time, part of the Huddersfield management structure.

'Yeah, that was obviously in my mind. You don't want to leave on bad terms as it could affect other people. But me and my dad have always tried to not get involved in each other's careers. The first thing he probably heard about it was when I told him that same day. But he was fine. He said, "You know what you need to do. It's just another person you have to prove wrong, so find yourself another club." That's always motivated me. It's just a game of opinions, so you try to prove as many people wrong as you can.'

Bunn's story wasn't unique at the John Smith's Stadium that summer. Other players were also shunted aside, cast off in the same boat. Eighteen others, in fact; eight leaving on loan and ten departing for ever. Thirteen new faces arrived, some of whom commanded the kind of transfer fees that could only be justified by them being in the starting line-up every week henceforth. Having scraped into the top flight through the escape hatch of the play-offs and via the lottery of a penalty shoot-out, Huddersfield boss David Wagner felt a substantial overhaul of his squad was necessary to bring them to a standard required to eke out Premier League survival.

Among the incoming players was the left-sided Tom Ince, a capture from Derby with a reported eight-figure price tag attached. His arrival in early July knocked Bunn even further down the pecking order. Exactly a month later, and just a week before the new Premier League season began, Bunn was on his way. And not just anywhere. He was on his way down to League Two.

'I still had two years left on my contract at Huddersfield and I had a few loan offers from Championship clubs. On reflection, one of those would probably have been a better move for me. I could have come back from a loan move to Huddersfield, who might have been relegated, and I'd still be in the Championship. But Huddersfield were adamant that they didn't want me to go out on loan. They wanted to get rid of me on a permanent.

'I could have played hardball with them, but I just saw it as another opportunity to play some more games. As long as you're playing games, there's always going to be someone watching. And the longer you're out of the game, the quicker people forget about you. Bury were the first to really come in. It was close to home for me and they offered me a three-year contract, so it was another year in the game above my Huddersfield contract. And Bury were having a go. They'd signed a few Championship players, so if they got promotion, I'd have back-to-back promotions on my CV. That was my thinking.'

That first season at Bury didn't go according to plan ('I could give you a few excuses and a few reasons why') and, when we speak, Bunn is halfway through a season-long loan at Southend, where he's been reunited with his old Huddersfield boss, Chris Powell. For someone who – had he not injured his hamstring and lost his place in the Terriers' side – could expect to now be gracing the Premier League, is being in loanee limbo not a dispiriting experience?

'When I was younger, I saw it as a free hit. You have the safety net of going back to your parent club, but you're going on loan to these clubs thinking, "I might as well just give it everything I've got. I've got nothing to lose." For me, it's miles better than playing in the reserves. You're playing in front of a few thousand every week and there's no better feeling than that. If I could give any advice to a young player, it would be to go and play in men's football, whether it be Conference, Conference North, Conference South – whatever league. If you go along to a League One club and score fifteen goals that season, there are going to be Championship clubs wanting to sign you for the following season. But if you score fifteen goals for the reserve side, you might only have League Two clubs after you.'

The pain of his Huddersfield departure – and his subsequent slide down the football pyramid – might not have stung so much if it wasn't the second time that Bunn had been within grabbing distance of becoming a Premier League footballer. He's been denied a shot at the big time earlier in his career. In 2012, two months after Manchester City had snatched the title from their Stretford neighbours with virtually the last kick of the season, Bunn was flying to Austria with the first-team squad on their pre-season tour. While there, he would line up alongside the likes of Vincent Kompany, Sergio Aguero, Yaya Touré and Carlos Tevez as he gained valuable game time in friendlies against Al Hilal of Saudi Arabia and Dynamo Dresden.

At the time, Bunn was working his way up the ranks at the Etihad, having been with the club since he was nine years old. His inclusion on the tour was down to the absence of some senior pros whose national sides had progressed to the latter stages of the European Championships. Rubbing shoulders with City's world-class elite thus couldn't be interpreted as the dress rehearsal for an imminent ascension into the senior squad. It was, nonetheless, proof that his progress with the Premier League champions was moving in a forward direction.

'I was with City at nine years old, when they were in the Championship. I was twenty when I left, nearly two seasons after they won the Premier League. It was pretty much from one end of the scale to the other while I was there. I was about fifteen or sixteen when the money started coming in. I started noticing quite a few changes around the place, in terms of the facilities. To be fair, the academy was probably already one of the better ones in the country and was well-known for producing players. I would have preferred to come through earlier, before the money came in, as I would probably have had a better chance. After then, if you hadn't got into the first team by the age of eighteen or nineteen, they'd be on to the next one. It was like a conveyor belt of players. It was relentless. In the past, you probably wouldn't break into the first team until you were twenty-one, twenty-two. They'd hold onto players longer, meaning you'd get a better chance of getting into the first team.'

If it was a conveyor belt, Bunn was a stand-out product as the belt delivered the next generation to the powers-that-be. Not only had he scooped that scholar of the year accolade and had been captain of the youth team, he had also broken into the elite development squad, the only one in his age group to be offered a professional deal. The clear upward trajectory of his career leads Bunn to conclude that, when he was released by City in January 2014 after a series of short loan spells at half a dozen clubs, he was jettisoned prematurely. 'I've looked at lads from other clubs who were also scholars of the year and they were probably kept hold of a little longer than I was. I did feel that, if I had been somewhere else, maybe I would have had a better chance, a longer chance. That's just my opinion. Perhaps someone else might have seen it differently.'

While gaining experience in men's football on loan at Crewe, Bunn seriously injured his anterior cruciate ligament and was out for a season. At one point, it wasn't certain that he'd play again. 'That was a long time to miss as a nineteen-year-old. To miss a full year when everyone else is developing around that age means you're playing catch-up with them. You'd hopefully usually be playing thirty to forty league games and that's a massive chunk to miss out on. When I came back from the injury, I felt my time at City was up, that they had already made their decision on whether to keep me or let me go. It was pretty much a matter of me getting fit and as soon as I was, they were then happy to let me leave.'

Even without the injured knee, the odds on Bunn becoming a first-team regular at the Etihad remained slight when City's seemingly infinite petrochem dollars were filling every position on the pitch twice over with the highest-grade players. In the way that Tom Ince's arrival at Huddersfield shrank Bunn's chances of playing in the Premier League, the regularity with which new big-money arrivals stepped through the players' entrance at City had already done likewise. Reading the transfer gossip columns and seeing your club being linked to the world's best players on a daily basis must knock the confidence of all but the most precocious teenagers. Indeed, the path to glory at City, from academy player to first-team regular, was a relatively untrodden one. The club's recruitment policy was based on immediate need. Cultivating and nurturing takes time. Football, or at least football in the Premier League, is impatient.

'You're always aware of transfer gossip. You always see who your club want to sign. But when I was at Man City, I didn't see Samir Nasri coming in and think, "Oh no, I'm not going to get into the firsts. He's going to be there for years." I didn't really look at it like that. He was a proven top-flight player and I understood that if a Premier League manager has got millions to spend, he's going to spend them. It's his job that's at risk and if he needs results, he's going to bring in people who are proven at that level. As I got into the first team at Huddersfield, and saw players who played in my position being linked with the club, that was when I knew I'd have to come back in the summer better and fitter than ever, that there was competition.' Transfer tittle-tattle is taken most notice of when there's something to protect.

'I still had six months left on my deal at City, but they said they weren't going to offer me another deal after that, so it was up to me whether I went there and then, or sat around for the rest of the season and went to another club in the summer. There wouldn't be many lads who'd just sit around at that age, so I decided to leave in the January. I probably only played a handful of games after coming back. I had a short loan at Sheffield United just before that – I only played about two games there before David Weir got sacked, about two weeks after I joined. I had a couple of options, but I was still trying to get fit after the knee injury, so I left to go to Huddersfield on a free transfer to play for their under-twenty-three team for the rest of the season and to get fit.'

Bunn appears both thick-skinned and philosophical when talking about being released by his boyhood club, about how his long-cherished dreams had been erased. Perhaps this resoluteness was made even stronger because of, not despite, having had the ACL injury. 'I was aware of "What if?" I was aware of what could happen either way. From an early age, I knew football wasn't plain sailing. My dad's career was cut short. He was twenty-seven when he had to retire through injury, so I knew all about the negative things that can happen. My injury definitely helped me mentally. It was a tough time, but it made me realise how much I missed football, how much I missed playing. It was refreshing and it gave me more hunger when I returned.

'And I needed to make it work. If I wasn't playing football, there wasn't a lot else that I was interested in doing. I knew it was what I wanted to do. I didn't care who I was playing for. I just wanted an opportunity.'

If there's any bitterness about his departure from east Manchester – and it's microscopic if it does exist – his goal in the FA Cup on his return to the Etihad, an arrowed drive through Caludio Bravo's legs that gave Huddersfield a seventh-minute lead, offered a light dusting of redemption and revenge. 'That was one of the best moments for me. That's right up there. My mum and dad were there too. My mum used to take me to training at City three times a week, and then to a game on Sunday, right from when I was nine until I was eighteen. So it was nice that she was there watching.'

Bunn's strike was interpreted as a message to City about the talent they let go, possibly prematurely, possibly impatiently. It felt good. Not that City were unduly fussed. Their high-price superstars just went down the other end and scored five.

* * *

If the wearing of shorts on an extremity-freezing winter's day in Lancashire isn't sufficient sign of someone's innate fortitude, then the bone-crushing handshake confirms it. When Sean Dyche's hand extends towards you in greeting, you justifiably fear that you'll lose use of your own for the rest of the day.

Dyche's physical toughness isn't in doubt, as shown over the course of more than five hundred matches as a blood-and-fire centre-back for Chesterfield, Bristol City, Luton, Millwall, Watford and Northampton. In his more conspicuous second career as a manager, it's been his mental fortitude that's come to the fore, twice taking Burnley into the Premier League, either side of a relegation that might have weakened lesser souls.

In turning the Clarets into a credible top-flight outfit, Dyche has had to make difficult decisions, decisions that have directly impacted on careers and dreams and aspirations. He's had to be the one to deliver the bad news to those Burnley players who found themselves in the same position as Harry Bunn and Jonny Williams and Ollie Norwood, on the cusp of becoming Premier League players. Thanks for helping us reach the promised land, but we've got it from here on in. Have a nice life.

Making these unkind cuts isn't easy. Playing the role of executioner isn't one that any manager would voluntarily sign up for if it wasn't on the job description. The world of football can be a very brutal and unforgiving place, and looking from the outside in, with nose pressed against the glass, the swift jettisoning of players who've not done anything fundamentally wrong – and who have actually contributed to that game-changing promotion – might suggest a vacuum where sentimentality is concerned. Dyche contests this view.

'I'm sentimental, but not to the point where I won't make a decision. I care for every player coming in and for every player going out. I give care and attention to all of them. I personally care a lot about players' welfare. Are they leaving in a better state, mentally and physically? Is their life pretty good? It's just that eventually I have to make a decision. That's my job. I'm the manager of a football club.'

When Phil Brown clinched Premier League status with Hull in 2008, he couldn't be quite as ruthless and efficient in releasing players, penned in as he was by a promise he'd made his players during that promotion-winning season. He had guaranteed that each and every member of his dressing room would have a chance to play in the Premier League. It was a carrot he'd successfully used to lure them. Now he couldn't go back on his word.

'I'm an honest guy,' Brown defends, a decade later. 'I'm an honest coach. I cannot for one minute stand up in front of a group of people in a changing-room environment and say, "I am promising you … " and then don't. I had to fulfil that. Plus, I doubled everybody's wage.

'The only player who really had a gripe with me was Wayne Brown. I gave him one game and we were beaten 5–0 at home by Wigan, who had Emile Heskey and Amr Zaki running things up top for them. Wayne read the game well, but unfortunately just didn't have the legs. But I gave him a chance. He may not think that was a good chance and I'll hold up my hands to that. But I did give him a chance to play in the Premier League. And what makes a Premier League player? One game? Fifty games? A hundred games? I wasn't a top-flight player. I played seven-hundred-odd games in the third and fourth tiers, but never played in the top two divisions. So what makes a Premier League player? Just one opportunity or more? I gave Wayne a chance. We got beat five nil and I had to make changes.

'Not only had I given everyone an opportunity, but we had four players in that changing room who had played for Hull in all four divisions. It was phenomenal. A fairy tale.'

Since those times, fairy tales have been in short supply when it comes to clubs achieving promotion to the Premier League. Because of the cash saturating the top flight since BT Sport became a broadcast partner in 2012, hard economics have replaced romantic sentimentality – if, of course, there was ever that much sentimentality involved, Phil Brown notwithstanding. When Aston Villa met Fulham in the Championship play-off final at the end of the 2017–18 season, the accountancy firm Deloitte – a company not known for reckless hyperbole – billed the game as a battle for 'the biggest financial prize in world football'. Its analysts calculated that promotion to the Premier League would be worth around £160m to the successful club over the next three years, even if they were relegated in twelve months' time, such were both the revenue levels of a single Premier League season and the parachute payments doled out over the two subsequent years. Should the promoted club survive their first season back in the top flight, that figure would rise to an estimated £280m over the same time period.

When presented with such eye-watering numbers, when the prize turns out to be even more valuable in financial terms than lifting the Champions League trophy, it's much easier to understand why promoted sides subject themselves to a little surgery come summertime. A nip here, a tuck there. More often than not over the past few close seasons, though, clubs have undertaken complete face-lifts.

We've already learned about Huddersfield and their nineteen-out, thirteen-in summer business. They're far from alone. Plenty of other promoted clubs have done likewise. Their players, either loaned, sold or simply released, represent the collateral damage that's absorbed in the winning of a greater war. And that war is Premier League survival.

Prior to the 2017–18 season, their first in the top flight since 1982–83, Brighton recruited thirteen new players, while the same number headed for the exit door at the Amex Stadium, either temporarily or permanently. These were hardly like-for-like exchanges. The summer spend was in the region of £50m, while income on the departing players was negligible. But it was a calculated gamble that paid off, with the radically changed new side – now featuring instant heroes like Pascal Gross and Davy Pröpper – avoiding the drop in that first season back and thus earning a serious cash injection into the club's coffers.

It was a similar story at Bournemouth as they prepared for top-flight football a couple of years earlier. They had a net spend of around £54m for the 2015–16 season, as twenty-seven new arrivals landed at Vitality Stadium and twenty-six departed.

In recent times, Wolves and Fulham have spent even larger amounts upgrading their respective first-team squads for life in the Premier League. Being promoted the same season, their subsequent twelve months couldn't have been more different. Despite substantial summer purchases that totted up just over the £100m mark, Fulham endured an abject season, rooted at or near the foot of the table for the vast majority of it, a position that none of its three managers that season could improve. Wolves on the other hand, who themselves also spent a near-identical figure before and during the 2018–19 season, had an absolute breeze, comfortably making themselves at home in the top half of the table and reaching the FA Cup semi-final.

The difference? It was probably less to do with the *amount* each club coughed up and more about *how* those small fortunes were spent. To what degree did the respective managers have input into who was signed? How much experience of top-flight football did each squad now have? And how well did those new signings gel with the existing, promotion-winning players (or, at least, those who were still at either club)? Merely waving a chequebook clearly wasn't enough. The turnover of players – who should be signed, who should be let go – needed more careful scrutiny before the spending spree began. That said, the breaking-up of a just-promoted squad usually starts soon after the cheers and celebrations have gone quiet, as double promotion-winning Sean Dyche confirms.

'You look at who you've got and you look at who probably needs to go. You feel that this player and this player are maybe not going to help us in this different league, whereas that player and that player possibly could. We had to sign players who could add to what we were doing and keep us in the Premier League on an ongoing basis, and that's really, really difficult.

'If you go back to the summer of 2014, there were some obvious ones who we knew were going to go. So that was a cleaner situation. Sometimes, "outs" are very simple – someone just pays a fortune and so the club's business model says, "They've got to go." That's easy. The harder ones are when a player's gone past their sell-by date and are trickier to remove. They don't really want to go anywhere and you can't really find a home for them. A player might be sitting on a contract that's too healthy to get out to another club.'

While space in the squad needs to be made quickly in order to ensure the earliest possible signing of new arrivals, at the same time those players from the promotion-winning side who are being retained need some attention and TLC. If they've performed well enough during a high-profile season to stay with the club into the top division, chances are they've attracted plenty of attention from other clubs over the previous nine months. A smart manager will act swiftly to avoid heads being turned.

'Before you go outside to recruit, you've got to re-engage with those who've done well for you because they'll get poached otherwise. And you have to get on with that quickly. The numbers, of course, change radically from the Championship to the Premier League, so that changes everything with your existing players, let alone those looking at coming in. You have to find a balance to their contracts that is enough to make it work for them as individuals, but which also includes some caveats that, if certain things happen, allow them an opportunity to go and spread their wings.'

Once some players are given the vote of confidence and others given their cards, the process of bringing in new talent begins. Dyche finds it an exasperating exercise. 'Here's the honest truth. You have a big meeting, sitting there in a room with the key football staff – chief exec, head of recruitment, sometimes the chairman – pow-wowing down. "Where's our market? What have we got? Who's out there?" You can have a list of twenty players and you sit in this room, thinking, "I'm going to get all twenty." He'll go out, he'll come in. That chess piece will move there, that chess piece will move here, and it'll all go swimmingly. Very quickly, you get down to the last player. "Where did they all go? What happened?"

'That's life in football. And equally that's life at Burnley. We're not the number-one payer in terms of wages. We're not the number-one payer in terms of transfer fees. And we're not everyone's desirable choice. So therefore it's not always probable we're going to get the number-one draft picks. You quickly learn this.

'Let's be black and white about it. Finance is virtually always the key. But we can't just look at finance. We have to look at age, at saleability in the future, at the development potential of the player, at the background of the player … Are they the right type? Will they understand Burnley? Will they understand the work ethic? Will they understand how the team plays? Will they understand living in the north-west? There's a lot of things going on. Most clubs do a version of this. They might tick some boxes and leave others. We have to more or less tick all those boxes, which obviously narrows our market once again. Some clubs don't have to worry because they've got enough money to go out and get whoever they want. So when people say,

"Why don't you sign him?", there's often a reason why not. It's not because we don't think he's a good player. It's because he doesn't fit the model.'

During the close season of 2014, the summer before Dyche's first Premier League season with Burnley, the club spent less than £10m on new recruits. Two years later, after an immediate relegation was followed by an immediate return to the top tier, the summer spend more than doubled. An easy conclusion could be drawn here: that the club now understood the rules of engagement a little more intimately, that more money had to be spent to maximise the chances of Premier League survival. Dyche disagrees.

'We spent more money because the market had gone north. It was irrelevant if we wanted to or not. We *had* to. It was like buying your house in 1980 and buying your house in 1985. It was considerably different. The second time we came up, people presupposed we spent more money to have more of a go. But it was the market saying we had to spend more. The first time we came up, I think we spent nine million. The second time I think we spent nineteen. It wasn't about getting better quality. The three-bedroom semi was still the three-bedroom semi. It was just that the market had shifted. To get in front of the market, we'd have had to spend forty, not twenty. That's been one of our biggest challenges. We're constantly chasing a market that keeps running away.'

And this increased spending, of course, carries absolutely no guarantee of survival, as Fulham's calamitous 2018–19 campaign proves. 'Trust me. For any team that gets promoted to any division, their first port of call is, "Right, what rough points tally do we need to be in this division for the next season?" The second port of call is, "If we hit that target, how can we move that forward?" People said we had no chance in 2013–14 and that we were going to get relegated from the Championship, because we'd sold Charlie Austin two days before the beginning of the season. It was, "Whoa! Whoa! Whoa! What's going on? Disaster." But we got promoted instead. I told the team to forget all the outside noise, and these players came of age right in front of our eyes. It's not a given that success like that happens, but it can grow out of nowhere. Whether spending money or not spending money, a club can still grow. But money helps. You can jump quicker with the finance. It's no guarantee of success, but it gives you a better chance.'

Born out of need, Dyche runs a tight ship here in landlocked Burnley. His net spend over the last four transfer windows stands at around £10m. His current rivals – those jockeying for positions in and around the bottom third of the Premier League – can't boast anything like such tidy book-keeping. Two clubs each have a net spend over the same period that is seven times greater than that of Dyche. A couple of other clubs' spending dwarfs it by a factor of ten.

These are different approaches with the same goal for promoted sides: survival. Consolidating, or bettering, that position the following season, and being regarded as an ongoing Premier League club rather than a one-season blunder, is an even more elusive trick to pull off, as Dyche knows only too well.

'Once you hit that forty points or whatever's needed, how do you grow from there? There's a big stream of money coming in for the second year so, in theory, you can try to catch the market up. But don't be surprised if, every year, it moves again.

'Because that's what's happened every year.'

CHAPTER SIX

AGENTS OF FORTUNE

'Imagine if they deregulated black cab drivers. I could go and buy a black cab and go, "Right, where do you want to go, mate? By the way, there's no guarantee I'm going to get you there"'

– Pete Smith

In August 2015, it was reported that Cristiano Ronaldo had forked out for one of the most lavish wedding gifts in history: an entire Greek island. The recipient of this largesse? His agent, Jorge Mendes.

Jonathan Barnett, the chairman of leading football agency Stellar and the agent who brokered Gareth Bale's world record transfer to Real Madrid, spends much of his time, as you'd expect, shuttling between his London base and various European cities in the service of his clients. This he does in his own private jet.

The whistle-blowing book *Football Leaks* reported that the deal that took Paul Pogba back to Old Trafford in the summer of 2016 represented something of a payday for his agent Mino Raiola, a tracksuit-wearing, former pizzeria waiter. As part of the agreement that initially took Pogba away from United to Juventus four years earlier for a paltry £1.5m, Raiola stood to pocket 50 per cent of any subsequent transfer fee above £40m. So when Pogba's £89m return to Manchester eclipsed the Bale record, it was reported that, once Raiola's fees from both United and Pogba were factored into the equation, the agent was personally better off to the tune of £41m.

Forty-one million pounds.

As the *Observer*'s Ed Aarons has noted about football's super-agents, 'Mr Ten Per Cent has increasingly become Mr Name Your Price.' And when such stories hog the head-lines, it's easy for the footballing public to deride the growing interference by and influence – possibly, even, the mere existence – of such agents. The belief is that the vast sums of money that are hitting the personal bank accounts of the leading practitioners of the art could be more wisely reinvested in the game itself.

The ever-accumulating wealth and conspicuous con-sumption of these super-agents doesn't help the public image of their less successful, less ambitious brethren. They all receive a tarring from the same brush. At best, they might be regarded as a necessary evil. At worst, they're cynically siphoning off a chunky cut of any deal, turning the national sport into an exercise in mere economics, while callously removing its soul. As such, they breathe the same air as those with equally derided professions – traffic wardens, perhaps, or estate agents.

Pete Smith wouldn't recognise that description. As one of the directors of New Era Global Sports, he knows the true lie of the land. 'The Jorge Mendeses are few and far between,' he cautions. 'If they've got the talent – if they've got Ronaldo, if they've got Messi – it is what it is. It's all relative. If the players are getting five hundred grand a week, the commission fees are going to be high, but no different than if you're working in the City as a banker. There are a lot more poor agents than rich agents. Everyone's chasing the dream. Everyone's chasing to get that player, the ultimate player.'

On the evidence of the New Era meeting-room, here on the ground floor of their offices down a Bermondsey side-street, this is a company that's neither flashily rich nor dirty poor. Somewhere pleasantly in the middle.

The agency has both household-name clients and future household-name clients. They handle the commercial activities of Rio Ferdinand, a close pal of New Era's managing director, the former Millwall and Watford striker Jamie Moralee (the pair had a shared upbringing on the estates of south London). Also looking after the broadcasting work of the likes of Harry Redknapp, Robbie Savage, John Hartson and Alex Scott, they're justifiably proud of their clients' success. One of Scott's old England shirts has been framed and hangs on the wall, across from a glass cabinet displaying a collection of Rio-branded baseball caps. Evidence that New Era work in a mildly unconventional industry is conspicuous. Not too many meeting rooms are dominated by a pool table, nor have a signed Kasabian guitar hanging from the wall.

But New Era's activity is far from confined to the post-retirement needs and ambitions of those who've seen it and done it. It's a fundamental that the company faces forward, that it focuses on the future. It's all about hope and promise. So, alongside a healthy roster of established Premier League and Championship players (among them Ashley Williams, Chris Gunter, Michael Keane, Neil Taylor, and the Murphy twins, Jacob and Josh), comes a veritable squadron of young players either gaining experience in League One or Two or progressing through a higher club's academy system.

These younger players, especially, can take advantage of the combined wisdom of Moralee and Smith. They can learn from the bruises suffered by the pair during their playing days. Smith was a full-back for Brighton for several seasons, having been plucked from Greenwich University where, at the advanced age of twenty-three, he was two years into a degree. Signed by Liam Brady in 1993, Smith played under an endless procession of managers, including Jimmy Case, Steve Gritt, Brian Horton and Micky Adams. The office door seemed to be constantly revolving. 'We had a manager about every nine months or so,' he explains. Turning out week in, week out for such an unsteady club made him very familiar with the ebbs and flows of the professional game.

As his career later began its descent into the semi-pro ranks, Smith started working for the PFA where he helped start a small satellite agency – the not exactly thrillingly named Player Management Agency – to represent those footballers whom agents had yet to get their hooks into. Among the PMA's clients were Marlon Harewood, Curtis Davies and James Milner. He discovered, though, that working within the bounds of union practice was a little restricting.

Still playing on Saturdays and midweek for Chelmsford City, Smith found himself sharing a lift with Moralee, a former teammate from his Brighton days. As they shuttled up and down the A12 to and from matches and training, an idea was hatched: they'd start their own agency. 'We both knew the peaks and troughs of football and we felt that the players could benefit from our experience not just on the pitch but off it as well – financial help, day-to-day living, those sort of things. Jamie had a good career, but probably could have had a better career had he better guidance from his agent at that time and wasn't left to his own devices. So between us, we felt we could build a better environment, an incubator, where we could advise our players for the future, for life after football.

'Rio came on as a commercial partner, rather than on the management side of things, which helped us quite a lot. We earned no money at all on our initial five or six players for the first two or three years. But we started to build Rio's commercial and intellectual property and launched his online magazine 5 in 2009. That was born here. It was fantastic for him. It got him in front and behind the camera, and it really taught him how to communicate with people.'

Smith's belated entry into the professional playing ranks means he's ideally suited to sprinkle some real-life grit onto the worldviews of young players hitherto cocooned in the academy system. 'I worked on building sites, I worked in factories. I went back to university to try to get an education and then fell into football. Then went back to college and then went back into football at the PFA. I've done the full three sixty.

'It's hard to go onto civvy street. What are you going to do? Most will have no qualifications, so they can't go and get a job as a banker or something. But where they've been in their lives, they feel they should be able to get one of those kind of jobs because of the status and revenue they've had as a footballer. They're actually coming out at the bottom rung, if they haven't prepared themselves for life after football.

'They've been in the sheltered environment of academies. They're not worldly. They're not streetwise in terms of everyday living, in terms of the fundamental basics of life. They lack that and this is what we try to implement from an early age.'

We're joined by another of New Era's agents, Chris Gankerseer, who joined the company in its early days as Smith's assistant. Ropes learned, he then put together his own roster of around fifteen players to represent. In that time, he's seen plenty of ex-pros struggle to adapt to life when the final whistle blows on their careers.

'It's not just about what you're going to do to earn a living. It's about having a purpose to get out of bed, especially when you're used to that feeling on a Saturday playing in front of twenty, thirty, fifty thousand people. These guys, if they finish at around thirty-five, they've still got fifty or sixty years left, touch wood. That's a long time to live if you've not prepared.

'Some players go into the club at the same time every morning, they have breakfast there, their kit is laid out for them, they train, they have their lunch. It's all handled for them. We've spoken to players who've retired who don't even know how to book a doctor's appointment. All they've done for fifteen years is knock on the club doctor's door when they're ill. It's completely different when you're inside that football bubble.'

The New Era ethos is far removed from the notion that an agent merely steps into the breach come contract renewal time, trying to either prise a new, more lucrative deal out of their client's existing club or to manoeuvre a high-earning move elsewhere. Gankerseer is keen to confirm their philosophy. 'We didn't want to be an agency that turns up, signs people's deals and says, "Thank you very much. See you in twelve months." We try to put everything in place from day dot, like having the right accountant. They might start out earning five hundred pounds a week when they first go pro, but within two years they can jump up to twenty grand a week. That's a massive change in how you live your life and what goes with it.'

The public perception of agents' working lives is almost certainly an unsubtle, and at times unfair, one: negotiate the contract, bank a fat wedge for themselves, job done. Negotiation is, at least going by New Era's approach, a mere fraction of the 24/7 attention given. 'I drove to Manchester United–Reading on Saturday,' says Smith, 'then drove to Sheffield for Sheffield United against Barnet, got home at half-eleven on Sunday night. That was my weekend and straight into work on Monday.'

'We don't just go to games but try to see our players during the week,' says Gankerseer. 'You might be lucky and get a Sunday off, but even then if you're not at a game, you're still on your phone, whether it's during the transfer window or not. You might be seen on social media signing a player's new deal, but if you've had that player for ten years, no one knows what's gone into those ten years you've looked after him. People don't see that.'

'We're like social workers as well as agents,' agrees Smith. 'We're at their beck and call. As well as a client, a player becomes a friend to a certain extent. And you need good relationships with the parents too. Ninety-nine per cent of parents have not been in the position of earning a million pounds a year. It's a lot of money. The parents won't necessarily know what to do with it, how to invest it.'

Gankerseer nods. 'I have clients where I speak to the dad more than I speak to the player. I might speak to the player once or twice a week, but I might speak to the dad three or four times. You spend time with them. You travel to games with them. You get to know their families, their partners, their children.'

It's all about the emotional involvement, the care, the attention, the human touch. It's the antithesis of the approach favoured by the jet-set Jonathan Barnett. 'I'm not looking to be their best friend,' he once candidly declared of his clients. 'I'm not going to their parties.'

'The biggest agencies have to play a numbers game,' explains Smith. 'The company's so big that you have to have five or six hundred footballers. Could we cope with that? I don't think I'd want to go down that route. It's a bit like the *Jerry Maguire* scenario. That film is so close to the mark. He's saying that it's about relationships – your relationship with your clients and with managers and so on. You'd rather have a small client base and look after them rather than it being a numbers game. Upstairs, there are ten of us and we're all working to move the same players.

At the biggest agencies, it's every man for himself. I've heard of an agent pitching for a player, but the guy behind him already pitched to him last week. That's in the same company.'

Gankerseer appreciates the New Era environment. 'You can go to a lot of agencies and they're quite fragmented. People are sitting on their own and just looking after their own clients. As an agency, we're slightly different. Here we work together, which benefits the player more. If I know I need to move a player on, but I feel that Pete has a better relationship with that club's manager or chief exec or director of football, it might be better being put across by Pete.'

This considered, collegiate approach bears fruit in the boardroom. Those patrolling the corridors of power at a football club know they're not dealing with opportunists out to make the fastest buck and the hastiest exit. That's not to say, though, that New Era won't strive for the best deal possible for each and every client of theirs.

'The key element is knowing what your player's actual worth is,' explains Smith. 'A lot of agents who haven't got the knowledge will go in and sell their player so high that the deal won't actually get done. The chairman or chief exec will say, "No, don't think so. Can't work with you." Myself and Chris and Jamie know the value of our players. Ninety-nine per cent of the time we get it right because we've got knowledge of the game, because we've got knowledge of that player. We can sit with the director of football and have a conversation that's credible. It won't be a conversation where we're far apart. But if we get that much, plus a little over and above, we're punching the air.

'It's always a hard negotiation process. It's never done in a day. Or very rarely so. It can take a week or two – sometimes three or four weeks – until you get to where you want to be. We never do it for greed. We always do it for what we feel the player's value is in relation to the squad of players that they're playing with. At the end of the day, a club will have a limit they can stretch to – it's just a case of how far you can prise them. But it's not all about the basic salary. It's about the caveats in there to protect the player in the short, the medium and the long term of his contract.

'If you've got a player who's unhappy, who's not in the team, the first port of call is to speak to the director of football to see what the situation is. The conversation you have with a player and the conversation you have with the director of football or the manager can be totally different. It normally doesn't mirror.

'You say to the club: "What do you want to do with him? He's not played the last five or six games. Is he in your plans? Do you want him in the squad? Should he go out on loan to get a few games under his belt and come back in the next window? What are your thoughts?" And they may say: "Look, yeah, he's not in our plans. He's got two years left on his contract. We're happy for him to stay. However, if you can get any opportunities for him, come back to us. This is what we want for him." Me and Chris will then sit down, write a list of potential clubs and call them all up.

'It may be that we have to convince the CEO or sporting director to let the player go. When Joel Lynch was leaving Huddersfield, they didn't want him to go. They wanted him to stay for another year. So he had to go in and see the manager and say, "It's been great, but I want to go to pastures new. I want to go back to London." I can't say to a manager, "My player wants to go." Well, I can, but for me it needs to come from the player. The manager might otherwise be thinking I'm saying it for my benefit. We always say the benefit is always for the player. That's our priority. Get the deal done, get the move done, get the financials done. We come after.

'We can't tell the football club to sell a player. We can request it and have the conversation. We can put the case forward. Ashley Williams going to Everton was a prime example. He'd been at Swansea for many years. He was their captain, their leader. They had great success under Ash. [Swansea chairman] Huw Jenkins didn't want to let Ash go and I could see why. Why would he want to lose his captain? Ash had been their spearhead for the previous eight years, but he was at that age when he needed to go to pastures new, to have the last few years of his career in a different environment. Ash, Jamie and myself all had conversations with Huw. And Huw saw the light in the end and granted him the move.'

This very afternoon, as Smith explains the respectful and diligent procedures New Era operate by, another method is in full effect. Marko Arnautović's agent has been busy informing the media that his client, who just happens to be his brother, wants to leave West Ham for a move to China. Danijel Arnautović talks in terms of the striker wanting 'to go to a new market and challenge for titles'. There's no mention of the financial lure, of the wallet-plumping personal terms being offered to a player who's on the brink of his thirtieth birthday. The reported package of £200,000 a week is an amount that equates to more than £40m across the length of the four-year contract.

The planting of stories in the press by agents might be a commonplace practice, but Smith casts doubts on their effectiveness in getting what a player wants. 'Personally, I'm not sure stories that journalists print have any bearing or any movement on a player. It goes out into the public domain and people pick it up, but does that make a difference whether a player moves or not? I can't think of an example where that's happened.' Indeed, in this particular window Arnautović elects not to leave for China. Smith's analysis seems to be spot-on.

Arnautović is far from the only family member currently representing a top-flight player. A glance at the FA's list of registered agents – or intermediaries, as they're now referred to – throws up some familiar surnames. It's not tricky to deduce the main clients of Dane Rashford, Tyler Alexander-Arnold or David Robson-Kanu.

Brothers, fathers and uncles might believe themselves to be best placed to further – to maximise, in fact – the possibilities and progress of their sibling, son or nephew, but as Smith argues, more often than not, this self-belief is woefully misguided.

'There are many dads who want to be their son's intermediary. Nine times out of ten, though, they'll end up doing a disservice to their son. Not intentionally, but because they just don't understand or know the game. It's great if you're at Chelsea and the deals do themselves, but it's when players are released that's important. Where's their network? Who's going to work on their behalf? Who's going to phone up eighty-odd clubs? Is their dad going to do that for them? Has he got those contacts? Can he just pick up the phone to CEOs?'

The ease with which not only family members, but any Tom, Dick or Harry can currently set themselves up as agents is a source of ire to Smith and Gankerseer. In 2015, FIFA deregulated the profession. Previously, a tough entrance exam had to be passed, and insurance cover taken out, before anyone could represent a player. With deregulation, that exam was ripped up. Now, to be accepted by the FA as an agent in the UK (or intermediary – the job title altered at the same time), you simply have to have no criminal record, no bankruptcy history and be able to pay the initial £500 fee. It proved attractive: twelve months after deregulation, the number of agents registered with the FA had almost trebled, from 518 to 1,516. Industry observers and existing agents alike likened it to the Wild West, a lawless free-for-all ripe for unscrupulous behaviour and banditry.

As Dan Chapman, the regional officer of the Association of Football Agents, noted at the time, 'because a player sees that a person is an FA-endorsed intermediary – and they are on the official list when they check it up – the player thinks that person has an understanding of how the job works.'

Four years on, Smith continues to scratch his head. 'I still can't, to this day, think why they would deregulate it and what the positives could be. What was the purpose of it? You've given carte blanche to everybody in the world to be an intermediary without needing to know any of the rules and regulations set out by their federations. Imagine if they deregulated black cab drivers. I could go and buy a black cab and go, "Right, where do you want to go, mate? By the way, there's no guarantee I'm going to get you there…" It's the same principle. In fact, it's worse, because you're dealing with millions and millions of pounds. A small percentage of these intermediaries are qualified. The rest have no experience or knowledge of the industry.'

Smith gently pounds his fist into his thigh. All this time later, a mixture of incredulity and anger continues to simmer. 'It can't be right.'

It's not the first time he's been annoyed by the regulations (or lack of them) governing how agents operate. Even in the era of the agent's exam, there were anomalies in the system that gave advantages to some. 'Solicitors and lawyers never had to do the exam before deregulation. They automatically received an agent's licence. So even if they had no knowledge of football, just because they were lawyers, they could go and conduct a negotiation for a footballer. They wouldn't necessarily know where a player was in his career, so they wouldn't know which clauses would be beneficial to the player. For example, after the tenth game he gets an uplift, or after fifteen games he gets a renegotiation of his contract. They would have had no knowledge or experience of that. I never understood why the FA allowed them to be agents, just because they'd qualified as lawyers. They weren't qualified in the football industry. That was always a bugbear for me.'

Whether the change from 'agents' to 'intermediaries' was an attempt for the FA to smudge and blur the reputation some agents had soiled the profession with, is unclear. 'Personally, I'd rather be called an agent than an intermediary. I'm a football agent who represents players and managers. "Intermediary" cheapens the role. We passed the exam, which wasn't easy, and have been successful in the marketplace, only to be brought down to the same level as everybody else.'

Many of these newly minted intermediaries will have little understanding about the subtleties of the football industry, while also not having had carefully cultivated relationships over a period of time with those who matter in the game. In cold-calling the decision-makers, their overtures are likely to be clumsy and indelicate. Bulls in a china shop.

'I imagine the phones of managers and directors of football and chief execs don't stop with messages and calls from people,' says Gankerseer. 'Before it was a few hundred licensed agents and everyone would largely know each other. Now it's into the thousands. Nathan Jones has taken over at Stoke today and his phone must be going absolutely mad.' Smith shoots his colleague a smile. 'It will be on fire. He will have a thousand calls a day.'

Judging by Smith's on-silent phone, which has been vibrating away on the coffee table between us for the last hour, he gets no shortage of calls throughout the waking hours of the day either. The phone's especially busy as we're halfway through January, but you suspect it never stays silent for long during the other eleven months of the year.

'We didn't start this window on the first of January. We've been doing it throughout November and December, talking to clubs to see what they're looking for when it comes to January. Loans? Permanents? Centre-forwards? Centre-halves? We'll then start a spreadsheet of "club wants" and try to fill those in with what we've got. We'll then try to get a deal done by getting the two CEOs together. They don't really speak all that much. In my opinion, they don't speak enough. We end up being the intermediary. "Tell him I want three million." "Well then tell him we've only got two million." We end up being the negotiator when really they should just have a chat. We end up going back and forth. We're the glue.'

Gankerseer agrees. 'Typically on a transfer you'd be talking to six, seven, eight people who are involved. It's not just a case of one person on one side, one person on the other.' Accordingly, swift deals are rare; mostly it's treading backwards through treacle, with everything taking longer than everyone wants. 'If you're going to the Premier League, a medical can last two days,' says Smith. 'You get there thinking, "Get this done and I'll be out of here by six." Then you end up staying overnight. And possibly the next night as well. The paperwork's easier these days, though. It used to be horrendous. I did Jonny Williams' move from Palace to Charlton last week. It was literally two pieces of paper.

'In this window, we're looking at around twenty or so of our players to either move or go on loan. The vast majority will be loan deals, without a doubt. If you're a mid-table club and you just need someone to tide you over, or if you're bottom of the league and you're after someone to help get you out, it's the cheaper option. Why go and buy a player for two million when you can spend five hundred grand on his wages for twenty-four weeks? If it's successful, you can then consider bringing him in permanently. But then the chairman's thinking, "Hmmm, are we actually going to keep this manager? Are we going to have a change?" So a lot of these deals will be based on loans.'

While the next few weeks will be extremely busy at New Era, January 31st will be the true day of reckoning. All the while that the window remains even slightly ajar, there's the chance of deals being done. As well as last-minute over-spending favouring the agent and his percentage, the cut and thrust of that last day of trading emits a definite, life-affirming buzz.

The diligent agent, one who's open all hours for his clients, has to be prepared for any eventuality in these closing hours, for any sudden move that reveals itself. Whether a player's career is a success or failure may depend on it. Curveballs might yet be thrown, and multiple destinations might be on the itinerary. But Smith is well versed in reacting swiftly. 'You keep your suit in the car and if something happens, you bang up the motorway.'

This is life at the sharp end. Who needs a Greek island anyway?

* * *

Smith and Moralee are far from alone in being former players who've gone down the agenting route. Another glance at the FA's list of licensed intermediaries throws up plenty of familiar names. And there's a pattern to those that jump out. The playing days of most of them pre-date the cash-rich times of English football, an era when a player wasn't financially set up for the rest of his life upon retirement. These are players who haven't gone down the avenues of coaching or punditry, but who want to retain that connection to the game while paying the bills.

The names are the kind that are staples of the where-are-they-now features in the printed press. And where the likes of David Hodgson and Ian Harte and Julian Joachim and Marco Gabbiadini and Paul Peschisolido and Paul Warhurst are is in the agents' quarters.

There are even a couple of ex-players who, while no strangers to the pundits' couch, have elected to lend their expertise to another branch of the game and become registered agents. And right now they're walking across the reception area of this country hotel on the outskirts of Southampton. One's tall and looking decidedly smart-casual, ready for a date later this morning on the nearby golf course. The other is shorter and more sharply dressed than anyone needs to be at ten in the morning. The knowing nods they're receiving from the hotel staff suggest them to be well-known faces round this part of the world. And they are. Legends, in fact. Their names are Matt Le Tissier and Francis Benali.

The pair's latest venture is 73 Management, a small agency that aims to have a decidedly hands-on approach with its clients (the name is a combination of their favoured shirt numbers). Its formation wasn't just a response to the changing, increasingly mercenary landscape of football, but was also driven by the knowledge they've accumulated over the course of a combined sixty-plus years since they first signed professional forms. Punditry is all well and good, but they needed another outlet to impart this wisdom onto players more directly.

When they turned professional in the late eighties, agents were both less conspicuous and less numerous. Some players had them, some players didn't. 'I had an agent from the age of around twenty,' explains Le Tissier. 'I was looked after by Jerome Anderson throughout my whole career. Obviously he didn't make a lot of money out of me because I didn't go anywhere, but he did other stuff for me – boot deals and newspaper articles and that kind of stuff. It worked fine for me. He would probably have preferred it if I'd moved on and he'd made a bit more money out of me. I don't think everybody had agents back in the early nineties. It was possibly a fifty-fifty split. And there weren't that many agents around.'

Benali was one of the other 50 per cent. 'I was born and raised in the city and never had any desire to leave. Playing for my hometown club, the challenge for me was to stay in the team. Players came in over the years to compete with, but there was never a desire to leave. I wanted to achieve success here. So I only had one agent do one contract for me. All the other times, it would have been a case of me sitting down in front of the manager and pretty much just accepting the terms that were slid across the table. There was almost no negotiation on that first contract. You pretty much signed what was offered. And I never once asked what Matt or my other teammates were earning. What other players were on never interested me. If I was happy with the terms of my contract, that was all that mattered. Over the years, the terms probably reflected the fact that the club always knew I never wanted to leave. Having said that, I never signed anything I didn't want to.'

The idea that players wouldn't have had a clue of what money their teammates were on now seems so alien at a time where, for instance, Alexis Sanchez's £400,000 weekly wage is splashed across every back page. Le Tissier shakes his head at Sanchez's reported salary. 'I always take that kind of stuff with a pinch of salt. Towards the end of my career, I'll never forget Sky Sports News did a piece on players' wages and my name got put on the board as earning twenty-five grand a week. "Shit! I'm being seriously underpaid here!" They were nowhere near. I was on three-and-a-half thousand pounds a week. They must have just plucked a figure out of the air and were absolutely a million miles away. So whenever I read in the papers that someone's going to be on three hundred and fifty grand a week or whatever, I know they're guessing.

'The Bosman ruling definitely helped the players in their negotiations. To have the option of running down their contracts and going for free was something the clubs were obviously going to be pretty wary of. If you were a player, anything that helped you in your negotiations was a good thing. But I'm not sure the rise of the agent was just down to Bosman. I think it came along with the rise in players' wages as a result of the money coming into the Premier League. People saw this was a league that would be awash with money and there was an opportunity to go and make some. The Premier League transformed the game, let's be honest. When we first started our careers in the mid-eighties, it wasn't a particularly great time for English football. Clubs were banned from Europe and hooliganism was still around. The Premier League did grab it by the throat, changed it round and made it into a desirable product that's now sold around the world for billions and billions of pounds.'

'There are a number of reasons for becoming agents,' explains Benali. 'We've come through the sport as players in very much a different era. We've been in that scenario as an individual in discussion with a manager or whoever over terms and sometimes that can be a little uncomfortable for the player.'

Le Tissier agrees. 'It's to take the conflict away. You don't want the player being in conflict with the club. The guy in the middle can do all the stuff and the player can concentrate on his football, not worried that he's upset someone in the boardroom because he's demanding too much. That's one of the reasons why players have agents, to take that worry out of their minds. What we wanted to do, with our experience in the game, is to be mentors for the boys that we're looking after. We can pass on our experiences. I didn't want to coach. I had no interest in coaching. But I built up a lot of experience after seventeen years at the football club and I felt it would be a nice idea to pass that on in some way, if it wasn't through coaching.

'I saw too many transfers of players – young English players, mainly – who were being taken to football clubs by their agents, knowing they weren't going to get in that team. They were going there for the payday. Perhaps the agent was getting a bigger payday out of that move. I wanted to be able to look after players, and do the best for their career, and not move them somewhere just because we'd make an extra few quid out of it. That's not what we're about and never have been. We want to make sure that players get the most out of their careers and don't just come out of it with the biggest bank balance they possibly could. I want them to come out of it thinking, "Do you know what? I've done eighteen years in the game, I've played more than five hundred games. I couldn't have done more. I haven't just sat on the bench for four or five years, picking up my money and doing nothing for it. I've had a fulfilling career."

'The best thing for me about being a footballer was that, at three o'clock on Saturday afternoon, I was walking out in front of all those people to do what I did best. The more often you do that in your career, the more fulfilled you'll feel at the end of it. You have just won at life if you have just spent eighteen years of your life getting paid for something that you love. No better feeling.'

It sounds like the pair view themselves much more as advisers than negotiators. They readily admit that they charge a smaller percentage on their clients' earnings than other agents. Yes, it's a commercial venture, but there's a streak of altruism running through the whole endeavour.

'The four of us, the four shareholders who are involved in it, we've all got good jobs. We don't rely on 73 Management for an income and that puts us in the nice position where we don't have to charge extortionate amounts of money for our services.'

Knowing that the percentages from whatever deals being negotiated aren't going towards repayments on overpriced cars or second homes, their clients are reassured. The players know that the enterprise, while not simply born out of love, isn't born out of necessity either, as Benali explains.

'Hopefully the players who are interested in us representing them are fully aware that we've got their best interests at heart. It's not for the reason of moving them to other clubs to line our own pockets. Yes, there are contracts to negotiate, but there are many other aspects to what we provide, and to what we want to provide. Ultimately, we want players who are going to trust us. That's paramount to us. That's our philosophy.

'I think there's a negative association with the word "agent". We prefer to be known as mentors. Seeing how some players were being taken care of – or not in certain cases – was a big part of it. We look to have input on every element that requires the services of a management team, but the mentoring side was a large part of it.'

Le Tissier takes up the baton. 'If you're going to be looked after by somebody, why not be looked after by somebody who's been in your position, who can give you first-hand advice? Not your mate from around the corner who's done nothing and just wants to take a little piece of what you're earning. Do it properly and go with somebody you look up to, someone who'd make you think, "You know what? I could learn something from him." That's the sensible way to go.'

The agency has seven clients at present and focuses on those in their late teens – either academy players or graduates – and they're scattered around the country. Unsurprisingly, a couple of them are with Southampton, but Swansea, Huddersfield, Ipswich and Dundee United currently have 73 Management players on their books. Benali notes, though, that they wouldn't be averse to signing established pros – 'as long as it was right for both parties'.

Their respective long careers can only mean that parents of possible future clients will be reassured by what they have to say to them – and the reasons for saying it. It's a question of both sides trusting the other that their motivation isn't money. Leave that to the others.

'Players have their own opinions about their wishes about what they want to do,' says Benali. But behind the scenes, what are they being told? How are they being guided? How are they being advised? And if it's a commercial and monetary reason for moving a player, and they're being fed that by their agent, then you're going to see these scenarios where deals happen more because of the agent being a greater influence on the player.'

Le Tissier rebalances the argument slightly. 'I wouldn't be quick to tar every agent with the same brush. I think players can be pretty mercenary too, but aren't willing to admit that and will use their agent as the cover for the deal. You have to appreciate that football is a short business and that some players are just in it for the money. But they'll never come out and say, "I've signed for this club because they're paying me fifty per cent more than another club has offered me."'

They both acknowledge that the removal of the agents' exam has both flattened and widened the playing field. 'It wasn't just the exam,' notes Le Tissier, 'but there was also a hundred grand bond that had to be put down, which would have scuppered a lot of people's hopes of becoming agents. Now any man and his dog can pay his five hundred quid and away he goes. It is very much a boom business.'

The occasional bad practices adopted by those untutored, unexamined newer agents are alien to this particular agency. 'I'd rather not have a player than have to pay his parents, or offer his parents a job somewhere in the company, to get him on our books. That's not the kind of person we're looking for.'

Nor will Benali and Le Tissier be the kind of agents who try to ship players on in every transfer window for the sake of their personal cashflow. Playing the long game is key, although they acknowledge that transfers happen more frequently, and that players move around to a greater extent, than they did in their day.

'I think one-club men will become rarer and rarer,' declares Le Tissier. 'You will get the odd one at a big club who will be good enough to spend his entire career there, who wins trophies and doesn't feel the need to move on, but I certainly think when it comes to the likes of people like myself – at a smaller club but turning down bigger clubs – that day has probably gone. If you asked me honestly now if I was at Southampton – where the average wage might be, say, fifty or sixty grand a week – and another club offered me two hundred and fifty grand a week, you know what? I'd probably think about that! And

I was as loyal as anybody. The figures are so astronomical these days that it must be difficult for the players to think, "You know what? I'm going to stay here and earn that much less when I could be a multimillionaire and sorted for life elsewhere."'

Even Benali, who only ever had eyes for his hometown club, might have been tempted elsewhere were he playing in this era. 'The sums of money now are just on a completely different level to what they were when we were playing. Players quite naturally want to look out for themselves and their families, and it's a big dilemma and a big decision. If there are any one-club men in the future, it'll be just one or two.'

Now it's time to tackle that stinkingly large elephant in the room. Critics might look at Le Tissier and Benali and conclude that, because they were almost exclusively one-club men themselves (both had post-Southampton spells at non-league Eastleigh, while Benali also played fifteen games on loan at Nottingham Forest towards the end of his Saints career), they're grossly under-qualified to offer advice on, let alone handle, big-money transfers. Le Tissier doesn't see it as a disadvantage and plays a straight bat back. 'We've had mates who have been transferred and we've spoken at length with them about that kind of stuff. The agent I used throughout my career is at the end of a phone for any advice on situations that we're not particularly certain about. Plus, one of our other partners is a sports lawyer who will deal with the legal side of the contracts, so we're pretty covered in that department. I don't think that there's anything we have to worry about.'

Keeping the agency a modest enterprise is paramount. 73 Management won't be jostling with the big boys for market share, nor will Le Tissier or Benali have the likes of Mendes, Barnett or Raiola in their crosshairs as part of football's own game of thrones.

'We've always set out for it to be a bespoke agency. We never wanted to have eighty or a hundred players on our books. We want a manageable amount of players that both Fran and I can mentor properly and give enough time to. In five years' time, hopefully the boys we've got on our books currently will all be plying their trade successfully in the top division, perhaps even trying to force their way into the England squad, if their careers go really well. That would be fantastic for everyone involved. We keep our fingers crossed that the boys have got the right mental attitude and want to work hard, because it doesn't just take ability to make it as a professional footballer. Probably what's more important than your physical abilities and your skills is what's going on between your ears.'

The uncommitted need not apply.

* * *

'This is my health warning. I don't want to sugar-coat how difficult a business it is. It's really, really tough.'

It's a Thursday evening at Molineux and Tony Sharkey is addressing thirty people sat around a horseshoe of tables here in the voluminous Hayward Suite, named after Wolves' late benefactor, Sir Jack. Through the picture windows, hydroponic lights glow yellow over the pitch. Next to the windows is a generous selection of biscuits on a side table. But neither the view, nor the light refreshments, distract the gathering. Sharkey and his words receive uninterrupted attention.

The audience – twenty-eight men and two women – are mainly in their thirties and early forties. Some are suited and booted; some are smart-casual; a couple of them look like puffer-jacketed football scouts. What unites them is that they're at the stage in their working lives where they're considering a gear change, a left turn in their career path. Thanks to Sharkey's ASA Football Agent Level 1 course, they're taking their first steps towards becoming players' representatives. £59 – or £44 for fast-moving early birds – gets them a few hours of invaluable insight.

Tonight's course is the entry-level session, so it's a general, fairly broad-brush overview of what's needed to become successful in the trade. The wannabes diligently jot down Sharkey's take-home messages, statements that'll be chewed over in the next few days as they consider their options. 'Unless you're really lucky, you're going to earn very little in the first few years' ... 'You're likely to be working with young players to start off with' ... 'If the guy in front of you doesn't trust you, you're in trouble.'

Hearing the lie of the land from Sharkey is indeed a health warning. Were it a successful ex-pro delivering tonight's course, someone whose passage into agenthood was smooth and untroubled, the assembled gathering might not be getting the full picture. Sharkey's route was rougher and more circuitous.

While he did play at a decent level – lining up in the same Leeds youth side as Denis Irwin and Scott Sellars – Sharkey was released early and forced to re-evaluate his life goals. 'I only ever wanted to be a footballer. I came back to Middlesbrough where I'm from and didn't know what to do. I played locally in the Northern League for cash in hand, and I did a PE degree, but didn't want to teach. Then I worked in sports development in Middlesbrough and Easington in County Durham, before I got sick of local authorities. I thought, "What do I know? Football." So I decided to give myself a job and learned the trade over two years. Suck it and see.

'In 2002 I took the agents exam and passed it, when it was a very low pass rate, and I went on my merry way. I actually went back to do supply teaching to get the business off the ground. It was one hundred and twenty quid a day for working nine am to three pm. I could do a bit of work in my lunchtime and after school, and my evenings and weekends were all free. And in 2005, I got a deal that paid me enough to go full-time.'

That deal was moving the Georgian defender Zurab Khizanishvili from Rangers to Blackburn. Sharkey had to sort out plenty for the player – house, car, tax, passport – which proved to be a steep learning curve. Up until then, he'd been dealing exclusively with young players from the north-east, sending them on trials to clubs and hoping that the dice rolled favourably.

One of Sharkey's tips to his students is to find a niche. The theory comes with evidence. Finding his own niche was how his career properly took off. 'I realised that working with foreign agents was quite a lucrative thing to do. I networked with foreign agents to get their players over here and to sort deals out for them. Everyone wanted to come to England, and they still do, but not many of the overseas agents knew the clubs here.

'The beauty of that was that the players were already established players. The first one I did was twenty-eight and came from Feyenoord to Southampton. Since the agent was close to him, as I was in Newcastle, I didn't have to look after him. I'd see him when Southampton came up to play Newcastle and that was it.'

One of Sharkey's best war stories comes from this period when he was the go-between for European agents wanting to place their players in the Premier League and the Championship. 'I got a call from this Spanish agent. Pep Guardiola had been playing in Qatar for a couple of years at the end of his career, but wanted to experience the Premier League. But I had trouble finding him a club because he was thirty-four. Stuart Pearce took him for a week at Man City, and Pep flew into Manchester with his agent. Pep was an unbelievable guy. I was absolutely blown away by him and he had a great week at City.

'When he came back to Manchester to manage, talk-SPORT asked me on to talk about it. Just as I was about to go on the radio, they played a clip of Stuart Pearce saying, "Pep Guardiola came to Man City but we didn't offer him anything." But they did, so I was conflicted straightaway. "What do I do now?" Well, I told the truth. They did make an offer and he turned it down.' Guardiola would have been a Man City player had the club offered him a one-year contract, not a six-month one.

The fact that Sharkey – who could pass for Mark Chapman's fifty-something, north-eastern brother – can spice up his courses with head-turning anecdotes like this ensures his every word is clung on to, shot through credibility that real-life experience can bring. He's been providing these courses for a couple of years, hosting them at various football grounds across the country – the Etihad, Elland Road, Vicarage Road, Easter Road, and Broadhurst Park, home of FC United of Manchester. Tonight's venue is an inadvertently appropriate one for those seeking to become successful agents, bearing in mind the controversial proximity of super-agent Jorge Mendes to the hierarchy here at Wolves, with the Chinese owners having a stake in the holding company behind Mendes's agency.

The Level 1 course has welcomed several hundred attendees over the past two years. It works well as a taster, giving wannabe agents a chance to consider whether they have the necessary attributes for the profession. Sharkey offers very specific practical advice – the importance of mobile phone etiquette, the effectiveness of LinkedIn – along with more general observations. These include how crucial it is to understand the culture and philosophy of individual clubs, along with being able to recognise their decision-makers at twenty paces ('They are your customers').

The over-arching lesson from this initial evening is to not underestimate the complexity of the industry. 'I tell them how it is. It's a tough business. Not everyone comes and still wants to be an agent. Some of them go, "You know what? It's not for me." But some will. They'll go on to do the Level two and Level three.'

Sharkey qualified as a licensed agent the same year that the transfer window was introduced. Having always worked within its confines, he's an advocate. 'I like how it works. It makes people make decisions. Clubs have to get their squads together by such and such a date, and once the window's closed, players know where they are.

'In our Level two course, we do a negotiation exercise and there are prizes for who gets the best price. One time, they were negotiating over a leather jacket – who bought it for the least and who sold it for the most. Towards the end, there were a couple of people who hadn't agreed a deal, so I started counting down from ten. Ten, nine, eight … The clock was ticking and they did a deal. It ended up being the best deal for one and the worst for the other. I said to them "Isn't this the transfer window?"

'In the last moments, there's always someone who does a deal. And sometimes it can be the best or worst deal, depending on which side of the fence you're on. And when we went round the room, each pair had agreed slightly different prices for the same thing, for the same leather jacket. It was a great exercise for them.'

Sharkey hit upon the idea of training prospective agents when deregulation was brought in back in 2015. The influx of new agents meant a heavily crowded marketplace. 'There was more competition for players, with more people trying to get their slice of the pie. I probably shot myself in the foot a little by concentrating on my contacts with clubs and not recruiting players. But brokering deals is harder now, too. The overseas agents have the contacts now. And there are a lot of foreign managers and sporting directors in English clubs now. The Premier League is a world league.

'There had always been talk about education and training, but the industry never got round to doing it. I saw there was a need. The market's dominated by the bigger agencies and they train their own, but when deregulation came in, so did everyone – brothers, hangers-on, people who hadn't a clue about doing a deal ...

'One club's sporting director once had to deal with the brother of a big player.

'"Why do you think you can represent your brother?"

'"Well, I know a lot about football. I watch it all the time."

'"Do you watch films?"

'"Yeah, I watch films."

'"So you'd be OK representing an actor, would you? You might watch football on a Saturday night, but do you know the business of football?"

'To the player's credit, he did start working with another agent. The dad–player relationship is a tough one, too. If your dad's your agent, that can be difficult. He might have your best interests at heart, but does he know the business? Some of them do. Some of them get the best deals you've ever heard of. Neymar's dad is quite wealthy, isn't he ...?'

Big-earning anomalies aside, Sharkey is correct about the family connection, echoing the words of Pete Smith and Chris Gankerseer. Is the person next to you on the sofa at home, the one who shares your DNA, really the best to represent you? It's a hell of a coincidence if so.

Looking around the Hayward Suite tonight, the make-up of those attending might be a little surprising. If the new landscape of player representation does resemble the Wild West, you might expect a few flashier types to have pulled their chairs up to the tables, those who see this career path as a fast-track to untold riches. Instead, it's a uniformly professional assembly of sober, sensible types, diligently making notes and asking pertinent questions at the right juncture. Among them are plenty who work in both the law and the financial sector.

In the tea break, I grab a handful of attendees to better understand their motivations. Ever since his mid-teens, Marco has always wanted to be an agent – at least after he realised that he was never going to make it as a professional sportsman. As part of a degree in sports marketing, he completed an internship with a rugby agency and now holds a salaried position there. The agency's clients range from British Lions to first-year academy players, but it's his hope to also bring some footballers into the fold. Ultimately he wants to be running his own boutique agency, one that values quality ahead of quantity, representing 'maybe a couple of Premier League international players. I'd love to see kids wearing shirts with my clients' names on the back.' He's not shy in putting in the work. 'I haven't got kids. I don't have anyone pinning me down. So I'll happily drive to Darlington or to Brighton for a game. If that's what it's got to be, that's what it will be. The harder you work, the luckier you get.'

One of the two women on tonight's course, Georgina is currently a student at the University Campus of Football Business at Wembley, where she's a second year studying Sports Business and Coaching. Her career path isn't quite as well defined as Marco's. 'I don't know exactly where I want to go career-wise, so I'm here to get educated in areas all across the football industry.' As a woman, and as almost certainly the youngest person in the room tonight, as an agent she would certainly stand out in a world that's largely middle-aged and almost exclusively male. She stresses that she wouldn't be a corner-cutting, only-in-it-for-the-money addition to the industry. 'There is the idea that agents are the bad guys in football. One of my goals is if I could be an agent who changes that perception. I'd like to make a good, positive impression, for sure.'

Myles currently works in the financial services industry, but has a strong football background, having previously earned a scholarship to the US where 'I got as close as I could to being a professional'. Being an agent would be the perfect fusion of his twin loves of football and finance. Like Marco, the end – if still distant – objective of running his own agency is Myles' ultimate prize: 'That's what my end goal is in life.' He's certainly not put off by the reputation that continues to discolour the profession. 'I used to work at an investment bank and I believe that's the second-most hated profession. So that's not a problem at all. In fact, this would be a step up ...'

In fact, neither Marco, Georgina nor Myles appear to be too concerned by the public perception of agents. 'We do get a bad press,' says Sharkey, 'but not from players. Players see the value. In any business, there are bad apples. There are going to be some people who are more in it for them-selves than for their clients. Obviously when you do see big, big numbers and agents earning big, big amounts, you've got to question it. But that's the game we're in at the moment. I don't know how much Tom Cruise's agent makes, but I expect it's a tidy sum. These top-level players are the Tom Cruises of this particular industry. The people who help them to get there, and to stay there, deserve paying.

'Clubs would prefer it if agents didn't exist. It used to be that clubs were all-powerful and the players were just puppets who had to get jobs in pubs when they retired. Now the lads retiring don't necessarily have to work again. They do need a purpose, though. You can't finish your life at thirty-five and just be on the golf course, can you?'

Plenty of this evening's attendees came in search of similar mid-life recalibration. Throughout, they've been a dedicated gathering – focused, engaged and undistracted. The amount of bourbons and custard creams still left on the tray suggests Tony Sharkey has hit the mark tonight. On a chilly February evening in Wolverhampton, a few new agents might have just been minted.

CHAPTER SEVEN

HERE IS THE NEWS

'I don't like the baloney that goes with it. I just like dealing in the facts'

– Ian Dennis

January is a busy time for Ian Dennis.

Being one of 5 Live's lead commentators, as well as the station's chief football reporter, he is pulled in opposing directions: the pile-up of matches that heralds a new calendar year takes him one way, while the gathering pace of a transfer window tugs him the other. Last night, Dennis was at Wembley commentating on the first leg of the Spurs–Chelsea semi-final of the Carabao Cup. A few hours later, he popped up on the *Today* programme on Radio 4, offering up his thoughts on both last night's VAR decisions and the escalation of Bayern Munich's bids for Chelsea winger Callum Hudson-Odoi. And before he could get into his car to head back home to his northern retreat, Dennis still had to find time to update the nation on the continuing delays to Spurs' return to White Hart Lane.

He's now finally behind the wheel, making steady progress up the West Yorkshire portion of the A1(M). With the cruise control set at 70mph to avoid the avaricious speed-traps of Britain's road network, this is Dennis's me-time, a few hours of peaceful, calm contemplation, perhaps even a podcast or two. After all, his working life is only going to get busier and more frantic as the end of the month rapidly approaches in his wing mirror. Enjoy the quiet before the storm erupts.

Over the past decade, Dennis has evolved into the BBC's most-recognised reporter on the transfer window. This is especially apparent on deadline day when he's usually found shuttling between radio mic and television studio as he chronicles the latest twists and turns of the closing hours of trading. 'Deadline Denno', some call him. But this current profile is merely the latest manifestation of a career-long relationship with the world of the football transfer.

'Before I joined the BBC, I worked for a company called TeamTalk. It was an 0898 number and all their calls were generated because every supporter wants to see their club linked with another player. That transfer tittle-tattle is what football fans thrive on. "Oh, we're being linked with so-and-so." "We're going to make a move for him." "So-and-so's on his way out." And this is why supporters couldn't get enough of transfer deadline day. That constant need for stories. And that's why transfer deadline day became the success it was. Every media outlet thrived on that speculation.'

Dennis joined the BBC in 2002, the same year that FIFA announced the transfer window's imminent arrival. 'Before I was a journalist, the transfer window ended on the third Thursday in March, so there was a continual build-up of speculation throughout the season until that date. It was constant. "So-and-so is going to sign Player X." "Player X wants to move there." The introduction of transfer deadline day focused the minds.'

Although initially Dennis wasn't involved on the day itself, his upward passage through the echelons of 5 Live's sports broadcasters saw him take on the mantle and become synonymous with the BBC's deadline-day coverage, both on radio and television. This was possibly a curious development; Dennis isn't one for succumbing to hype. 'Sensationalist' isn't a word that could ever be used to describe his methodical, near-forensic approach. There's no loose talk with Ian Dennis. The frippery applied to deadline day by other channels, and their occasional attendant goofball behaviour, is ignored. He is a defiant, card-carrying alumnus of the old school. 'I don't like the baloney that goes with the whole thing,' he cautions. 'I just like dealing in the facts.'

These facts are carefully jotted down, not on some large-memory electronic device, but on some distinctly pre-twenty-first-century apparatus. 'I struggle with modern technology,' he admits, 'so I've got a tatty old book that I use. Whenever I get briefed throughout the year – by a club or an agent or whatever – I write it in this A4 book. It's in a right old state. The back of it is falling off and it's held together by a piece of duct tape. But it contains countless stories of what I've been told, all my scrawls and scribbles. On deadline day, I open it up and write everything down on two pages as I go along throughout the day. 'Could move' gets a tick; a done deal gets a circle in red. Dan Walker calls it The Book of Destiny.

'I refer to this book the whole day. There's no script. I just adlib it. But it's a fourteen-hour day for me and, because I'm repeating the same old stories, by the end someone could ask "What business have Tottenham done?" and I will know the ins and the outs because they've been constantly in my head throughout the day.

'Deadline day often begins for me the night before when I'll start texting chief execs, chairmen, managers, scouts and sometimes players. I'll just say, "If you hear anything, let me know." It's a scattergun approach. Invariably, if a club is doing business, the people at the heart of the deal haven't got time to contact a journalist. That just doesn't happen. They've got so much paperwork to do. But occasionally you strike lucky.

'For instance, one time I called somebody at Hull City and they said, "Well, Steve Bruce is in the room. He's next to me." So he passed me on to Steve. I've known Steve for a number of years and he's good as gold. He marked my card that day and told me what Hull were likely to do and what they wanted to do. And that was it. I didn't have a chance to speak to Steve again throughout that day because he'd have been busy, but I'd been given an idea of what was going on. There are a number of chief execs who are equally as good as gold and it's now become a standing joke that I will contact them on deadline day. Even the PA is expecting the call. "Is it that time of year again? That's gone fast." But sometimes it's not possible for them to talk. I get that. They get that. We both know where we're coming from.

'At the start of the day, it'll be this scattergun approach. If you get lucky, then great. It's like a slot machine. If the three golden bells all align, you get yourself a story. And if they don't, you can be frustrated. I once broke a story on the Victoria Derbyshire programme on 5 Live. I got a phone call from somebody who just said, "I can't talk, but Robbie Keane is going back to Tottenham" and the phone went dead. I knew the source and trusted him impeccably. Normally I would want two sources to a story, but I can trust certain individuals with my life. So I just went onto the programme. Victoria said, "Ooh, breaking news" and I said, "Yep, Robbie Keane is on his way back to Tottenham." That was it. A short little snippet.

'I'll never get a bigger story than the time I broke the news that Andy Carroll was going from Newcastle to Liverpool. It was a genuine exclusive and I couldn't believe it. I was fortunate to get a call from someone in the north-east who told me that Liverpool had made a bid of thirty million. Wow! You took your phone away from your ear – it was one of those moments. The call wasn't from anybody from either club, but it was from somebody who was close to the situation. I knew straightaway that I could run with it, so I went and reported it. But as soon as I got back to my desk, I heard from my source that Newcastle had rejected the offer. "But don't worry. Liverpool are going to come back in with another bid."

'So I then reported that Liverpool were increasing their offer to thirty-five million. And once the bid was accepted, I was able to both break the story that Carroll was definitely on his way to Anfield and to deduce that the likelihood was that Fernando Torres was going to Chelsea. I've since found out that Newcastle knew he was heading to

London and were able to operate from a position of strength and turn down the original thirty million. They knew Liverpool had fifty million to play with and they knew Liverpool needed a reinforcement. That really was astute and shrewd.

'That was my biggest story, one I probably won't beat. Those genuine exclusives are so hard to find these days, especially with the way that social media has come on leaps and bounds. Clubs now have their own media channels and they want to keep the information for themselves – for their own website or social media platforms or TV channel.'

Like Mike McGrath at the *Sun*, the quality of the stories Dennis breaks traces a direct correlation with the quality of his contacts. With both the Keane and Carroll exclusives, the inherent faith he had in those respective contacts was proven to be a sound investment. In both cases – and in plenty of others –– Dennis was placing his reputation as one of the leading football reporters of his age into the hands of others. He didn't bat an eyelid, didn't flinch an inch.

'All my relationships are built up over a number of years. Trust is one of those things that is very hard to build but very easy to lose. I always establish what's on and off the record. You know the people you can trust in life, and it's the same in football. Equally, the people I speak to on deadline day know that they can trust me. They wouldn't take my phone call otherwise. Sometimes they're too busy to respond, so you might get a text twenty-four or forty-eight hours later. "Sorry, I wasn't able to get back to you. It was just manic." "Don't worry. It's fine."

'There is a lot of misinformation as well. But there always used to be. You'd get the phone calls into the radio station – "So-and-so has been spotted in a taxi." We still get that, but it's largely been transferred to social media. Sometimes if you get a tip-off, it might be a bit of a wild-goose chase. But I always like to check stories out. Sometimes it'll be, "No, it's safe to report that that's not going to happen." Last summer, I got a call from a director of football, from a club I can't name, saying that they'd been linked with a particular striker. "Can you put it out that it's bollocks? It's just not true." The club might be being used as a pawn for a player to orchestrate a move away from another club and to generate interest.

'Sometimes it's the things that go on behind the scenes that I find more interesting, like Charlie Adam hitching a lift in a white Transit van to take him to Liverpool.' Adam's arrival on Merseyside from Blackpool in 2011 was notable for Kenny Dalglish driving the midfielder into the Melwood training ground to sign the contract. However, the bulk of the journey down the M6 was actually spent in the cab of a builder friend's grubby work van. When real life infringes on the fantasy world of the transfer market, gold dust is sprinkled on those journalists agonisingly starved of a story. They'd bite their arm off for one as rich as that.

Dennis seems to apply the traits of his commentating – methodical, diligent, conscientious – to his news-gathering. This is a man whose pursuit of a good news story is impervious to outlandish grandstanding. He reserves getting excited for the moments that truly require it. Again, it's all about the simple things – and doing them well. His long-time 5 Live producer Phil Wye once noted that Dennis 'works harder at the behind-the-scenes PR than any commentator I've ever encountered. He's very well liked – and totally trusted – by anyone from club owners, board members, managers, coaches, players, press officers, journalists. The list goes on.'

This networking can bear rich, ripe fruit – rewards that often see parity between the BBC and Sky when it comes to breaking exclusives, despite the latter's deployment of reporters at all major stadiums and training grounds throughout the window. Dennis and his colleagues won't be battered by the January rain and cold winds come deadline day, unlike their Sky counterparts. Instead, this small team will work on their stories in the warm isolation of BBC Sport's headquarters at Salford. And for a team so diminutive, their hit-rate is impressively strong.

'We do it differently to Sky. On deadline day at the Beeb, there'll be four or five of us who will sit round the desk. Between us, we phone-bash to get the stories. It's a small, tight-knit group. The BBC is blessed in having David Ornstein, who is fantastic on Arsenal matters, Simon Stone, who is well-connected at Manchester United, and Phil McNulty, who has strong connections on Merseyside. Juliette Ferrington would be someone else I'd throw into the mix.'

Even though this set-up only convenes on two days of the year, to most football fans it sounds a highly enviable way to make a living. But there's a pressure there. Due diligence must be applied. The corporation's reputation could take a dent if true journalistic principles are not in force.

'I'm a firm believer in the BBC's values. It's not a race to be first with the news, but it is important to be accurate. Whether it's David or Simon or Phil or Juliette or myself, we can all reflect on deadline day and say that nine times out of ten, we got it right. We don't take fliers – and that's the most important thing. There might be deadline days where you strike lucky in breaking a story and there might be deadline days when you don't. But I'd prefer it to be that way rather than try to make up stories just for the sake of gaining an extra thousand followers on Twitter. I pride myself on being accurate, rather than dealing in tittle-tattle. I'm not driven by ego. I just want to be right.

'Sometimes there'll be mitigating circumstances where you know you're right but the club will say you're wrong. I can't name him, but I once contacted a player. I sent him a direct message on Twitter. I knew he was in the process of a move and for whatever reason it didn't come off. We then had the owner on 5 Live later that night and I asked him if there was any movement on that player. "Oh no, he was never going." But I knew that wasn't the case because I'd got it from the horse's mouth that there was a possible move.'

For every signature on the dotted line, every new shirt raised to the cameras, there's a collapsed deal. These, says Dennis, hold just as much intrigue for a broadcaster beguiled by the mechanisms of football.

'I find the stories where moves don't happen, and the reasons for them not happening, just as fascinating as when moves are successful. For instance, when Fulham signed Kostas Mitroglou from Olympiacos, I know for a fact that there was another Premier League club who tried to gazump the deal. But Fulham still managed to secure Mitroglou – although they probably wished they hadn't because he was such a flop. Sometimes those stories are equally fascinating for what doesn't happen than for what does. There are a lot of things that go on behind the scenes that the everyday fan maybe isn't aware of. They'll just see that Fulham signed Mitroglou, but won't be aware that another Premier League club came in and tried to hijack the deal. In that respect, it's become a lot more competitive now. It is dog eat dog. Another reason why clubs try to keep things hush-hush until a deal is over the line is the fear of being gazumped. An agent might be able to tout Player X to another club, or another club might get wind of the deal.'

This inter-club sense of competition is mirrored among the press corps, whether broadcast, print or online. 'The pressure, desire and appetite for instant stories is now also there from the newspapers through their online services. A newspaper journalist will now be as busy as a broadcast journalist to try to meet the demand for their paper's online output, whether it's the Mail Online, the *Telegraph*, the *Guardian* or whoever. They're competing with websites like those of the BBC and Sky now. All facets of the media are looking for the same crumbs, for their own story.'

In snuffling after those same crumbs, these outlets do things differently. For instance, there is a marked difference between the reporting style of Sky Sports News – which can, on occasion, resemble a branch of light entertainment – and that of the BBC, which employs the straighter, more noble art of the newsroom. Part of this can be explained by airtime. Not only does Sky Sports News need as many stories as possible to help ensure they're putting out meaningful content round the clock and round the calendar, in January the channel has a whole month of bulletins – 744 hours, to be precise – to fill with whatever transfer morsels its reporters can dig up. In contrast, the BBC, with way fewer hours dedicated to the window, has to be more selective in what stories it covers. Time is tight, so stay on brief.

Dennis concedes that Sky is the main engine of the window, and always has been since its introduction. That's not necessarily a problem for the BBC; the corporation has always been content with taking a more junior role in this particular aspect of football life. 'Obviously Sky with their resources have turned transfer deadline day into what it is. On the back of that, the BBC probably thought there was mileage in it and that they should do their own programme. At 5 Live, we've always done a deals show from seven pm until eleven pm. But in recent years, because the deals aren't as frenetic as they once were, it's become more of a discussion programme. And that can be hard to fill because there hasn't been that same level of activity.

'By and large, the big clubs have never tended to do their business in January. It's always those clubs who are looking for a bit of a fix to spark something to avoid relegation. But I'm still amazed by the amount of business that's still conducted on the last day. I still find it astonishing after all these years that clubs, or individuals, can't resist that temptation for a late deal – whether it's an adrenalin thing or it's the opportunity to gamble for one last time. Sometimes it's the nature of the beast, that element of brinkmanship. It continues to fascinate for that reason alone. And there'll always be that interest because of the nature of it. You can bet, at eleven o'clock at the end of this window, there will be deal sheets going through that buy clubs an additional couple of hours. A deal sheet isn't a legally binding contract, but it serves the intention that they're willing to do the deal. They will have had all month and yet they're still trying to get deals through.'

If deal sheets soften the slamming shut of the transfer window, some poor souls still get their fingers caught in the mechanism. No one felt that pain more than Adrien Silva. On the last day of August 2017, Silva sealed a £22m move from Sporting Lisbon to Leicester City. Only it wasn't sealed. The documents reached FIFA a full *fourteen seconds* after the deadline. The move couldn't then be completed until the following January, leaving the Portuguese international, eager for a strong season before the World Cup squads were finalised the following spring, unable to kick a ball in Leicester blue until the new year. By the time he finally did grace the King Power Stadium pitch, Silva wore number fourteen on his back, an undisguised riposte to what many interpreted as FIFA obstinacy. (This moment of not-exactly-biting satire later gained an additional level of irony. Eighteen months after his arrival at Leicester, Silva left the King Power for Monaco on loan after appearing in the Premier League on, you guessed it, just fourteen occasions.)

The Silva affair was an anomaly, certainly at top-flight level. There are now very few Premier League clubs who would leave their business so late. And this caution is replicated in how tightly the purse strings are pulled by those clubs outside the top six, despite the abundance of cash in Europe's most affluent league. 'The clubs now are more reluctant to spend the money,' Dennis observes. 'Owners are now taking a more pragmatic approach to the transfer window. Before, they were prepared to gamble. And while the money in the Premier League is as rich as it's ever been, where you get a hundred million for finishing bottom, they're also aware of the consequences if they were to get relegated. You've seen what happens to other clubs who've struggled to adapt to life in the Football League – Birmingham, QPR, Sunderland, Leeds … It can unravel quite quickly and I think the owners are aware of that.

'I also think there's been a noticeable change in not wanting to pay unrealistic prices. Clubs don't want to go over the odds. The nature of it is that you probably always pay over the top because that's the economics, that's the market forces. But I do think the owners are looking to take a step back from paying silly money. And the wages are a factor as well. Sometimes a loan deal – which might include a fee and a percentage of the player's wages – can cost a lot of money.'

But if a club refuses to play the cash-heavy transfer game, they will almost certainly be drawing up new objectives, a new *raison d'être*. There's a high-definition example of this near to Dennis's own doorstep in his adopted north-east.

'Newcastle United are no longer a competitive force in the transfer market because Mike Ashley will not be dictated to. He's got a rigid business model that he sticks to and, as a result of that, where they used to be a top-six club challenging for Champions League positions, Newcastle can't compete with a newly promoted club like Fulham spending a hundred million, simply because Ashley won't do it. Where Newcastle used to be able to attract players like Shearer and Ferdinand and Ginola and Asprilla, they're in the bottom three of the Premier League when it comes to wages. Ashley refuses to do business where others, such as Fulham if they got relegated, are going to have to count the cost. Look at Stoke and Swansea. They'd have been looking at bouncing straight back to the Premier League. It doesn't happen. There's no divine right.

'Mike Ashley is not going to spend an extra sixty or seventy million to try to gain Newcastle an extra three or four places up the Premier League. Moving up an extra three or four places actually adds no value to Newcastle United as a football club. He's putting all his faith in the manager keeping the club up. Last season, they got whatever prize money it is for finishing tenth, but more importantly he kept them in the top flight. Spending money on a couple of new players wouldn't propel Newcastle United to challenge for a European place. The Premier League is now much of a muchness outside of the top six or seven clubs. The objective, for Leicester City downwards, is to stay in the Premier League.'

Another change that the transfer window's evolution has brought about is the increased strain on managers of having just two periods of trading in a twelve-month time-frame. It's a simple, hard-to-refute logic that Dennis applies, echoing the earlier words of John Barnwell. 'Managers have come under greater pressure to help fill the void of the media. Before the transfer window was introduced, clubs had until the third Thursday in March and all the papers were always full of transfer speculation. But because that speculation is now squeezed into the two windows, managers have come under greater pressure to fill the column inches. There has to be another talking point.

'Also, I'm not too sure nowadays how many managers have a one hundred per cent say in who's being signed. I think it's become much more of a collaborative effort. Some clubs have transfer committees, while others will have a director of football or an operations director who's more hands-on with recruitment. For instance, when Slavisa Jokanovic was still the manager at Fulham, how many signings was he responsible for? You'd probably say Aleksandar Mitrovic for one, but in bringing in twelve new players, how many were down to the manager?

'The manager might say to the transfer committee that they need to strengthen in certain areas, but then it'll be left for a director of football or a chief executive to then deliver those players. Tony Pulis at Middlesbrough was frustrated last summer because they didn't land their targets and it's not easy. The chief executive might have to divvy up the figures to make it work, but there might be other players and agents holding the club to ransom by saying, "We want this because we can get this amount of money at another club." There is a lot going on. It's like a juggler trying to keep all the balls in the air. You might be dependent on getting a player out in order to get one in. Cause and effect is at play.'

For Dennis, the transfer window has mutated into something very different from when it was first announced in 2002, just as he stepped over the threshold into the BBC for the first time. 'Sky deserve a lot of credit for turning deadline day into what it is. They are the ones that have created the monster of transfer deadline day. They saw a niche and they had the vehicle for it with their rolling sports news service. It has become what it has because of Sky, and others have latched on to it and followed suit. Deadline day has become this all-singing, all-dancing affair.

'It is an adrenalin-fuelled day when you've got stories happening and you're constantly on the phone. You still get the last-minute rush, but it's not as chaotic as it once was. It's been a lame duck of late, a little bit limp. It needs an aphrodisiac to try to give it a pep up.

'To a degree, it's become a parody of itself. It's become too showbiz. I'm not knocking Sky. They've got a product and in many ways they've enhanced deadline day through their coverage. But has it gone too far? Has it become too much when the presenters are the star attraction when realistically it should be the news that people are tuning in for?

'Personally, I'm not a fan of deadline day. I don't enjoy working it – and that's nothing to do with it being a double shift. I don't enjoy the hype that goes around it. It's become this charade, this circus. For instance, there are some outlets that peddle the need for a reporter having three phones because they're so busy. It's a myth. It's nonsense. You don't need three phones. It's a sham and it doesn't happen. I just get wound up by the idea of TV producers saying, "Pretend that you're busy. Pretend that your phone's ringing."'

If Ian Dennis is an old-fashioned news man, then full praise to him for sticking to his guns as he goes about his work, for staying on the straight and narrow. Patience, discipline and the application of unwavering journalistic instinct are his tools when reporting on a month's worth of transfer news. He has no time for, or truck with, pantomime or cabaret. The story is all.

'Ultimately there's no right or wrong way to report deadline day,' he concludes as the car continues its steady progress towards the north-east, eating up exactly seventy miles of motorway with each hour that passes.

'I just do it the way I like to do it.'

* * *

On this grey Friday in mid-January, the sleepy Surrey village of Stoke d'Abernon doesn't appear to be a hotbed of gossip and rumour. A nearly-done-for-the-day postman strides down the street whistling a rough approximation of the Carpenters' *Close To You*, while a modest queue in the delicatessen patiently waits to place their orders for quiches and cheeses and olives. But this charming tableau is disturbed when the 11.41am from London Waterloo pulls into the station and off step representatives of Her Majesty's Press, newshounds hungry for stories, hungry for headlines.

They're admirable multi-taskers, able to alight from the train while simultaneously talking on their phones and tapping into laptops. They're also shooting furtive glances at each other, second-guessing which story each is working on, and whether their grasp of the realité is at a more advanced stage.

Their destination is Chelsea's Cobham training ground, 140 acres of football pitches located half a mile down the road. Their mission is to squeeze out, at this lunchtime's press conference, as much information as possible about the club's transfer activity as head coach Maurizio Sarri will reveal – or, as it turns out, as much as he actually knows.

There's always plenty of raw material for a reporter sent to cover Chelsea during the transfer window. Not only does the club currently have forty-one players out on loan, but it has a reputation for spending at will, for finding solutions – often short-term in nature – through the splashing of cash, redistributing their wealth into the bank accounts of clubs across Europe. Over the course of the five summer transfer windows between 2014 and 2018, no fewer than sixteen players were signed by Chelsea at a fee in excess of €20m apiece. Some were pricier than others, most notably the comparatively inexperienced Atlético Madrid goalkeeper Kepa Arrizabalaga whose release clause was met when Chelsea coughed up a cool €80m.

Unsurprisingly, given this long-standing, big-spending acquisition policy, the morning transfer gossip columns would be somewhat skinnier without the Blues' existence. To what extent Sarri would be putting meat on the bone of this speculation at the imminent press conference, though, was questionable. And there were plenty of Chelsea-related rumours doing the rounds this particular morning.

Imminent arrivals might include Gonzalo Higuaín on a loan deal from Juventus, although the Italians reportedly prefer a permanent cash sale, perhaps to help cover the reported weekly post-tax salary of $538,000 of a certain Cristiano Ronaldo. Different sources claim that different midfielders were en route to Stamford Bridge, among them Watford's Roberto Pereyra, Cagliari's Nicolò Barella and Zenit St Petersburg's Leandro Paredes. On the outgoing side, the hot overnight news was that Barcelona were attempting to lure Brazilian winger Willian to Catalonia, trying to catch Roman Abramovich's attention by waving £50m in his direction. Meanwhile, the departing Cesc Fàbregas had still to confirm his next destination, Álvaro Morata apparently had a straight choice between Seville or Atlético Madrid, Gary Cahill looked to be the answer to Fulham's defensive woes, and Tammy Abraham had turned down a loan spell with Wolves. And then there was the ongoing saga of Callum Hudson-Odoi, with Bayern's bids supposedly increasing by the hour.

In short, there are plenty of transfer-related enquiries to be made at a Chelsea press conference. While the club will ration the number of such questions, and would surely prefer comparatively benign interrogation that largely relates to tomorrow's match against Newcastle, the press pack can't be denied their right to ask. There's a clear pecking order among the gathered journalists. The man who leads off, cameras rolling, is one of the most recognised of Sky Sports News's reporters. His name is Gary Cotterill.

Cotterill is a veteran in this arena. It's too genial a set-up to be described as a bear pit, but there are tactics to be deployed in order to grab as much flesh as possible. He begins by softening Sarri with belated wishes for his sixtieth birthday the day before ('Too many years, I think,' sighs the Italian) and an innocuous opening question about current injuries. Cotterill's second question adroitly points out that Chelsea haven't scored in their last two home Premier League matches and that the last time they went three without a goal was all the way back in the nineties when Glenn Hoddle was boss. It's a smart manoeuvre on the Sky man's part, one that then allows him to smoothly segue into a direct question about the arrival or otherwise of Higuaín, a proven striker at the highest level who once bagged thirty-six goals in a season under Sarri's management at Napoli.

As an interviewee, Sarri is preferred by the press pack over his predecessor Antonio Conte. While Conte offered lengthy quotes, they often contained minimal substance. Talking loud but saying little. Sarri is much blunter, to the point. He doesn't prevaricate and filibuster like a politician. He'll give a straight answer. One of these straight answers is that he freely admits he's relatively toothless when it comes to Chelsea's recruitment. The previous weekend, when quizzed in front of the *Match of the Day* cameras about the confirmed signing of the United States winger Christian Pulisic earlier that day, he displayed a candour rarely heard in football circles. 'I didn't know anything about Pulisic yesterday,' he revealed to the nation. 'The club asked me about my opinion of him about one month ago. My opinion was positive. Today I knew the deal was done. I didn't know anything [before].'

If Sarri was a little surprised by the signing of the Borussia Dortmund player, the German newspaper *Bild* was flabbergasted by the price tag. 'It's on the border of crazy. The whole thing is madness from Chelsea's perspective. It shows once again that Dortmund have profited from the irrationality of the Premier League as Chelsea splashed out €64m on a positionally limited player that as a substitute more recently has stagnated.'

Sarri's answer to Cotterill's Higuaín question again made clear his comparative non-involvement in Chelsea's acquisition policy: 'As you know very well, I am not involved in the market.' The sharpness of Cotterill's questions increases with each one he asks. He's now raising the fact that Cesc Fàbregas, despite clearly having said goodbye to the fans at the last home game, remains at the club. 'He needs to go,' admits Sarri with a shrug, readjusting his glasses on his forehead.

Cotterill's most acute enquiry, though, is reserved for the transfer story most troubling Chelsea fans during this particular window: the Hudson-Odoi Question.

'I know you've made it clear you're not selling him, that you don't want him to go. But are you annoyed that a big, classy club like Bayern Munich would go public and say that they want him?'

The bait is laid. The bite is taken.

'I think that it's not professional because they are talking about a player under contract with Chelsea. They didn't respect our club.'

It's Sarri's most newsworthy response of the entire press conference, the take-home quote that will create headlines on Sky Sports News all afternoon and into the evening. Job done.

Cotterill is at the head of the food chain when it comes to the hierarchy here inside the press room. With his half-dozen questions asked, the baton is handed to John Southall from 5 Live to take his turn. His subjects – the timing of Morata's expected departure; whether a midfielder has been targeted to replace Fàbregas; if Sarri actually enjoys the transfer window – complement those of his Sky counterpart. It's then the turn of the talkSPORT reporter to ask anything that's not yet been ventured.

The broadcasters' questions are then followed by those of the print journalists, with TV cameras switched off and Sarri's answers here embargoed so as to offer the newspapermen some exclusive material. Sarri visibly relaxes more with the filming having ended and his answers are a little lighter in tone – especially when he's asked if his newly shaved head was to look smart for his birthday. Not so. It turns out he always cuts his hair when his team loses. With Chelsea still smarting from the Carabao Cup defeat to Spurs less than forty-eight hours earlier, it's small wonder why he looks sharp.

As Sarri exits stage left, flanked by press officer and translator, many in the room start to write their pieces, putting some context around his quotes before filing their copy. With the footage already heading down the line back to Sky HQ in Isleworth, Cotterill is largely done here – or, at least, he will be once he's sent a couple of emails suggesting which of Sarri's answers the production team should run with.

'If this had been yesterday and Sarri had said what he said today about the lack of respect shown to the club by Bayern Munich over Hudson-Odoi, I'd have been told to do a few live reports off the back of it. But because there are so many press conferences on a Friday – they've got stuff coming in from Klopp and Pep and Roy Hodgson – they haven't really got time for the live reports. I was at Watford yesterday and the production team told me they might want a live throughout the afternoon if Javi Garcia said something interesting. He didn't and they didn't. Of primary importance is who they are. Secondarily, it's what they said. Javi Gracia criticising Bayern Munich isn't going to be that exciting, but Chelsea doing it is.'

Cotterill has thirty-odd years of experience with the broadcaster under his belt, first with Sky News before switching over to Sky Sports News. He's thus ideally placed to offer chapter and verse on how the transfer window has evolved, and his employers' role in that.

'It took a while for us to realise it was going to be quite as exciting and rewarding as it turned out to be. It put Sky Sports News on the map as a channel and it got better as time moved on. It was very different at the start. We got the fans involved but we didn't get a lot of cooperation from the clubs. And maybe we ran stories that were in the papers rather than checking them out ourselves. As the window has come of age and got older, so has the coverage. It now needs to be a lot more professional, with stories getting checked out. We now like to find our own stories and react to our own stories. In the old days, maybe we saw a headline on the back page of the *Sun* and reported it without checking it out fully.

'Accuracy is important. It's all very well to be entertaining, but if you keep getting stuff wrong, people aren't going
to tune in any more. In the old days, we were probably
guilty of going with stories before we checked them. A new
procedure was brought in about three years ago. Every
story that comes in – whether from an agent, or a club that
wants a player or a club that wants to get rid of a player or a
player themselves – has to be checked with the player if you
can, or more likely the agent, or the press officer at each
club. If they don't respond or say, "No comment", you have
to put that in the story. If you've got a relationship with
them, they might say, "There's no truth in it but it might
happen" or "Yeah, we're looking at a loan with an option to
buy." You get a little meat on the bone, then you can go
with it.'

Just like Ian Dennis, Cotterill appreciates that cultivating long-lasting relationships with key personnel across the
football landscape is crucial for the on-their-toes reporter
who wants the scent of a scoop in their nostrils. 'We started
with different reporters going to different clubs, based on
who was working and what the news desk decided that day.
Then people started to form relationships with particular
clubs and with particular managers. Harry at Spurs became
my gig while he was there. And then, when he went to QPR,
I went to QPR.

'Now, when a transfer window opens, each reporter is
assigned a club and if there's a rumour about a player, either
coming or going, I have to ring the press officer. "This is
what the agent is telling us. This is what the other club is
telling us. Is it true? Isn't it true?" He'll give me a steer, I'll

put that steer back to our transfer desk and they'll put that into whatever story they report. This window I've got Watford. It's not necessarily the club I'll cover on the day, but for the whole of that month you'll cover that club and you'll be the one that they go to if they want to check a story out.'

Playing a successful long game is vital – working with, not against, press officers. Vindication might be a little exclusive further down the line. 'To me, if when it really counts on deadline day, I get something back as a result of playing ball earlier in the window, to me that's "Bingo!" That's worked. The whole month has been worth it.

'When Mido signed for West Ham, there was a good press officer there called Greg Demetriou, who's now at the FA. I got on well with him and he was kind enough to tell me what was happening, where it was going to happen and when it was going to happen. Back then, Mido was quite a big name. Greg called me.

'"Where are you?"

'"At the training ground."

'"Get to the stadium."

'Twenty minutes later, I was there.

'"We're signing Mido. He's about to arrive. You can ask him two questions on his way in."

'I asked him those two questions, but the cameraman had switched the camera off instead of on. But, Greg being Greg, he let me have another go on Mido's way out.

'"But if I let you do this, Guillermo Franco's about to arrive with his little boy. Is it OK not to film them?"

'"Yeah, no problem."

'That's the way it works.'

Such an approach extends beyond press officers. 'I've always had a fairly decent relationship with José Mourinho. I've never been around to his house for dinner, but I've always treated him with respect. I think he deserves respect for what he's done. And I think he has respect for me. Whenever I've done one-on-ones with him, and at press conferences too, he's always given me a straight answer to a straight question. I know recently he's been surly and grumpy, but I've never had a go at him publicly. I tend to think that one day, my relationship with José might help me. And so it came to pass. The morning after he got sacked at Old Trafford, having gone back to London, he came out of his house and did a little turn for me. All those years of not stitching him up when I had the chance paid dividends.'

It's this professionalism that's given Cotterill such tenure in front of an outside broadcast camera, seeing the transfer window evolve from the closest of quarters. Was there one particular window when he realised that it had taken a life force of its own? 'The one for me was two or three windows before we started having difficulties with the fans. I was outside Spurs, Rob Dorsett was outside Stoke, and Dharmesh Sheth was outside Arsenal. The fans were joining in, but in a good way, in an excited way. It was like *It's A Knockout*. I was having particular fun because Harry was always particularly helpful – "Hello, come in, have a cup of tea, have a bacon sandwich."

'Those days of him at Spurs, with the wound-down car window, were when I realised it was turning into something amazing. Then we started bringing in the yellow.

There was one year when all the reporters had to wear yellow ties as well as Jim White, but that only lasted one year. The public started getting excited about it too, taking days off work. It was turning into a carnival.

'In Harry's first summer window at QPR, my editor had the bright idea of using the referee's spray that had just been introduced at the Euros. "Gaz, take this can of spray down to Loftus Road with you and try to use it." This was still when the fans were getting involved. All the fans were standing behind me down there. "OK, lads. What we're going to do is you're going to be standing too close to me and I'll turn around saying, "Lads, lads. You know the rules. Ten yards! I'll spray a line and you'll stay behind it." It worked like a dream.'

The fan trouble that Cotterill alludes to has undeniably altered the complexion and consumption of Sky's live transfer updates. Previously, he and his colleagues would report from outside the compound of stadium or training ground. Even if very little of actual substance was happening, the presence of a handful of spotty youths helped to keep things buoyant. Until that incident in 2014, that is, involving Alan Irwin and that dildo. By the time the next window came round, Sky's reporters were safely ensconced on the other side of the security fence.

'There was some bad language and there were some sex toys. It's no secret – everyone knows it. In the end, the powers-that-be at Sky Sports News said we couldn't do that any more. It was for health and safety reasons as much as anything. If someone can hold a sex toy to a reporter's ear, how far away is something worse? Even though ratings were at their highest, the excitement was at its highest, and there were some good stories around, the bosses – with the support of everyone around, including the reporters – quite rightly realised they had to find a different way. The clubs were also aware things needed to change. If an Everton fan turns up brandishing a sex toy, it's as bad for Everton as it is for us.

'Now it's a little more controlled, but it looks better to be inside the Emirates Stadium or the Manchester City training complex, rather than outside next to some security hut. There is a downside, though. The clubs know where we are at any given time. For instance, on deadline day, Chelsea create a little space for us next to the Stamford Bridge sign. I was there when Olivier Giroud signed and they brought him into the stadium a different way. We're not really getting these shots of people in dark cars or going through the back door.

'I think something has disappeared. The unexpected has been lost. One time at Spurs, I remember Clint Dempsey arriving out of absolutely nowhere. There had been no talk whatsoever of him joining Spurs. Now he was there, with one hour to go. A fan said to me: "That was Clint Dempsey in that car." I double-checked with the club: "We're not saying it wasn't."

'Now, though, Spurs – very kindly, don't get me wrong – put you in a little space in their car park at their new training ground. They know where you are and control what you see. But that's no criticism of anybody. It's the way it had to go.'

Without the supporting cast of fans to add extra colour should stories be few and far between on the ground, it's a challenge journalistically for Sky's field reporters to keep the levels of enthusiasm and intrigue high for the watching public, hour after hour. After all, just how many ways are there of saying that nothing's happening?

'First of all, you have to admit that if you're at Fulham or Watford or Swansea or Bournemouth or Southampton, you need to keep it short. If there's nothing happening, say something like, "There's nothing happening, but on deadline day you never know." Or try to come up with something a bit different – almost entertain rather than inform. Usually there's some deal that might be in the offing – perhaps a defender from a second division Turkish team who's coming in as the third-choice left-back and whose name might be something you can play with.

'But we've got better at this. Nowadays, if you're at Bournemouth and there's nothing happening, you tell the production team and they won't come to you. They won't let you leave just in case, but they won't come to you. In the early days, it was "How great are we? We're everywhere!" And in those days we could get away with nothing happening because at least there were some fans behind you or perhaps a dog with a Bournemouth shirt on. But if it's just you in an empty training ground or an empty stadium, they are now a lot better in not coming to you. When you're at Man City or Man United or Liverpool though, they'll come to you more often, even if nothing's happening.

'Even so, I remember a recent transfer window where City weren't going to be doing any business. We had someone there, but I think they only got on air four times during the whole day. It is now driven much more by what's actually happening. We're probably still not quite as good as we should be at admitting that some windows can be dull, but I think we're getting there ...'

The *Guardian* journalist Barry Glendenning has previously highlighted the stoicism of Sky's reporters. 'Apart from their microphones,' he wrote, 'enthusiasm is often the only weapon. Faking excitement and intrigue after suffering the spirit-crushing humiliation of being blanked by a sullen, young multimillionaire in his agent's Range Rover can't be easy, but these transfer-window warriors remain consistently inquisitive and upbeat.'

It's undoubtedly the tumultuous conclusions to transfer windows that make the best war stories. Cotterill has a bagful of them, including the time that Manchester United keeper David de Gea believed he had secured his dream move to the Bernabéu. 'I was in Belgium the day before deadline day and so the team thought it would be easier for me to get to Madrid from Brussels rather than to send someone from London. Sometimes they think a bit like that, like any news desk. While I was at Brussels Airport, I listened to Guillem Balague say, "The deal's done. It's going to be announced in ten minutes' time." United were happy, Real Madrid were happy and de Gea was jumping through hoops because it was the move he'd wanted all along.

'I got to Madrid at eleven in the evening. We were already off-air because it was the day before deadline day – the Spanish window was closing a day earlier than ours. But the next morning, the deal had fallen through. For some reason, de Gea's paperwork hadn't arrived at the La Liga offices on time. So I spent the whole day talking about de

Gea and made some calls to find out that the paperwork did arrive but it wasn't the right bit of paperwork. And by the time that the right bit of paperwork did arrive, it was too late.

'Real Madrid said it did arrive on time, but I got someone from La Liga to show me the arrival time for the paperwork, which was ten minutes after it should have been. De Gea was distraught and Real Madrid and Man United fell out. The biggest transfer story of the whole window didn't happen. But I was in the right place to report it. The unexpected turned out to be a really good story.'

Again, what went wrong with a deal is generally of more interest than merely reporting 'Man puts signature on piece of paper. Gets paid lots of money'. The value is in watching the inquest unfold. 'It's "What the hell went wrong?"' agrees Cotterill. 'How can these two powerful clubs get it so wrong when it comes to hitting a fax machine button? And it was a fax machine, even in this day and age. That's the bizarre thing.'

January is one of the genuine red-letter months for Cotterill, a chance to be reporting on something other than the recovery progress of injuries or speculating about managerial insecurities. There will always be some tasty, potentially dramatic transfer stories to sink his teeth into.

'The journalistic instinct certainly comes to the fore during that month. But it's deadline day itself for me. As a news journalist by training, I love the adrenalin of the actual day. Starting at six in the morning and if it is an eleven o'clock or midnight window, staying on until then – and afterwards, because as we know the window doesn't slam shut then. If you've got a big one, or you've potentially got a big one, or you're finding out that there might be a big one, it is the highlight.

'It's like a general election is for a political journalist. It's what everyone's been talking about for three or four weeks and you're there on the day and you don't know what's going to happen. But nothing's better than when you do know what's going to happen and you've been at the heart of it.'

And, over the fifteen or so years riding the undulating currents of the transfer window, Cotterill was most at the pumping heart of things when he was in the company of a certain Mr Redknapp.

'I remember one year with Harry at Spurs when not a lot was happening. We knew a few things might be, but weren't sure what. It was mid-afternoon and Kevin Bond, his long-time assistant, was hitting a few golf balls at the training ground.

'"What's happening?"

'"I don't know. Go and speak to H."

'I walked in and Harry was sitting there, watching TV and devouring pizza.

'"It's great, innit? I love deadline day."

'"So what's happening?"

'"Jermaine Jenas is going to Villa on loan and Alan Hutton's going there on a permanent. Peter Crouch is going to Stoke on a permanent, as is Wilson Palacios. I'm signing Scott Parker from West Ham on a permanent and David Bentley's going the other way on loan. These are all happening."

'So I went out and did this report, just as the afternoon was quietening down a bit.

'"Sources close to the club say Parker in, Crouch out, Palacios out, Hutton out, Jenas and Bentley out on loan. They're all going to happen imminently – if not, then certainly by deadline."

'I crossed back to Jim White in the studio.

'"Wow! Gary right across it there at Spurs …"

CHAPTER EIGHT

D-DAY VETERANS

'I remember the boss telling me, "I kind of need you there to control Jim"'

– Natalie Sawyer

One man above anyone else has become synonymous with transfer deadline day – one man whose voice rings louder, and more excitedly, than all others. He barks his lines with gusto and certainty, even when the news is unconfirmed. Sketchy rumours receive the same delivery. He is the physical manifestation of the closing of the window, his excitement level going up as the clock ticks down. He is a volcano just about to erupt. He is Jim White of Sky Sports News.

One woman in particular was charged with calming the volcano. Natalie Sawyer has spent more deadline days sat on White's left-hand side than any of her colleagues. As his long-time co-presenter, she was the brake, the counterweight, to White's more untrammelled moments.

When she left Sky in the spring of 2018, Sawyer swapped the small screen for radio, and now presents the early-evening show on talkSPORT. We meet at the station's offices, finding a quiet corner in the cafeteria while all hell breaks loose in the newsroom upstairs. José Mourinho has just been served his cards at Old Trafford.

It's here that she reveals the on-screen duties at Sky that went beyond her job description. 'I was there to – erm, how can I say it? – *control* Jim. Jim is wonderful and I love him, but I'd have to rein him in. He can go off-piste a little and forget where we're supposed to be going. He fully admits that. I remember the boss telling me, "I kind of need you there to control Jim."' Aside from gathering the breaking news at Goodison Park or St Mary's or the Stadium of Light, Sawyer had this additional role. She was the anchor of the anchorman.

Having joined Sky in 2002 as a runner – making teas, running errands, doing the dirty work – Sawyer is perfectly placed to trace deadline day's evolution as shaped by Sky, from its modest origins to the mini-industry it is today. 'I don't want to say the first one was a normal day, because it obviously wasn't a normal day. But it grew to become such an event. It's always been a busy day, but it seems to have ramped up over the last few years. A newsroom is always buzzing, but it just goes up a few notches on deadline day. Towards the end of my time at Sky, you'd have journalists and newspapers and magazines coming in from mainland Europe wanting to sit in and watch how it all works. It has become a TV phenomenon.

'Every year it's got bigger and bigger, but I think the year it really kicked off was in 2008 when both Dimitar Berbatov and Robinho had their very late transfers. Suddenly people realised that late deals do happen. And not just any old transfers, but big deals. It seemed to steamroll after then. That window really stuck in my mind. I can still picture Berbatov in those shots of him walking along that corridor at Old Trafford. That's an image I can still remember.

'After then, we knew that anything could happen, so on the last shift we always had to mention that although the deadline had been reached, there were always deals coming through because paperwork was still being filed. We always knew something might happen. Whether it always did was another thing ...'

If Sky's adoption and subsequent stewardship of deadline day has been steadfast and unwavering, much of this has been down to the identity and branding they've given the day. It's an identity simply based around one colour. Yellow. But no matter how many yellow ties Jim White has bought and worn on deadline day, no matter how closely he's identified with this particular garment, Sawyer reveals that he wasn't the instigator of the dominant colour.

'The first time I did deadline day, I decided to wear an orange dress on air. It was bright and colourful, and I thought it was a bit different. For the next window, I thought I'd wear a different colour. So I just went online and found a yellow dress. And that was it. The stylists on the show loved the yellow, so it stuck. People assume Jim picked out a yellow tie and it just happened to match my dress. Not so.

'Yellow then became synonymous with deadline day. BT Sport did a spoof advert where they were all wearing bright yellow – Robbie Savage had a yellow suit on. I ended up having loads of yellow dresses that I wouldn't wear to any other occasion. If I wore yellow on air on a normal day, people would be say, "It's not deadline day. Why are you wearing yellow?" So there came a point where I couldn't wear yellow on a day other than August 31st or January 31st. But I don't think they're using it as much these days. Hayley McQueen, who does the late shift now, tends to wear black with perhaps a little bit of yellow – a belt or shoes or something.'

But deadline day's appeal on Sky goes way beyond the visual. It's also about information, about giving the viewer plenty of titbits to snack on and chew over, even at times when there wasn't necessarily plenty to give. Having made the co-presenting seat on the final shift of the transfer window her own, Sawyer learned the secret to keeping things lively, to making sure the ball stayed in the air during the day's quieter moments. 'I think I went on at seven pm and I wouldn't be done until one. I've done the middle-of-the-day shift too and found that to always be busy. There were always stories you could generate. Whether they ever came to anything was another matter. By the evening, you knew those stories weren't coming true, so that was always hard. How do you keep it going? You just do because you have to. You want people to be excited by it. And you want to be excited by it yourself.'

Being a twenty-four-hour rolling sports news service – the *only* twenty-four-hour rolling sports news service – Sky were able to take complete ownership of the transfer window, especially deadline day, and totally make it their own. It wouldn't be anything like as big as it is, certainly from a fan's point of view, without the channel.

'I agree. I think Sky do it very well and manage to keep it going, even on days when it's not as busy as you'd hope it would be, because they have reporters based everywhere. You can cross to them in order to find out if anything's going on. And if a club isn't doing business, that's a story in itself. They get great access. Most clubs – I say most clubs, but I think it's pretty much all of them – are quite happy for a reporter to be stationed there and to be fed information, or for them to garner information whenever they can.

'The report can be a cabaret in itself. It's obviously more sterilised now, probably for the right reasons. I was on that night when Dildogate occurred. I didn't even see it – I was looking ahead to the next story. I remember I was on with Paul Merson and he was like "Oh my God! It's a dildo!" and I was like "What? No!"

'I'm not going to blame fans because they get excited and lots of people do silly things in front of a camera, but people took advantage. And the comedian Simon Brodkin did stuff as well. There's reporter safety to consider too. Some reporters did get drenched in beer or whatever. I can under-stand the decision, but it did lose that element of crossing to a reporter and it all being wild. That's the sad part.'

If the deadline days of the present aren't quite as explo-sive as the deadline days of the past, that's also because clubs increasingly do their business early, detracting from the spectacle. The eleventh-hour panic is what provides the most entertainment. Sawyer nods enthusiastically. 'Abso-lutely, absolutely. We all want to see Peter Odemwingie sitting in his car thinking he's about to get a move to QPR. Yes, clubs do tend to do their business earlier, but there's still always one or two who leave it late. Even when clubs come out and say they're done for the window, you never know if they are. There's always drama.

'There's usually a deal late on that you haven't seen coming. And Sky aren't slow. It's not "We'll go across to this reporter" and, ten minutes later, "Now we'll go across to this reporter." It's bang, bang, bang, bang, bang – trying to get out the information as quickly as possible, even if it's "Nothing's happening." At least the viewer has had their fix. Their team's been covered.'

Through its unbreakable bonds with the transfer window, Sky has been a major contributor to the hype machine, both feeding it and being fuelled by it. 'There was a time when Sky would film adverts especially for deadline day. I remember having to get up silly early and go to this army training base. No yellow dresses. We were all in camouflage gear and had to do an assault course, while being shouted at. It wasn't just me and Jim. There were loads of other presenters too. It was all to tell everyone that we were getting into shape for deadline day. This was how it was built up into a great day. And they've all turned out to be great, even if there wasn't any big news. That sometimes would be the story in itself – if a club doesn't buy anyone.

'In January, the countdown clock starts running from the first of the month, so you're constantly reminding everybody, "We're getting closer!" And as it gets closer, you're ramping it up every time. If a club hasn't done business but you know they're after, for example, a centre-back, that's one that you're going to highlight as you build up to deadline day itself. You naturally ramp it up. But, of course, you can't peak too soon.'

The hype machine both reflects and drives the level of enthusiastic consumption, allowing the *delivery* of news stories to be as significant to viewers as the news stories themselves. 'Bookmakers will even take bets on the first word Jim will say. I've seen things like that. It's crazy. That just shows how big a day it's become.'

As exciting as the breaking stories themselves might be, and as important as keeping ringmaster White in check was, the most rewarding aspect of the day itself for Sawyer was the journalistic challenge. 'A lot of the day is unscripted. It's "Can you throw to this person?" or "Can you fill for ten minutes talking to your guest?" It's all down to you and that's brilliant. That's what you want. You want to lead it, not just read it. You want to show that you do know what you're talking about. But a lot of it is down to the production team, don't get me wrong. They're brilliant and they work tirelessly. It's a collective thing.'

It was also an irresistible thing. 'On a typical deadline day when I was on the late shift, I'd be at home in the morning watching it, glued to it. I'd need to know what's happened and what's happening. Normally I'd get into work three hours before the shift started at seven pm, but on deadline day I might have got in a bit earlier. You just want to get in to feel part of it and get that buzz.'

We're fast approaching Sawyer's first January deadline day as a talkSPORT presenter. There are whispers at this stage that she and White might join forces together again, co-presenting over the airwaves for one day only – an unexpected development in her post-Sky life that naturally excites her. But as charged as the transfer window makes

Sawyer as a broadcaster, she adopts a different worldview as a diehard Brentford supporter. With a metaphorical scarf around her neck, she treats deadline day with caution, and sometimes disdain.

'We are a club that sadly, for the feasible, will be a selling club. In the summer 2017 window, we lost three players on deadline day – all of them to Birmingham. It was a kick in the teeth. I knew two were going to go, but the third came out of nowhere. We knew he was leaving, but not that he was going to Birmingham as well. Three players going to our rivals! But that's who we are at the moment – a selling club. So a more successful window for us is one where we've retained players rather than recruited.'

It's a week before Christmas, but any festive cheer is compromised by Sawyer's fear that there will be more key departures from Griffin Park when the window opens in a fortnight. 'This coming January, we're looking at our old manager Dean Smith, who's now at Aston Villa, who we know loves some of our players. There's already that fear that he's going to come in for Romaine Sawyers or Ollie Watkins or Chris Mepham or whoever. Every player does have a price, after all.'

For someone so sharp, responsive and enthusiastic on air, a dark cloud now hovers above. 'It's always a turbulent time as a Brentford fan during the transfer window.'

Not every day can be a bright yellow one.

* * *

The Wikipedia page for 'brinkmanship' was once doctored, presumably by a contributor from the red quarter of north

London. After using the threat of nuclear war as an example of the concept's deployment, the page noted it was 'also used by Daniel Levy in negotiating deals to buy or loan players for Tottenham Hotspur. He inevitably fails and in desperation buys a Frazier Campbell-type player in the last minutes of the transfer window'.

The Tottenham chairman is known as English football's toughest negotiator – and possibly world football's, too. Alex Ferguson memorably observed that dealing with Levy was 'more painful than my hip replacement', while the *Guardian*'s David Hytner neatly refers to him as 'the iron fist within an iron glove'. Hytner goes further: 'The very mention of his name can have agents and players letting out mournful sighs before they launch into stories about how they thought they had a deal, only for Levy to make an eleventh-hour revision to his demands.'

That reputation has been slightly revised in recent times; two successive acquisition-free windows failed to affect Spurs' passage to their first-ever Champions League final. Not a single deal was done, But it wasn't always thus. Back in October 2008, Levy appointed Harry Redknapp as Spurs manager and, for the next three years and eight months, the pair formed a formidable double act when it came to the club's recruitment. Their character types complemented each other. Levy – softly spoken, inscrutable, economic with his words; Redknapp – outgoing, fidgety, the affable raconteur.

Well, not always affable. During a TV interview after Spurs' home win over Wigan on the evening of deadline day in January 2012, a reporter asked why there had been such little transfer activity from Spurs, bearing in mind 'you've made your name as a wheeler-dealer'. Redknapp was distinctly unimpressed and unleashed twin barrels of Anglo-Saxon rarely heard in the usually asinine world of the post-match interview. 'No, I'm not a wheeler-dealer. No, fuck off.' Redknapp marched off camera, but was still clearly audible. 'I'm not a fucking wheeler-dealer. Don't say that. I'm a fucking football manager.'

His point was crystal-clear and perfectly justified. At that point, Spurs held third place in the ever-fierce Premier League behind the two Manchester clubs – so only behind Roberto Mancini and Alex Ferguson. Suggesting Redknapp to be football's own Arthur Daley blithely ignored his managerial acumen, both as a tactician and a motivator.

That Levy's recruitment decisions are often described as shrewd while Redknapp's are likened to that of a market trader clearly has its roots in class. Levy is a graduate, with first-class honours, of Sidney Sussex College, Cambridge. Redknapp is an alumnus of Sir Humphrey Gilbert School in Stepney; 'the worst school in the East End, without a doubt,' says its most famous son.

Nonetheless, the pair seemed to find some common ground where Spurs' recruitment was concerned. 'People think Daniel and I were always clashing over players,' Redknapp later wrote, 'but it was never like that. Yes, he had his own views, but we never made a signing that wasn't run by me first – and even though I knew he didn't fancy some of my choices, I got most of them.

'I know that I became synonymous with transfer deadline day in my later years, but the reality was that it was usually a nightmare because I had been brought into a club in trouble. The experience at Tottenham, where we had such a good squad already, was far preferable. Yet, even then, Daniel would always be in the market for late deals. I already knew what he was like because, when I was at Portsmouth, he would ring me at nine thirty pm or ten pm on deadline day to see what was going on.'

The later in the window, the higher the price for a player in demand. But, conversely, the cheaper a player whom a club is desperate to offload, hence Levy's eleventh-hour sorties. You could possibly liken him to an astute grocery shopper, monitoring the supermarket aisles for the late-in-the-day markdowns – snooping around in the closing hours of a transfer window when some yellow-stickered players could be found.

If Redknapp was indelibly linked to deadline day – and specifically TV interviews conducted through the open window of his car – he was also hardwired to signing certain players on or around the final twenty-four hours of the window. The Croatian midfielder Niko Kranjčar is a member of this intimate club, as are Jermaine Defoe and Peter Crouch. The latter, though, has been keen to show it went both ways with Redknapp; he might have been signed by Harry twice, but he's been sold by him on two occasions too. 'I was never his teacher's pet,' Crouch later wrote, 'and I was never immune to being moved on if he felt he could do better without me.'

Tottenham's offloading of Crouch on the final day of August 2011 was proof of this – and of Levy's ruthlessness. Having enjoyed a successful season at White Hart Lane just a few months before – he played in forty-five matches and scored the winner against AC Milan at the San Siro – Crouch was all geared up for more of the same. But then he walked into Redknapp's office and, unbeknownst to him, straight into a conference call with Levy. The upshot was that Redknapp liked the cut of Emmanuel Adebayor's jib. Signing the man from Togo would make Crouch surplus to requirements, despite having two years left on his contract. Levy bluntly informed him he wasn't being given a squad number. Plus, the big money being offered for Crouch by Stoke – it was a £16m double swoop for him and Wilson Palacios – made it a no-brainer for the Spurs hierarchy. Crouch was understandably miffed, but what happened next that day, though, did lighten the tone and soften the striker's mood.

'I went home to meet my dad,' he revealed to the *Daily Mail*, 'and we jumped in the car to head to Stoke. First, we stopped to get something to eat. The restaurant of choice? McDonald's at the Target roundabout on the A40. It was here, though, that things became a bit surreal. We were watching Sky Sports News as we ate and the yellow strip comes across the bottom of the screen. "PETER CROUCH IS IN A HELICOPTER ON HIS WAY TO STOKE".

'Dad and I were in stitches.'

That August 2011 deadline day was a properly busy one for Redknapp; it was the one that Gary Cotterill described, when Harry confided all that day's intentions to the Sky Sports News reporter. But it didn't compare to a decidedly dysfunctional and infamous day less than eighteen months later, by which time Redknapp had taken over at an ailing QPR, rooted to the foot of the Premier League.

The cash of QPR owner Tony Fernandes was being spent in serious quantity in order to give the club as much chance as possible of avoiding the drop. This was the ultimate trolley dash against the clock. The arrivals kept coming, the entrance door to Loftus Road permanently propped open. Having already signed the French striker Loïc Rémy from Marseille, deadline-day arrivals included Chris Samba, Jermaine Jenas and Andros Townsend.

Samba's deal in particular came in for sizeable scorn. At the age of twenty-nine, he'd been offered – and had gratefully accepted – a four-and-a-half-year deal of £100,000 a week, making him one of the world's best-paid footballers. This was crazy, unsustainable overspending underwritten by a club staring deep into the abyss. The financial burden was likely to be crippling for a Championship club, and the odds were very much suggesting that would be their status in five months' time.

As the then between-jobs manager Owen Coyle told BBC Sport, 'If the worst happens, the financial position QPR will be in doesn't bear thinking about. This feels like a club panicking.' The *Daily Mail* was equally dismissive, describing them as 'a club who have spent this transfer window in the last-chance saloon attempting to buy anything with a pulse that can put in a tackle'.

Indeed, were this level of speculation taking place in a Monte Carlo casino, there would have been a collective intake of breath from the onlookers gathered around the roulette table. The stakes were high, the gamble enormous, the fall potentially fatal.

Even an experienced operator like Redknapp seemed bewildered by the frantic fury of that particular deadline day. 'Every agent is out to screw the other agent. It's a bit like the ice cream wars in Glasgow. They're all at each other's throats. It's as if someone is going to shoot them. It's crazy.' Three years later, as he contemplated his life's work for another volume of memoirs, Redknapp set that evening's events, and the club's recruitment in general, into a more considered context. 'QPR were naïve initially with agents and paid a heavy price for very average players. It tied them into situations that became difficult to reverse at any sort of speed.'

No amount of the majority shareholder's money could arrest the slide into the Championship – and poorly negotiated contracts somewhat hamstrung the club. 'I think I allowed myself to be exploited,' Tony Fernandes confessed to the BBC, 'but that's my choice. Agents are trying to get the best contracts and there are no two ways about it – I had to pay premiums. I've seen all parts that make football quite – maybe immoral is a strong word – but they would sell their grandmother to do something. It's all part of the football ecosystem.'

Premier League status had evaporated, as had a wedge of Fernandes cash. 'This has been a tragic season in many ways. It is a Shakespearean play in the making.'

But the events of 31 January 2013 at Loftus Road that evening have been immortalised in the annals of deadline-day history for another reason – for a player who *didn't* join QPR that day. Writing about the advent of the transfer window in *When Saturday Comes* back in 2003, Barney Ronay had shown fabulous prescience. 'Jean-Marc Bosman publicised his case by juggling a football while wearing a set of rubber manacles,' he observed. 'How long will it be before unemployed footballers stage sit-ins at service stations the length of the country demanding that Harry Redknapp sign them?'

Ronay's words proved prophetic when, ten years later – and with three and a half hours left of the January window – a car pulled up outside Loftus Road in west London. Its driver was instantly recognisable and the Sky Sports News cameraman and reporter swarmed straight to the driver's side window, like eager, honeypot-visiting bees. In the driving seat was West Brom striker Peter Odemwingie. There hadn't been word thus far of him becoming a QPR player, but going by his conversation with the man from Sky, Odemwingie thought it a formality.

Sky: 'Peter, do you feel disappointed how you've been treated by West Brom?'

Odemwingie: 'No, no, [it's] fine. West Brom is my home. This is a new chapter to start in my life, you know. I love West Brom and I always will.'

Sky: 'How excited are you about this challenge?'

Odemwingie: 'Oh, I think every football fan is interested to see if we're going to make it or not. I'm very optimistic about it. A few good players have already arrived here and I'm happy with the trust that the manager Harry Redknapp has given me.'

Sky: 'Do you think QPR can stay up now?'

Odemwingie: 'Yes, of course I believe. The last few results have shown there's a chance to stay up. I don't think the owners would bring so many quality players and spend so much money if they didn't believe it could happen. So I believe as well as they believe.'

Sky: 'Will you definitely be a QPR player as of this evening?'

Odemwingie: 'It's not one hundred per cent. It's not sorted yet, but I hope West Brom will be happy with what they will get. And, of course, they're hoping to get players themselves. I just hope things will go well in the last few hours.'

Sky: 'And you finally got your wish after speaking on Twitter at the weekend.'

Odemwingie: 'Well, you know, I had to push a little bit, so ...'

From the Sky studios a few miles west in Isleworth, Natalie Sawyer watched the Odemwingie saga unfold before her astonished eyes. It's still a redolent memory today. 'It was such a good story. I'm a mum, so my maternal instinct kicked in. I just wanted to give him a hug and tell him to go home. Who told him to get in his car and drive there? Who thought it was a good idea? He was there in public view. Everyone knew who he was. And he was probably driving something like a Range Rover or something. It wouldn't have been a discreet car. Maybe it had a "Peter Loves QPR" bumper sticker too ...'

Discretion could have been the better part of valour. If the deal still showed at least a faint pulse, why not just park up somewhere relatively close by – the nearest motorway services perhaps, or a hotel – under cover of darkness and ride it out away from prying eyes? Instead, Odemwingie drove straight into the eye of the storm. It became a tale that, 130 appearances and a good few goals aside, ultimately defined the Nigerian striker's playing days in English football.

That's undoubtedly harsh on Odemwingie. The collective verdict of what he did that evening was no doubt coloured by a recent social media pop he had at the powers-that-be at West Brom. A logical conclusion to draw was that the want-away player was showing more petulance, trying to push through a transfer by turning up at his preferred place of future employment.

A more reasonable analysis has subsequently emerged. It may have just been a breakdown in communication between the various parties. Odemwingie has subsequently revealed that it was only after he arrived in London that he discovered the deal was dependent on QPR striker Junior Hoilett travelling in the opposite direction to The Hawthorns. Hoilett had turned the move down. But no one had told Odemwingie.

'I believed the deal was done,' Odemwingie explained to Sky Sports a couple of years later. 'I had nothing to hide and when the cameras came, I didn't feel awkward to say what I thought. But until you see things on paper, then nothing is done.'

With Akron's 'Lonely' as apt musical accompaniment, Odemwingie drove back up the M40, ready to serve himself a large portion of humble pie upon his reunion with his West Brom teammates. Jermaine Jenas was more fortunate that day. He had successfully put his signature on a QPR contract earlier on. It was the third and final deadline-day move made by the midfielder.

The first, in 2005, saw him swap Newcastle for Spurs, a deal that only made itself known in the last couple of hours of the window. The young Jenas was away on England duty, relaxing in a St Albans hotel room around 10pm, when he got a call from his agent. One speedy car journey around the M25 later and he was putting pen to contract at the Spurs training ground in Chigwell, having pass the sketchiest of medicals. Desperate to escape Graeme Souness's reign at St James's Park, Jenas didn't return to Tyneside once. 'I never went back,' he confessed to the BBC. 'I was gone. I even had two houses there. I left everything that was in my locker, too – boots and shinpads.'

If that move to Spurs was of a young man in demand, his first departure from White Hart Lane – a season-long loan to Aston Villa in the summer of 2011 – was that of a player being voluntarily jettisoned by his parent club. The player at that stage of his career has fewer options. He can't necessarily pick and choose. He is limited to whichever clubs might be interested in him.

Jenas had been expecting that day's loan move to be taking him to the blue side of Manchester, after hearing favourable comments about himself from Roberto Mancini via the Italian's coach David Platt, his former manager at Nottingham Forest. But City plumped for Owen Hargreaves instead, leaving Jenas to mull over Villa's offer instead. When plans change on deadline day, there's no time for careful consideration. A player needs to think straight but to also think sharp. Ticking clocks and all that.

'In football,' Jenas observed, 'there are decisions you have to make, especially on deadline day. It is heightened by the fact that it has to happen *now*.

'Should I? Should I not? The decision is made and you are gone.'

* * *

Like Jermaine Jenas, Glenn Murray is another player who has also signed deals on three separate deadline days. In fact, he signed all three less than two and a half years apart.

The first time the Brighton striker moved on deadline day was in September 2014, when he went on loan to Reading from Crystal Palace. Until then – over the course of ten years as a pro, moving his way through the divisions right up to the Premier League – he'd always been a spectator on deadline day, never the protagonist. As such, he treated it just like Joe or Josephine Public does: a source of both intrigue and entertainment.

'I viewed it the exact same as everyone else. You're waiting for who's going to pop up on that tickertape on Sky Sports News. Or, as a player, you're waiting to see who's going to burst through the doors in the dressing-room or who you're going to walk in on having his medical. It's just as exciting for us.

'There will be a buzz around the training ground. There'll be a camera crew outside and on the road into the training ground, looking at the cars to see if anyone new is coming in. For the players, though, it's generally a pretty normal day. Whether you tune in to the TV or not depends on what you've got planned that day. If they aren't, they'll still be having sneaky looks on their phones. Or people will be sending them text updates.

'Sometimes, of course, it can be worrying – if there are rumours of somebody coming who could take your position. We all understand that clubs are always trying to evolve and become better. They always want a better eleven than the one they've already got. That's the nature of the beast. Players are aware of rumours, but I think it's down to the person how worried they are about someone coming in. Some people might worry, some people might have had a conversation with the manager and be waiting for someone to come in to allow them to move on. The manager might have said, "If I get a centre-half in, I'll let you look for another club." So some players will be willing it, some players won't. And, with the twenty-five-man squad in the Premier League, players on the fringes will be concerned that an incoming player will knock them out of the squad. There are all different kinds of scenarios for everyone.'

When Murray woke on the morning of 1 September 2014, the final day of that summer's window, he knew he was taking a sojourn away from Selhurst Park. Unlike Jenas having to reset his sat-nav towards Birmingham when Villa, not Manchester City, turned out to be his next destination, Murray knew what was going to unfold that particular day.

'Yes, I asked to leave the football club. I went in and asked Neil Warnock, the manager at the time, where he saw me for that year. He told me that, without doubt, I was his fifth-choice centre-forward, that there were four strikers above me. That was good, really. People might think that was a bad thing to hear – that you're fifth of five. But for a manager to be so open and frank with you was quite a blessing. That allowed me to go and try to get game time elsewhere.

'Quite often, a manager might err on the grey side a little bit. "Well, maybe you're third, maybe fourth, maybe fifth. But I want you to hang around. I want you to try to push your way in." Thankfully, Neil didn't do that to me. He was honest and that gave me a decision to make. I'd just come back from an ACL (anterior cruciate ligament) and hadn't played too much football. I wanted to really test my knee out for ninety minutes, week in, week out, and get used to the contact of the sport again. After having ten months out, and then a long period on the bench, I questioned my ability during that time. You question yourself a lot when you're staring at the walls of the physio's room or the gym. Or when you watch the squad train. I questioned whether I'd be the same player again, so I wanted to get back on the horse and head back out to get some games.

'It was pretty nailed on that I was going to Reading. It had been rumoured for a long time. Having the manager's blessing made it a lot easier – Reading wanted me and it was a pretty smooth process. They had some concerns about my injury and obviously didn't want to sign a player who was going to break down after three games. I went up to London to get a scan and after that a little medical and they were happy. It was pretty smooth.'

The smoothness of Murray's move down the M4 is in contrast to the uncertainty of other deadline-day transfers, where players will be sat at the breakfast table first thing in the morning with little or no clue about who they'll be contracted to by nightfall. Such scenarios, where the player is such a hostage to the whims and ways of others, are rare, says Murray.

'I have heard of that, but only on a couple of occasions for people close to me, to be honest. Normally a player will have a pretty educated guess. These things very rarely spring up without any prior conversations, either between the clubs or between the agents. The truth of the matter is, in ninety-nine per cent of deadline-day transfers, the player has a pretty good idea of where he's going. Obviously, there are those one per cent that I've heard about where a player will be in one medical room before getting changed, getting into the car and going to another club to have a medical there, because that club has matched his club's valuation.'

When it came to his second deadline-day move – exactly a year to the day that he'd gone to Reading – Murray had more than an educated guess that he was going to sign for Bournemouth on a permanent. Loud whispers about the proposed deal had been a staple of transfer gossip columns for the best part of the close season, after all.

'The move was rumoured for six to eight weeks. But again it came down to the last minute, when Crystal Palace decided to accept the offer. Clubs are very coy in the transfer market and this is why you can get some excitement on the last day. People hold their cards close to their chest for as long as possible – even long enough to miss out on what they actually want and sometimes what they actually need. If everyone was open and honest, it would be so much easier. If it was down to the player, a lot of the time he would be out of that club six weeks earlier. A player would prefer to start a pre-season with a club – get to know his teammates, get to know the philosophy, get settled in the area, and get fit. That would be a perfect start at a new club from a player's point of view.'

With the carrot of a desired move dangling tantalisingly just out of reach, those eight or so weeks must have been torture for the striker. As the transfer window entered its end-game without an agreed offer and thus without an inky squiggle on a contract, thoughts of this new challenge at a new club must have begun to evaporate. The longer that a club holds its cards close, the quicker that hopes and dreams disappear on the air.

'It all boils down to what type of person you are. Some guys might be really relaxed about the situation. Others may not be. You do start questioning the people who are in charge. I questioned my agent at times. He tells me Bournemouth are keen. I ask why they haven't come in. He says he doesn't know. So we go round and round in circles for six weeks, and it all gets a little bit tense in the end. Agents' phones must be red-hot with players asking "Has anyone put a bid in? Why has nothing happened? What's going on? Do they not want me?" Agents will get so many questions from insecure players over the course of the transfer window. It must make their heads spin.

'In the end, the deal was done the night before. That's when I got the call. I was up and off early the next morning down to Bournemouth. It was all pretty stress-free because we had the whole day to get the move over the line. But we needed the whole day because that was a permanent and, if it hadn't happened, I'd have been back to Crystal Palace until January the first.'

Of course, what looks like – and what has looked like for the past eight weeks – a well-suited move to a newly promoted club might not be such a snug fit. For all the pre-deal talk, there are no guarantees that it won't be a mismatch. And so it was for Murray down in Dorset. Over nineteen Premier League games that season for the Cherries, he found the net just three times. 'My time at Bournemouth wasn't great,' he concedes. 'Although it was a successful period for the club, it just wasn't quite the right fit for me personally.'

By now, at nearly thirty-three, Murray was entering the late afternoon of his life as a professional footballer. There was no time to calmly contemplate the future, to consider his career arc while staring at a wall, to merely go through the motions and warm the bench in return for a Premier League salary. He needed to grasp the nettle himself, to find a new challenge, to set his own agenda.

Murray would find it on his own doorstep. Still based in Brighton from his three-and-a-half seasons there before he joined Crystal Palace, the lure of returning to Albion and securing top-flight football for them for the first time since the early 1980s represented fat, juicy bait. He joined on a season-long loan in July 2016, but so well did the prodigal son play during the first half of the season – when he averaged more than a goal every two games – he signed a permanent deal in January. Naturally, this only finally went through on the last day of the window, following the now-established pattern.

'The Brighton permanent move was something I really pushed for and really wanted. It was going really well back there. I could see there was a big possibility that we'd get promoted and I obviously wanted to be part of that. Everything seemed to be right.'

Nonetheless, despite the deal suiting player and both clubs, it still went down to the wire. If it hadn't gone through that day, not only would Brighton not have been able to secure Murray's services permanently until the summer, but their promotion campaign could have been derailed if Bournemouth had fancied recalling their striker.

'It certainly would have been a lot less stressful for me if Bournemouth and Brighton had agreed a fee before then. It had been made apparent that Brighton wanted to sign me and they'd made noises that they'd sign me at the end of the season whatever the situation was. But as a footballer, you just want your situation to be settled so you can concentrate on football. And that's what I wanted. You never know what could happen in those six months. You could break down with an injury and the club wouldn't want you any more. Snap an Achilles tendon or something like that and you're looking at ten or twelve months out. Why would they sign a player with a really bad injury? There are lots of things that change the playing field.'

Is that much-longed-for job security the reason why players get so nervous during the window – and even more so on deadline day? 'Again,' cautions Murray, 'that's very much on a player-by-player basis. I've played alongside players who've loved playing on a one-year deal. They liked the challenge it gave them – it made them hungry for another year and they felt it got the best out of them. Me, personally, I'm much happier to be settled – and even more so now we've had children. It's nice to know where you're going to be for the foreseeable future.'

Over the course of a well-travelled career, a journey that's known a few potholes, there's been one constant guiding Murray each and every time he reached a junction: the direction he then went in was his decision. He's never been a puppet, submissive to a club's alternative agenda. He's kept his desired destination in clear focus. And the bottom line is that, although a footballer is a trading commodity, he's in a rare position: he's a trading commodity with a voice.

'A player always has the opportunity to turn a move down,' he concludes. 'It is optional. As long as you are sitting on a contract, a club can't force you to leave. They can nudge you in the right direction by, for example, saying that you're not going to play. But it's the player's prerogative if he doesn't want to move. For instance, if a club in, say, Sweden or Bulgaria came and offered ten million for me, Brighton would probably want to take it at my age. But I wouldn't want to go. And it would be down to me.

'The player has got a little bit of power. He can't make a move happen, but he can *stop* a move happening.'

CHAPTER NINE

THE LONGEST DAY

'I don't think deadline day is there to be enjoyed or not. It's part of the business. You have no choice about it'
– Sean Dyche

7am

Phil Jones's alarm clock goes off at the usual hour and, for the first couple of seconds of groggy confusion, he doesn't remember that it's the last day of January, that it's transfer deadline day. When the clouds do part and the significance of the day kicks in, he starts smiling. It's a red-letter day for him, one of the highlights of the year.

This isn't Phil Jones the footballer, waking up in a mansion in Alderley Edge in anticipation of welcoming a new teammate or two into the Old Trafford dressing room. This is Phil Jones the IT engineer, waking up in a modest semi in Towcester in anticipation of a day sat in front of the gogglebox.

Phil is a deadline-day addict and has been for years, going right back to his university days when he and his housemates would bunk off lectures to take in the high drama (or otherwise) of the transfer window's closure. These days, it's a solo pursuit. 'It's a different experience nowadays, but I still love it. I can get lost in it all without any distractions.'

Phil's partner works in Northampton and tonight is going out in town straight after work, leaving him the evening free. By 7am, he's taken up his position for the next sixteen hours – all day and some of the night. He's on the sofa in the front room. The TV is on and tuned to Sky Sports News. The laptop is on and tuned to Twitter. There's a large cafetière of steaming coffee before him. He's in for the duration.

Phil isn't just looking out for who his favoured club has jettisoned or recruited. If he were, he could be in for the dullest of days. He's a Newcastle fan and, over the previous thirty days, owner Mike Ashley appears not to have told Rafa Benitez whether he's got any cash to splash.

To spice up what could potentially be an anticlimactic day, Phil has devised a distraction to help him through until 11pm, to keep his interest sharp. When he used to be in the company of his college pals, drinking games were undertaken throughout the day, usually based around a game of deadline-day cliché bingo. As a solo pursuit, it's a little more sober. Each time a done deal is announced today, Phil will allow himself to pay a visit to the kitchen to raid the biscuit tin. While it's his own rule that's not subject to scrutiny from any whistle-blowing official, he's none-theless disciplined about it. Just one chocolate Hobnob for each confirmed permanent signing. Loan deals don't count; Phil gets nothing for one of those. But he seems optimistic that it's going to be a productive day with plenty of business. He's bought two packets of Hobnobs.

Today's diet might be a little suspect but, reassuringly, Phil has at least swapped his pyjamas for actual clothes. 'I'm not a complete hooligan ...'

10am

There's a reunion going on at talkSPORT's studio near Waterloo. Jim White and Natalie Sawyer, the dynamic duo of deadline day, are back together, broadcasting partners for the first time since their Sky days.

Back then, it was all about the yellow. This morning, it's all about the red. White is wearing a scarlet tie to chime with the station's Red Alert theme, ready to – among the shouty ads for van hire, plumbing materials and, incongruously, the *Times Literary Supplement* – be the first with the scoops and exclusives. Later in the day, presenter Andy Jacobs, one half of the celebrated Hawksbee & Jacobs broadcasting tag-team, will put everyone else at talkSPORT to shame with his bright-red three-piece suit, red tie and red tartan trainers. He'll point out that not everyone at the station observed the red dress code. Alan Brazil, for one, didn't – although, quips Jacobs, his face was already red enough.

It doesn't take long for some very interesting breaking news to emerge. Just four minutes into the show, in fact. The Wales striker Sam Vokes is reported to be on his way from Premier League Burnley to Championship Stoke City for a medical. Passing him on the motorway network in the opposite direction will be Peter Crouch, who's swapping the bet365 Stadium for Turf Moor – and a return to top-flight football. White is clearly excited by such a headline-grabbing move this early in the day. 'He was thirty-eight years of age yesterday. He's Peter Crouch and he's on the move. Let's get more on it …'

It's a transfer that gives the gathered panel something meaty to chew on. White asks Tony Cascarino about the wisdom of signing a thirty-eight-year-old, even if he is on a free. 'They're getting the great mentality of a pro. Peter's the kind of player who, if you bring him into a dressing room, you know he's going to bring character to the table. There's nothing better than getting a senior pro coming through the door. And he's a good pro. Sometimes it can rebound if you bring in one without the right mentality and who can kick up a stink. You definitely won't get that with Peter Crouch.'

Alongside Cascarino, Simon Jordan will be a particularly cogent, articulate observer of what will unfold today, a former club owner with plenty of deadline-day experience and someone who, he gleefully admits, now basks in 'the privilege of being able to sit down and watch other people have this indignation foisted upon them'. There's plenty of time to fill on air today, so the debate, for now at least, has room to stretch out, allowing Jordan to draw the clear differences between the calendar's two windows. You suspect that, during his days as proprietor of Crystal Palace, he may even have enjoyed trading during the summer window, viewing it as a time born of optimism, the filling-in of a blank slate. January's dark days represent something altogether different, when blinkered panic and ill-advised haste take charge. These thirty-one days, he declares, are nothing but 'the bastion of bad business'.

Brighton chief executive Paul Barber comes on air to offer his thoughts. For him, the January window has a definite use. He describes it as a time of 'backfill', when a club can repair any fissures in its squad. Perhaps a mistake was made during the summer spending spree, or maybe the club has accumulated too many injuries or suspensions in the first half of the season. It's the month, and the day, to try to correct what's gone wrong by the season's mid-point.

News comes in that the serial loanee, Chelsea's Lucas Piazon, is making another temporary move, this time to Chievo in Serie A. Cascarino tries to put a positive spin on the deal, but this is now the sixth club, and fifth country, that the Brazilian has been farmed out to. 'Obviously, when you're a Premier League player, you think you're at a higher status and going out on loan doesn't feel the right thing. But it's an opportunity to play. The one thing you want to do if you're a player is play football, and it's a time to find your career again. It's a platform to show what you can do.' What Piazon feels this time around, as his Chelsea career continues to be put on hold, remains undocumented.

11.30am

Mid-morning arrives and the pot, for now at least, seems to be simmering nicely. There are a few confirmed deals involving Premier League clubs. Marouane Fellaini has cashed in his chips and is leaving Old Trafford for an extremely lucrative sojourn in the Chinese Super League, while Wolves have turned their loan deal for Atlético Madrid wing-back Jonny Otto into an £18m permanent move. Down in north London, Arsenal have been linked with several players. The most likely of these to sign, Barcelona's Denis Suárez, tweets a picture of him saying farewell to his pals at the Camp Nou. But it's 'Hasta luego', rather than 'Adios para siempre'. It's another loan move.

And in what would surely be the scoop of the century, Sky Sports News relays a viewer's tip-off that Lionel Messi has been spotted in Tranmere.

1pm

At the Wham Stadium, home of Accrington Stanley of League One, the snow lies crisp and even in the car park, satisfyingly crunchy underfoot. However, there aren't any agents' or players' cars leaving tread marks. It's only builders' vans making an impression.

While it's busy (and warm) inside the club, it's not necessarily transfer business that's the main focus. For starters, the two-person media team are frantically trying to get the programme for this weekend's local-ish derby with Blackpool to press, all the while ignoring a frequently ringing phone, the ringtone of which is the jangly intro of 'This Charming Man'.

Dave Burgess, Stanley's chief executive, has just come in from the pitch. He's been mucking in with the ground staff trying to clear the snow from the playing surface ready for Saturday. On the TV set in the corner, Sky Sports News is showing a photo of Fellaini at the airport, ready to fly to the Far East. Burgess ignores it. He's right to do so. The annual £1.3m playing budget here at the Wham is what the Belgian will reportedly be earning per month in China. Instead, Burgess pulls off his snowy gloves and gets stuck into his packed lunch. He's ready to hold court on the limitations of the current transfer process.

'The window means we can't trade at any other time,' he sighs. 'It's like saying to Sainsbury's that they can open until Saturday dinner-time, but then they've got to shut until Monday morning. No other business would let you do that. Football does. It stops us from buying players, it stops us from selling players. It means that we panic towards the end of a window, because we haven't got who we wanted because we're down the food chain. What happens then is we'll have to get one or two loans in that we probably don't want, but we have to get in order to get the numbers in. Hopefully we get the right ones. I'd say that eight-and-a-half times out of ten, John [Coleman, manager] and Jimmy [Bell, assistant manager] do get the right ones and they improve what we've got.

'We want to trade all year round and the fact that we've got to stop today, and we've got what we've got for the rest of the season, means that we'll probably be working until last thing tonight bringing a couple of loans in. We can't buy anybody else. We're not Man United, we're not Arsenal, and we're certainly not Chelsea. We've got to get what we get. We've got to pick the scraps up. And that's not being detrimental to the players, either. Teams won't let their players go until they've got their replacements in. And it's normally the tiddlers at the bottom who miss out on the food. We've got less money to spend and we've got less pull than teams in higher divisions. We have to wait to get whatever's left at the end.

'We don't like the transfer window. Just because the Premier League stops on a certain day in August, why should that stop us? Why can't the Premier League and the Championship stop on a certain day and League One and League Two trade right through? I know it comes direct from UEFA, but it's stopping us trading. The EFL say we should be in line with the Premier League, but why? It's a different competition, it's a different entity, it's a different ball game altogether. We shouldn't have to follow like sheep because that's what the Premier League does. The EFL needs to stand on its own two feet and ask "What is the best for our membership?" But no one's come to me to ask what we want.'

Burgess has a point here. League One and League Two voted against adopting the new August 9th deadline for the summer window, but nineteen out of twenty-four Championship clubs approved the idea, so the EFL adopted it. The main reason the Premier League brought the deadline forward was so that the window would have closed before the season kicked off, which would have avoided unsettling teams after the first round of matches. However, Accrington's season kicked off on August 4th. It was of no benefit to them or their League One contemporaries.

Despite his loathing of the system, Burgess didn't wake up with a sense of dread this morning – nor does he ever on January 31st. 'I don't, because I can't affect it from where I sit in the club. I can't do anything about it, so it's a normal day in the office for me. I'll listen to the media guys and I'll listen with interest to Mark the club secretary about who might be coming in, but I can't affect what goes on, so it's pointless me getting worked up about it.

'I've no idea about which players we're looking at today. That's John's job. I'm not running the team. He doesn't come to me and ask how I'm doing on the business side today. I don't ask him what he's doing on the football side – as long as he sticks to his budget. And he does. He's really good at that.'

John Coleman is unlikely to be in today, but will be in touch with Mark the secretary to tell him who to get in. Mark will then meet them and get the signing done. 'It's not glamorous here,' says Burgess. 'He might meet them at Charnock Richard services on the M6. It could be anywhere.

'I don't even watch it on television, to be honest. It doesn't grab me at all. I'm one of the three signatories, so I'll be here to sign paperwork if anything happens. If it doesn't, I'll go home and – what is it, Thursday? – I'll go and watch whatever's on a Thursday night. *Question Time* and then bed!'

Burgess pops the lid back on the Tupperware and reaches for his gloves. He's heading back out into the sub-zero temperatures. You get the sense that shovelling snow off the pitch is, in his eyes, more preferable and pleasurable than dealing with deadline day. Which does he prefer? 'Shovelling snow,' he smiles, disappearing back outside. 'It's pure ...'

2.30pm

On the twenty-minute drive between the Wham Stadium and Burnley's training facilities in the grounds of the

National Trust-owned stately pile of Gawthorpe Hall, there's more news involving the Clarets. With Peter Crouch believed to be signing only until the end of the season, Burnley are almost certain to be in the market for a long-term replacement for Sam Vokes. Reports earlier in the day linked them to Vincent Janssen, the Dutch striker who's done little other than underwhelm in two-and-a-half years at Spurs. However, Lancashire seems low down on the priorities of want-away Janssen, with both Real Betis and Schalke more attractive possible destinations.

It appears that Burnley's attention is instead crystallising around Birmingham's free-scoring striker Che Adams, with talkSPORT reporting that a second bid from the Premier League club has been declined.

3.30pm

At Gawthorpe Hall, the squirrels are getting impatient waiting for Peter Crouch to arrive. Here, on this late winter afternoon, they sit in the skeletal trees, eyes towards the security barrier, before eventually losing interest and hurtling down to the ground to frantically dig for morsels they might have buried a couple of months ago.

The press pack are waiting, too. Their sustenance isn't found underground, but in the complimentary coffee machine that will help some of them get through today's double shift.

A dog-walking couple linger near the security barrier, looking down the lane to see if a certain former international striker is about to whizz past them. A pair of schoolkids who've taken a detour on their walk home have a similar idea. But, for now, the traffic is heading the other way, as a fast-moving, post-training motorcade of players' cars zips out of the car park, down the lane and off towards home.

Training is over and Sean Dyche is ready to meet the press corps. He's exceedingly relaxed, offering a straight bat when asked about other transfer targets ('I don't talk about other clubs' players'), but more than willing to talk about Crouch and Vokes now that both deals are very close to completion. He offers a tribute to Vokes and the service he's given Turf Moor, while clearly relishing the spark that Crouch will bring to the club, if only for a few months. (No one, though, asks Dyche about lining up against Crouch when he was still a player. In his most recent volume of autobiography, Crouch recalls the time he played for QPR against Millwall as a twig-like nineteen-year-old, with Dyche the enforcer happily 'tenderising any bit of my body he could reach'. Forgiveness clearly comes in the shape of a rejuvenated Premier League career.)

Once everyone's questions have been exhausted, Dyche and I decamp to a side room. It's little bigger than a box room in a standard semi and is cluttered with equipment ahead of recording Crouch's first interview as a Claret. The boss seems extraordinarily calm, despite it being deadline day and despite ongoing bids for at least one more player. If he's not remotely stressed by it, does he actually enjoy it?

'I don't think it's there to be enjoyed or not. It's part of the business. You have no choice about it. You can't govern it. The rules are laid down in front of you. I just get on with it. I'm pretty much like that about all my business. I don't get too emotional about it, I don't get too frustrated with it, I don't get too excited by it.

'I've had fantastic deals that have come out of the blue, and I've had deals that I thought were absolutely nailed on just disappear. Work hard, do what you can to get done and, if it doesn't get done, it's not always your fault. If it does get done, sometimes it's because of your good practice. And sometimes, you know, it's just a twist of fate. I've had them as well.'

While understandably not forthcoming at the press conference about the signing of a second striker, it was nonetheless quite rare for a manager to talk at length about the Crouch/Vokes switch, bearing in mind that both contracts, at this stage, remain unsigned. 'It is unusual, but it's a sense that all parties are on the same wavelength. Sometimes that's hard. This has been pretty straightforward, which is not always the case. Today's slightly different. I opened it up to the media, which I don't always do as I don't like talking about other people's players. But this is different because I spoke to Stoke. "I'm just about to do the media now. Are you happy that I suggest we're more or less there?" They said yes. Just a bit of respect.

'If all deals could be like this, that would be fantastic. But I'm afraid to say they're not. The main thing today is that the key people have spoken to the key people, which doesn't always happen. Stoke played a good part in that. Today has been a different day for us. There is speculation about others, but I don't speak about other people's players. I've never wanted to and I don't think it's correct to. That's not judging anyone else. Those are just my rules.

'Transfers can be very complex and sometimes less complex, which is the situation today. There might still be a twist and later on today we find that it didn't go through. Who knows? I've had that before, where at the last minute, something's happened in the medical and we've had to pull the deal. Maybe the i's didn't get dotted and the t's didn't get crossed ...'

4.45pm

Dyche leaves the room just as the car carrying Crouch arrives on site – straight through the two sets of security barriers and over the narrow bridge spanning the River Calder to the training ground's main building. He had his medical in Manchester earlier, the scans from which have been sent over for the scrutiny of the club's medical staff. Despite Crouch celebrating his thirty-eighth birthday yesterday, he's still in tremendously good nick. He's played in World Cups and has appeared for a still-lengthening list of top-flight clubs, but has stayed relatively injury-free. Dyche's confidence says it all. Those scans aren't expected to show anything untoward.

5.15pm

With the print reporters having long departed to meet deadlines and suggest headlines, Alan Myers from Sky Sports News stands in the darkening gloom, lit by a single flashbulb as he delivers his live report, updating the nation about the deals for the departing Vokes and the arriving Crouch.

Myers, though, has forgotten his *de rigueur* yellow tie today and has had to borrow a Burnley club tie from the man on the security gate. Decorum must be maintained, even if wearing it is the ultimate embarrassment for a former director of bitter rivals Blackburn Rovers.

6pm

Over on the continent, the Bundesliga window shuts. After all the column inches and airtime accorded him over the past month, Callum Hudson-Odoi is not on his way to Bavaria. Bayern Munich have failed to snare him – or to persuade Chelsea to part with him. The Blues have held on to their starlet. For now.

(The retention of Hudson-Odoi will take on extra significance twenty-two days later when FIFA ban Chelsea from making new signings for the next two transfer windows, citing a breach of regulations surrounding the recruitment and registration of players under the age of eighteen. With the club unable to open the chequebook and splash the cash in their usual fashion, the winger became an even more valuable commodity at Stamford Bridge, especially with the continual speculation linking Eden Hazard with Real Madrid. The ban also held significance for at least some of the sizeable Chelsea contingent out on loan. The likes of Michael Hector and Todd Kane were still unlikely to find their way into the following season's Premier League squad, but Tammy Abraham and Mason Mount – so influential in getting Aston Villa and Derby respectively to the Championship Play-Off Final – had the chance to finally cement themselves as permanent fixtures at their parent club.)

Meanwhile, back on deadline day, the results of the latest on-air Sky Sports News poll – 'Can Peter Crouch still be a success in the Premier League?' – are revealed. Fifty-four per cent of viewers are in the affirmative.

6.45pm

Crouch leaves the training ground, having fulfilled the obligatory demands made of a new signing: recording an interview for the club's website and being snapped holding aloft his new number fifteen shirt. Crouch, of course, holds a shirt more aloft than anyone else in football.

7pm

Even though Sean Dyche was giving candid interviews about the deal three hours before, the Crouch move is only now officially announced by Burnley. It comes in the form of a neat film that shows a robot making his way around the training ground, most of which was clearly filmed in daylight earlier in the day. The closing shot, though, is of a rolling football knocking the robot over before the camera pans upwards to reveal the man who kicked it: a certain smiling, lanky striker.

The video interview is published online too, a reminder to the Burnley faithful that their club has just signed one of the more self-deprecating footballers around. The hashtag #CrouchIsAClaret begins to trend on Twitter. 'You can sort of see the end,' Crouch admits of his career's mortality. 'My game has probably changed a little bit. I'm not twenty-five. But my attributes haven't waned. I never really had blistering pace, so I haven't lost that.'

Crouch has had the opportunity to join Burnley before. Early in his career – and in a pre-echo of that deadline day he spent in McDonalds on the A40 – the then twenty-year-old met the then Clarets manager Stan Ternent in a Little Chef on the M6, one equidistant between London and Burnley. That time, he opted to stay down south and signed for Portsmouth instead.

On 5 Live, Ian Dennis opens the dedicated deadline-day show with a brief summary of the transfer highlights so far, which, aside from Crouch stretching those long legs in the direction of Lancashire, include Fellaini being halfway to China for his payday and Newcastle's capture of the Paraguayan striker Miguel Almirón from MLS side Atlanta United for a club record fee in excess of £20m. But, ever the sober realist, Dennis refuses to get unnecessarily carried away. 'Forget the hype,' he cautions. 'The reality is that it's been an extremely quiet day.'

7.15pm

Just fifteen minutes into 5 Live's dedicated deadline-day show – and with four hours still left of the window – the inquest has started as to why today hasn't been, and why January windows aren't generally, the dramatic affairs they used to be.

Several theories are offered by the guest panel. One suggests there have been fewer deals because more of the available pie has gone on higher transfer fees and higher wages. With the average Premier League weekly wage now in the region of £60,000–£70,000, the loan-with-an-option-to-buy – as favoured by Allardyce and Brown all those years ago – is undeniably attractive. A big-money permanent transfer is much less of a gamble if a club has been able to try the goods out before committing. Recruitment on on-approval terms.

UEFA's Financial Fair Play regulations are invariably mentioned as a caution on reckless spending, even if clubs wriggle furiously to avoid the legislation's grasp. Elsewhere, Andy Townsend posits a perfectly credible theory about how the rise of sporting directors is shaping spending patterns. The argument goes that we're seeing more cautious behaviour because not only is decision-making increasingly more collective (as opposed to a single manager calling all the shots), sporting directors are also accountable for these decisions. Careless spending can cost them their jobs. The result is calmer, more professional purchasing during the summer window.

8pm

Having co-anchored this morning's show on talkSPORT, Jim White switches to the small screen and that late shift at Sky Sports News. His arrival on screen is the signal for football fans that we're entering the end-game. This is the sharp end. Were today a 1500-metre race, White's appearance is the equivalent of the bell announcing the last lap. Up until now, it's been cagey. But these metaphorical final four hundred metres are where the action should accelerate, ideally culminating in an explosive surge for the tape.

8.30pm

If the transfer window excitement was supposed to be a party that lasted until at least 11pm, no one told Accrington Stanley. Back at the Wham Stadium, the snowy car park is completely empty. The lights are out and there's no one home.

9pm

Jim White, with Hayley McQueen in Natalie Sawyer's old role, is an hour into the late shift. The studio in Isleworth is a far more welcoming and warm place than the frozen outposts from which various frozen reporters are filing their updates. Wrapped up as if prepared for a polar expedition, at the Cardiff City training ground, Michelle Owen is being plastered by the heavy snow that's arrived in south Wales. She's obliged to stay in position for at least another couple of hours, despite the club having already announced there will be no further arrivals.

In the studio, Hayley McQueen has no need for a fur-lined parka or woolly pom-pom hat. She's in her now-trademark black, albeit accessorised with a yellow belt, while Jim White's tie is of a paler yellow shade than normal. Perhaps he's actually playing down the hype. Perhaps it's an admission – from deadline day's most vocal, most vociferous champion – that today has been something of a damp squib. Few fizzes and minimal bangs.

9.30pm

Ian Dennis admits, a little sheepishly, that he left the sainted Book Of Destiny at home today and is thus strangely relieved that, without his main reference source to hand, it's been a decidedly quiet deadline day.

Will Grigg thinks it's going to be quiet for the remaining ninety minutes of the window. The Northern Ireland international's goalscoring abilities have been the subject of, according to reports, no fewer than seven bids from Sunderland across the month and in particular today, but it appears that his club, Wigan, remain dogged and unmoving, coolly refusing each and every one of the Black Cats' overtures for their man.

After a day of speculation and bids, the move seems to have flatlined. So sure is Grigg that he'll still be a Latic for at least the rest of the season that, once he's put his kids to bed, he's changed into his pyjamas and is getting an early night. But then he gets a text. The move to Sunderland could well be finally on; it appears an eighth bid of £3m (rising to £4m if Sunderland make it back to the Premier League) has been sufficient for Wigan to unlock the door marked 'Exit'. At this late hour, though, it's still not a certainty. Grigg needs to get himself to Wigan's Euxton training ground as quickly as possible. Immediately, in fact. Perhaps even in his pyjamas.

9.45pm

There's no such late excitement for Gary Cotterill. It's been a quiet deadline day for the Sky reporter, who has been on duty at Watford's training ground since first thing. There was but one deal done by the Hornets today, with the defender Ben Wilmot heading to Udinese on loan. Instead – and without any snowy conditions to brave – Cotterill's live report informs the nation about something else entirely: the three-course meal he's just been served by the club. A starter of lobster spaghetti, a main course of lamb with vegetables, and rhubarb crumble for dessert appears to have softened any disappointment he might have felt at a lack of transfers to report on.

Meanwhile, Cotterill's colleague Paul Gilmour, who's been seconded to report on Tottenham for the day, is in equally less-than-serious mood. Like five other Premier League clubs, including Liverpool and West Ham, Spurs have failed to sign any players in this entire window. This is the second trading period on the trot that the club have been inactive, making them the first club in history without any incoming signings for two successive windows. 'Deadline day,' begins Gilmour's latest live missive, 'or Thursday as Spurs like to call it …'

9.48pm

Earlier in the month, Pete Smith had explained how New Era were keen for around twenty of their clients to move, either permanently or temporarily, at some point in this window. He now reckons that around half of these have come off.

'It's all about supply and demand on the day, and whether the domino effect kicks in – whether a player goes out, allowing another to come in. This window has been quiet all round. There wasn't lots of activity.

'You're never disappointed. It is what it is. We know what to expect. But at the end of the day, we've got to get the players playing. That's the be-all and end-all. If you're not playing, you're not in the shop window and you're not going to get a move. The January window is historically mainly loans. It's about getting players playing football, getting them opportunities for the summer window.'

With seventy-two minutes left of this window, the highest profile move for a New Era client is announced when Jacob Murphy's loan move from Newcastle to West Brom is confirmed. You'd have got evens money earlier in the day on whether it was going to go through or not, but Miguel Almirón's arrival on Tyneside enabled Murphy to head for the West Midlands.

'It was always dependent on them bringing a player in,' says Smith. 'Rafa made that public knowledge to an extent, that he needed to bring a winger in. He believes that Jacob has done a great job and has developed really well, but that he still needs to continue to develop, and that's why he gave him the opportunity to go out on loan and continue playing football. And that's fair enough.'

That the deal was only confirmed with little more than an hour remaining of the window wasn't because of a race-against-the-clock drive down from the north-east. Murphy and his agent were positioned relatively close to The Hawthorns. 'We read between the lines,' says Smith, 'and stationed ourselves accordingly so we had no issues with travel or with getting the medical done. Medicals nowadays are not what they used to be. They're a lot more intense and the procedures are a lot more stringent. They give the guys a proper medical, even for a loan.'

9.54pm

After rumours have been flying around for the past fifteen minutes, Crystal Palace part-owner and chairman Steve Parish confirms to Sky Sports News that Michy Batshuayi is, as the whispers have it, indeed on his way to Selhurst Park. Following his loan to Borussia Dortmund twelve months ago, this will be the second successive January deadline day that Chelsea's Belgian striker has been on the move. In fact, he also switched clubs during the summer, swapping that temporary secondment in the Bundesliga with one in La Liga with Valencia. Batshuayi has been cropping up in rumours all day long; Palace is the fourth Premier League club he's been linked to today, after West Ham, Everton and Spurs were all reported to be interested in securing his services.

That a decent-sized name is on the move is the kind of eleventh-hour deal that the reputation of deadline day was built on. A deal sheet for Batshuayi has been submitted, giving Chelsea and Palace additional time to get all the requisite paperwork shipshape.

10pm

5 Live's deadline-day programme ends an hour before the window closes. The Adrian Chiles-presented *Question Time Extra Time* appears to be a higher priority for the station. It suggests – along with the absence of a late-night deadline-day presence on one of its TV channels – that it's of growing indifference to the corporation. It's certainly not as important or exciting enough to replace the regular politics show now that the UK is within two months of the original Brexit withdrawal date.

10.30pm

Into the last half hour and a show-stopping, gob-smacking final flourish of deals seems unlikely. The only news of late is that Wolves have allowed three marginal, and largely unknown, players to go out on loan to less-than-glamorous destinations: two have gone to third-tier football in Germany and Spain, the other to sample the Slovakian leagues.

10.55pm

Having started out at Turf Moor in sub-zero temperatures at first light this morning before transferring to Gawthorpe Hall, Alan Myers has returned to Burnley's ground as he files his final live report of the day. Aside from relaying the same information about Crouch's capture that he's been reciting for the past six-odd hours, he also reveals that the club today put in no fewer than four bids for Che Adams, the final offer being for £12.5m. But Birmingham demurred four times over; with a transfer ban in place, the Blues would have been unable to sign a replacement.

Palace appear to be having more success in adding to their forward line. Never mind the hearsay and guesswork around the Batshuayi situation. More concrete clarification comes from the club itself – or, at least, from their left-back Patrick van Aanholt. 'I'm driving to the training ground just so I can come say hi,' he tweets. Beauty sleep wouldn't be compromised were the striker not already at the training ground in Beckenham, presumably with stethoscope to chest or feet on pounding treadmill.

10.57pm

Will Grigg's deal sheet has been registered with the EFL, buying Sunderland more time. This they surely need when considering the triangular nature of the negotiations: Grigg is in Wigan, Black Cats boss Jack Ross is on Wearside, and the club's owner Stewart Donald is at home in Oxfordshire.

The deal won't actually be officially confirmed until mid-morning tomorrow, after Grigg arrives in the north-east to face the scrutiny of the press and the ardour of the fans. Aside from the beat-the-clock panic, the move makes a little history, too. It's the highest fee ever paid for a player by a third-tier English club.

11pm

The Sky Sports News countdown clock, ticking down for a whole month, has reached its final destination. 'The

January window is closed!' barks Jim White. But the late shift for him and Hayley McQueen isn't over yet. The mopping-up process continues, whether it's summarising the day's bigger moves for the umpteenth time or imparting further information concerning those extension-giving deal sheets. Two have apparently been lodged with the Premier League. One was the expected extension for the Batshuayi deal. But the other is an unidentified one from Fulham. An element of intrigue has belatedly entered the night's proceedings.

12:22am

Batshuayi's third loan move in twelve months is confirmed by Crystal Palace on their Twitter feed. 'Batsman Returns To London!' screams the tweet – when 'Batman Returns To London' would have been both perfectly correct and better. But it's late and eyes are tired. Time to cut Palace's social-media department some slack.

The identity of the player for whom that second deal sheet was submitted is revealed within seconds of the Batshuayi announcement. It's for Lazar Markovic, the winger frozen out at Liverpool, who leaves Anfield on a free to become a Fulham player for the rest of the season. Leftfield and unexpected.

12:31am

With those two deal sheet moves confirmed, Niall McVeigh, the *Guardian*'s man on their blow-by-blow, minute-by-minute deadline-day blog, signs off. 'I'm off to bed on a long-term deal,' he neatly announces.

In Towcester, Phil Jones is also heading up the wooden stairs to Bedfordshire. It's not been a vintage deadline day, as shown by the amount of uneaten chocolate Hobnobs still in his possession. But there's been enough activity to justify using up a day of his annual leave allowance, thanks largely to the late will-it-won't-it jeopardy of the Batshuayi deal.

It was certainly a good day for Phil as a Newcastle fan. A war chest was finally handed over to Rafa Benitez, a large chunk of which he invested in Miguel Almirón. However belated, it was quite a statement of intent. The £21m fee was not only the biggest of the Ashley era, it was the biggest in Newcastle's history, breaking their fourteen-year transfer record set when they signed Michael Owen from Real Madrid back in 2005. 'I'm not familiar with this Almirón,' shrugs Phil, 'and I'm not sure about spending that much on a player from MLS, but Rafa's no mug. He doesn't get a lot to spend, so let's hope he's used it wisely.'

Other than his partisan interests, Phil's favourite deal of the day was the Crouch move. 'Those are the kind of deadline-day stories we remember. That'll be the defining story of this one. It has so much romance about it. But that's it for now. I always go to bed a little deflated afterwards, just like on Christmas night. All the presents have been unwrapped. We're all done until August now.'

Shut down the laptop. Put the TV on standby. Shoot out the lights.

The longest day is over.

Extra time

Kevin Nolan and Harry Kewell weren't the only significant departures from Meadow Lane. In May 2019, following a 4–1 defeat to Swindon Town, **Notts County** became a non-league club for the first time in its 157-year history. Chairman/owner Alan Hardy also left when a Danish consortium took charge, saving the club from impending administration. 'It was the wrong sort of adventure,' Hardy admitted at the time of the relegation from League Two. 'On paper, it has cost me thirty-five million. My wife is not happy. She didn't want me to buy County in the first place.'

The nomadic existence of **Benik Afobe** continued into the summer of 2019. After a frustrating season at Stoke, in which he scored just eight times in forty-five league appearances, on deadline day the striker was farmed out to another Championship side, Bristol City, on a season-long loan with a view to a permanent deal. He described the move as a 'no-brainer', expressing his hope to 'get back to the Benik Afobe that has done well in the past'.

Life as a serial loanee became even more uncertain for **Harry Bunn**. Having completed his season-long spell at Southend, he returned to Lancashire and the turmoil of Bury Football Club. Its players never got to kick a ball for the club in League One, the division to which they had just been promoted. Off-field matters hadn't mirrored the on-field success and the club were expelled from the EFL in late August 2019 without fulfilling a single fixture. 'We have had some wages,' Bunn told the *Guardian* at the time of the expulsion. 'We got last month's, but we're still owed our pay for a few months before that. It looks like the owner had a fair few other businesses that were liquidated. It's beyond me and the other lads as to how you could allow him in to buy a football club.'

'The time has come to refer to myself as a former footballer.' **Peter Crouch** will be a fixture of deadline days no more. He's told his last tale of mad, cross-country dashes at the eleventh hour. Those five months at Turf Moor proved to be his last as a professional footballer. Crouch is no longer a Claret.

Acknowledgements

Hefty quantities of gratitude go to the various players, managers, chairmen, agents, scouts, analysts, fans, journalists, broadcasters and bookmakers who kindly gave up so much time and wisdom in interview.

For passing on names and numbers, and for unlocking doors, big thanks to Darren Bentley, Colin Burgess, Paul Camillin, Ryan Crompton, Matt Deacon, Mick Doherty, Matt Hall, Ben Hooke, Brendan McLoughlin, John Murray, Nick Richardson, John Simpson, Dale Tempest and Sean Watts.

Massive, massive thanks to Fran Jessop who not only came up with the original idea but also commissioned it. And big congratulations to her for the success of her own youth policy.

At Yellow Jersey, my editor/Burnley fanatic Tim Broughton kept an enthusiastic hand on the tiller, while Matt Broughton created a fabulous cover design. Thanks also to Joe Pickering, Konrad Kirkham and Tim Bainbridge.

For always being on the end of a phone, thanks go to my agent Kevin Pocklington at The North literary agency, supplying laughs and no-bullshit analysis in equal measure.

And finally to Jane, Finn and Ned, for their ever-present patience when, at times consumed by the book, I probably deserved to be stuck on the transfer list. Love you guys forever.